Sport in Consumer Culture

Also by John Horne

WORK AND UNEMPLOYMENT

UNDERSTANDING SPORT: An Introduction to the Sociological and Cultural Analysis of Sport (*co-author with A. Tomlinson and G. Whannel*)

SPORT, LEISURE AND SOCIAL RELATIONS (*co-editor with D. Jary and A. Tomlinson*)

MASCULINITIES: Leisure Cultures, Identities and Consumption (*co-editor with S. Fleming*)

LEISURE CULTURES, CONSUMPTION AND COMMODIFICATION

JAPAN, KOREA AND THE 2002 WORLD CUP (*co-editor with W. Manzenreiter*)

FOOTBALL GOES EAST: Business Culture and the People's Game in China, Japan and South Korea (*co-editor with W. Manzenreiter*)

Sport in Consumer Culture

John Horne

First published 2006 by
PALGRAVE MACMILLAN
Houndmills, Basingstoke, Hampshire RG21 6XS and
175 Fifth Avenue, New York, N.Y. 10010
Companies and representatives throughout the world

PALGRAVE MACMILLAN is the global academic imprint of the Palgrave
Macmillan division of St. Martin's Press, LLC and of Palgrave Macmillan Ltd.
Macmillan® is a registered trademark in the United States, United Kingdom
and other countries. Palgrave is a registered trademark in the European
Union and other countries.

ISBN-13: 978–0–333–91285–0 hardback
ISBN-10: 0–333–91285–3 hardback
ISBN-13: 978–0–333–91286–7 paperback
ISBN-10: 0–333–91286–1 paperback

This book is printed on paper suitable for recycling and made from fully
managed and sustained forest sources.

A catalogue record for this book is available from the British Library.

A catalog record for this book is available from the Library of Congress.

10   9   8   7   6   5   4   3   2   1
15 14 13 12 11 10 09 08 07 06

Printed in China

This book is dedicated to 'non-aspirational perfectionists' everywhere – you know who you are.

Contents

Part I
Globalisation, Consumerisation and the Mass Media

Part II
Commodification, Regulation and Power

List of Tables and Box

Tables

Box

Preface

This book is partly the product of teaching several cohorts of undergraduate and postgraduate students in the 1990s and early 2000s. In various modules, including leisure and consumer culture, physical culture, sport, media and society, and social theories of sport and leisure, we explored how and why has sport become so central to the advanced capitalist economies of signs and space. The book aims to help to answer the various questions that stem from this situation. How did it develop? Who is responsible? What mechanisms brought it about? Who is most affected by it? Are the impacts evenly spread and if not how are different social groups affected? When did it begin? It draws together material from several disciplines that inform the field of sports studies, but the main emphasis is on the sociological analysis of sport. If you don't want to know the score, look away now. If you do, then read on.

Acknowledgements

It would be remiss to fail to acknowledge the insights and other forms of assistance that I have received from the many people and organisations which indirectly or directly have informed this book. In alphabetical order these people include Alan Bairner, Ian Craib, Jean Harvey, David Jary, John MacInnes, Wolfram Manzenreiter, Atsuo Sugimoto, Yoshio Takahashi, Garry Whannel, Dave Whitson and last, but by no means least, Takayuki Yamashita. I am grateful to the library staff at the University of Edinburgh and **sport**scotland for help with accessing some of the material. There are others and apologies if I have not mentioned you personally.

1

Introduction

Introduction: Sport, Consumption and the Cultural Turn

The rationale of this book is to provide a distinctive introduction to sport in society drawing on recent developments in sociological research and theory, especially with reference to consumer culture, consumer society and consumption. It will also provide a deeper and more critical understanding of contemporary debates in Sociology after the 'cultural turn' applied to the Sociology of Sport. The 'cultural turn' refers to recognition of the cultural significance and importance of the growth of consumption (Ray and Sayer 1999, Roberts 1999, Ch. 7), the role of 'consumption as an activity in and through which identity is constructed' (Smart 2003, p. 74), and the reversal of the 'production paradigm' associated with postmodern social theory (Dodd 1999, p. 136). It is connected to debates about modernity, lifestyles and identities (Bauman 1998), concerning the shifting relationship between the state and the market, above and below the national level, the transformation of the meaning of citizenship and the implications of these developments for personal and social identities. The expansion of studies of consumption and consumerism in the last twenty years is also linked to debates about globalisation, postmodernity, identity and new forms of inequality along the lines of taste and distinction. The 'cultural turn' raises interesting questions for critical traditions in sociology and the sociology of sport (Blackshaw 2002). Two key issues are: Do the structures and organisation of consumerism exclude, dominate and marginalise other modes of provision of sport and leisure? And does consumer culture heighten the manipulation of consumer agency or are consumers able to exert a degree of control (if not sovereignty)? In short, are consumers dupes, victims, rational actors or heroic communicators in consumer society? (Aldridge 2003, pp. 15–23).

Sport can be seen as central to the 'economies of signs and space' (Lash and Urry 1994) in late capitalist modernity. In these economies the body is more than an instrument for producing material goods and getting things done – after all in the UK in May 2004 only 3.38 million people out of a total workforce of 28.3 million were in manufacturing employment (Moore 2004).

1

The body, including the sporting and physically active body, is now portrayed as an object of contemplation and improvement, in the spectacular discourses of the mass media, the regulatory discourses of the state and in people's everyday practices (sometimes referred to as 'body projects' – Shilling 1993). Moreover sport has become increasingly allied to the consumption of goods and services, which is now the structural basis of the advanced capitalist countries (Lash and Urry 1994, p. 296), through discourses about the model, (post)modern consumer-citizen. This person is an enterprising self who is also a calculating and reflexive self. Someone permanently ready to discipline himself or herself – through crash diets, gymnastics, aerobics, muscle toning, tanning, strip-waxing and cosmetic ('plastic') surgery (including breast enlargement and cellulite reduction) as well as sporting physical activity – in order to fit in with the demands of advanced liberalism (Rose 1992).

The relationship of sport (and active bodies) with consumer culture has been noted by several social commentators. For example McPherson et al. (1993, p. 81) suggest that 'in conjunction with the emergence of consumer culture was the progressive commercialisation and commodification of sport and sporting bodies'. John Hargreaves (1986, p. 134) argued that 'What links up consumer culture with sports culture so economically is their common concern with, and capacity to accommodate, the body as a means of expression.' Contemporary advertisements for commercial sport and leisure clubs in the UK (such as Next Generation and Fitness First) combine the discourses of both medical science and popular culture in such phrases as 'fitness regime', 'problem areas like the bottom or the stomach', 'consultation' and 'fix'. By exhorting potential consumers/members to 'Flatten your tum and perk up your bum' and reassuring us that 'Gym'll fix it', 'The regulatory control of the body is now experienced through consumerism and the fashion industry rather than through religion' (Turner 1996, p. 23).

Other recent attempts to discuss aspects of sport in consumer culture have focussed on: fandom and fans (Crawford 2004), advertising (Jackson and Andrews 2005), individual athletes (Andrews 2001, Andrews and Jackson 2001, Cashmore 2002), teams (Andrews 2004) or mega sports events (Jennings and Sambrook 2000, Sugden and Tomlinson 1998a, 2003, Dauncey and Hare 1999, Horne and Manzenreiter 2002a). This book not only incorporates this research but also attempts to bring together a much broader range of studies and interpretations of consumer culture. It also considers a wider dimension of sport by focussing on it as an active practice as well as a commercial spectacle. The main focus of this book is on sport in developed English-speaking countries, especially the UK and North America, although some references are included to experience in other societies. This book thus offers a partial focus, but one which is alert to the need to learn from experience elsewhere. When discussing sport in consumer culture it is necessary to think about the terms being used, even what is meant by 'in', and therefore we shall start with some definitions.

Sport: A Contested Concept

In 1984 the then Prime Minister Margaret Thatcher's statement that there were great industries in other people's pleasures was dismissed by critics as a reference to 'Mickey Mouse' jobs (she was thinking of places like Disney World, see Clarke and Critcher 1985, pp. 100–103). Since then, however, many more leisure activities have become job generators. 'Travel and tourism' has become the world's largest industry, responsible for '11.7 per cent of world GDP, 8 per cent of world exports and 8 per cent of all employment' (Urry 2002, p. 5). The number of jobs in 'sport and recreation' has likewise continued to grow, if not on such a great scale, leading to continuing high demand for courses in sport-related subjects in further and higher education throughout the advanced world. There is no longer much reticence about discussing the economics or marketing of sport as a business or an industry.

If sport is an industry, it is clearly a rather unorthodox one. As Whannel (2004, pp. 481–482) observes, where else would consumers (football fans) maintain high levels of consumption even if quality (success) declines and prices rise? Indeed continuing consumption (support) in the face of lack of success is seen as a sign of true commitment. Likewise otherwise rational entrepreneurs will invest vast sums of money into commercial teams in pursuit of sports success without serious expectation of financial return. Ego, vanity and self-aggrandisement appear to over-rule the rationality of the balance sheet. Sport is clearly much more than simply another industry. Miller et al. (2001, p. 132) define sport as 'recreational and professional competitive, rule-governed physical activity'. They also note that 'sport of a regular and organized kind is the product of a social institution with its origins in Victorian England'. Modern sport is just that – a *modernist* creation of the late 19th century, as opposed to the considerable number of physical game contests and play forms that have existed throughout the world over several centuries. Sport has its own cultural origins, but these are mixed up with the development of industrialism and capitalism, the spread of liberal democracy and the growth of mass communications.

As we will consider in Chapter 3, sport is one of those forms of culture that has increasingly been subject to 'mediazation' or 'mediatization' (Thompson 1990, pp. 12–20, 163–271) through which it has become part of media culture. As Blain (2002, p. 229) notes, 'Forms of culture that do not depend on the media for their reception and transmission are becoming more and more to resemble curiosities.' Sports that are not routinely covered by the media – and there are still many of those – are treated as discoveries when they do, however fleetingly, become part of a newsworthy story. Blain provides the example of the Great Britain (GB) Women's curling team's unexpected gold medal at the Salt Lake City Winter Olympics in 2002. In addition, however, he suggests that even the most commercialised or televised sports retain a degree of autonomy from both the media and capitalist consumer culture. Sport 'is best seen as exhibiting *both* modern and postmodern characteristics' (Blain 2002, p. 237). Athletes may lead (postmodern) celebrity lives as product sponsors, media commentators and even movie stars, but are also required to undergo the (modernist) discipline of specific dietary and training regimes in order to perform in their sport. Sports therefore have both postmodern (media saturated) and modern (sport practice) lives.

Twenty years ago, John Hargreaves (1986, pp. 10–14) observed that 'the realm of sport encompasses a bewildering diversity of radically different kinds of activity, which defies a watertight definition'. He identified six characteristics of sport that remain relevant to understanding its distinctive (or autonomous) culture. First, he noted that sports, in comparison with other types of social activity, consisted of *play*. Secondly, sports have been formalised and were 'governed by very elaborate codes and statutes'. Thirdly, the uncertainty of sports' contested outcomes, and the attendant tension it creates, lends a unique excitement to them. Fourthly, sports provide *drama* and 'regular public occasions for discourse on some of the basic themes of social life'. Fifthly, sport's rule-governed behaviour of a symbolic character 'draws the attention of its participants to objects of thought and feeling which are held to be of special significance', and provides much of its *ritual* quality (Hargreaves 1986). Sixthly, Hargreaves noted that *the body* constituted 'the most striking symbol as well as the material core of sporting activity'. He argued that in the second half of the 20th century, sporting activity of all kinds was increasingly linked with a particular pattern of consumption:

> The body is clearly an object of crucial importance in consumer culture and its supply industries; and sports, together with fashion, eating and drinking outside the home, cooking, dieting, keep fit therapy, other physically active leisure, advertising imagery, and a battery of aids to sexual attractiveness, are deployed in a constantly elaborating programme whose objective is the production of the new 'normalized' individual. (p. 14)

The 'normalized' body of the 21st century was clearly not the same as that of 100 years earlier.

Other academics and governmental agencies have also defined sport as more than just competitive team games. For example, both Gratton and Taylor (2000) and the UK Government have adopted the Council of Europe definition of sport as 'all forms of physical activity which, through casual or organised participation, aim at expressing or improving physical fitness and mental well-being, forming social relationships or obtaining results in competition at all levels' (Council of Europe 1993, *European Sports Charter*, Article 2). Sport can be understood not only as competitive physical activity, but also as other forms of physical activity, including recreational sport and physical exercise. Hence sport may conjure up images of spectacular forms of entertainment, but it can also refer to personal exercise routines. That physical health features as an important source of life satisfaction in surveys suggests that a broader definition of sport could see it as part of the solution to some of the problems generated by consumer culture rather than its servant.

We take the view that sport in all its forms needs to be considered in relationship to consumer culture. Whilst the search for growth in revenue streams in addition to gate money on the part of professional sports (such as television rights agreements, hospitality and merchandise) is important, we also need to understand the growth of sports services (private health clubs and gyms such as Next Generation and Fitness First) as enterprises. Moreover much sport still takes place because of its organisation through volunteer-run clubs, which have sometimes been considered to offer a degree of autonomy from commercial consumer culture. Sport may be both a commercial spectacle and used as a means of resisting commercial values. This is one of the reasons why it makes for such an interesting topic in connection with discussions of consumer culture. It is useful to recognise competing tendencies – the dominant, residual, oppositional and emergent (Williams 1977, pp. 121–127, 1981, pp. 203–205) – that have affected the development of cultural forms such as sport. Its history is a product of the interplay between these different influences and power relationships.

A final reason why consideration of sport in consumer culture is overdue is because there has been significant growth in the social, cultural and historical analysis of sport in society and consumer culture in the past twenty years, but little attempt to bring this material together. Early inspirations for considering sport in this way were writers such as Gruneau (1999/1983), Whannel (1983) and Hargreaves (1986, 1987). Recently both sports sociologists and historians (Dunning and Malcolm 2003, p. 5, Holt and Mason 2000, p. 94) have provided several measures of the growing importance of sport in contemporary society. In the second half of the 20th century in Britain, for example, the media has acted as a most important transforming force, turning sport into a 'male soap opera' (Holt and Mason 2000, p. 94). Not far behind were commercialisation, sponsors and celebrity following the 'drift towards the American TV model' (Holt and Mason 2000, p. 109). Whereas in the 1950s sport 'occupied a niche', by the end of the 1990s satellite television had 'democratised spectating and linked it to a globalising of consumption' (Holt and Mason 2000, p. 176). Sport has become an 'industry' and its goods widely worn as fashion items. Holt and Mason (2000, p. 177) note that divisions between 'the best and the rest' in sport have become greater, with rewards to the former reaching amounts only previously paid to film and other entertainment celebrities. Sport has been promoted like other commodities – as a consistent and quality product (Holt and Mason 2000, p. 177). To understand these developments in sport better, it is essential that we also know about consumer society and culture. It is to this subject we will now turn.

Consumer Society and Culture

In the past three decades, debates about consumption, consumer society and consumer culture have developed from a minority academic issue to a public concern (Featherstone 1991). Part of the debate about postmodernity was the suggestion that social scientists, especially sociologists, had focussed too much on the experience and effect of paid work and production and not enough on consumption (Dodd 1999, Edwards 2000). Are people increasingly addicted to spending and shopping? Does affluence create happiness? Is shopping the ultimate freedom? One suggestion is that affluence – like poverty – is relative, and hence as opportunities to spend increase so too do the comparisons with others. People may compare their position in society with celebrity lifestyles – of David and Victoria Beckham, for example. The fact that a professional football player (and his pop star wife) has become for some a central indicator of the good life is a development that will be considered in more detail in Chapter 4.

Other writers suggest that whilst shopping represents itself as the ultimate freedom, it may in fact destroy freedom. In the 1950s the so-called 'affluent society' was hailed as bringing about more free time. Some described it as the beginning of the leisure age. Today life is considered to be speeding up and lack of time is a core condition. According to research into life satisfaction, more durable sources of satisfaction are to be found in social connection, marital status and physical health rather than consumption (Lodziak 2002).

The 'buy now pay later' belief is one of several developments that are conceived of as peculiar to consumer culture. Others include a concentration on form or style over function and product disposability or planned obsolescence, which appears to have become embraced by consumers in the past fifty years. Is this the result of indoctrination or brainwashing, or more to do with changes in the availability of credit? In the 1970s designer labels or brands were introduced and these were met with apparent approval. People were prepared to pay more for a product just because it carried a label (even though as in the case of Calvin Klein's 'CK One' perfume, for example, the product was mass-produced by the multinational corporation Unilever). Branding was created by extensive marketing. Certain brands became 'cool' and helped to placate anxious consumers by providing them with reassurance that they had obtained goods of a certain quality, reliability or fashionable chic. In addition, as Frank (1997, p. 31) has shown, 'cool' itself has been harnessed since the 1970s to propel the 'cultural perpetual motion machine in which disgust with the falseness, shoddiness, and everyday oppressions of consumer society . . . (are) . . . enlisted to drive the ever-accelerating wheels of consumption'.

The extended credit facility associated today with credit cards was first introduced in the USA in the 1950s. In the UK it faced challenges from both social values with respect to indebtedness and government controls over the availability of credit. Today consumer credit drives and responds to ups and downs in national economies. In the UK, in the 1980s interest rates boomed, half a million houses were repossessed and unemployment reached 3 million. During the 1990s portable cell (USA) or mobile (UK) telephones have helped to stimulate another consumer boom. Now there is speeded-up obsolescence by which products rarely stay in the shops for longer than six weeks. Schor (1998, p. 40) cites research from the USA that suggests that 'the street life of a trendy athletic shoe has fallen in some cases to a month and even fifteen days'. It is suggested that 1 million people in the UK and 5 million people in the USA suffer from a shopping addiction. Reports of riots at the opening of a new IKEA store in north London and outside a New York store selling a limited edition Pigeon Dunk skateboarding trainer in February 2005 may just be the most visible aspects of these conditions (*The Guardian* 24 February 2005).

Theoretical Approaches to Consumption and Consumer Culture

How are we to make sense of these developments? There have been three main approaches to understanding consumption and consumer culture: the production of consumption approach, the modes of consumption approach and the pleasures of consumption approach. We will briefly consider the arguments of exemplars of each approach.

For critical theorists, as the 20th century developed, more aspects of culture became increasingly commodified – made into items for sale on the capitalist market place – and thus came to be just like any other 'industry' rather than offering an escape from (repressive and exploitative) capitalist relationships. As Adorno and Horkheimer (1977, p. 361) wrote, 'Amusement under late capitalism is the prolongation of work. It is sought after as an escape from the mechanised work process, and to recruit strength in order to be able to cope with it again.' Adorno and Horkheimer felt that, despite appearances to the contrary, leisure time activities were massively shaped by what happened at work, in the factory, or in the office. This had the consequences that most modern amusements were predictable, inevitably short-lived, lacking in challenge and therefore ultimately disappointing. Much of the critical theorists' argument revolved around the distinction between 'true' and 'false' needs.

They argued that in developed consumer capitalism 'wants' (desires) were turned into 'needs' (essentials), thus suggesting a shift from the 'authentic' to the 'inauthentic'. Moreover because of the impact of cultural intermediaries – market researchers and consumer analysts, for example – the 'triumph of advertising' in the culture industry is secured since 'consumers feel compelled to buy and use its products even though they see through them' (Adorno and Horkheimer 1977, p. 383). The choice of consumer goods is all that is left of freedom. 'What the philosophers once knew as life has become the sphere of private existence and now of mere consumption, dragged along as an appendage of the process of material production, without autonomy or substance of its own' (Adorno 1996/1951, p. 15). There is no need, or inclination, to rebel or overthrow capitalism since 'consumer culture is basically a lot of false compensations for the fundamental loss of human authenticity' (Slater 1997). At this point some students have been known to contemplate leaving my lecture room. But let us be clear, as Alan How (2003) remarks, 'Adorno may have been an old sourpuss but that does not mean he was wrong!' The important thing is to consider this as a perspective with which to think about sport in consumer culture. What are the implications if Theodor was correct in his assessment?

Despite its power and illuminating insights, the production of consumption perspective has been criticised for three main reasons. First, in its general form it appears to ignore the particularity and the specificity of different social contexts and sites of consumption and consumption practices. Secondly, it also appears too deterministic, negative and pessimistic about the ways that people respond to and use consumer goods and services. Thirdly, and related to the first two points, it underplays human agency and fails to see how active consumers are involved in personal resistance, subversiveness and the transgression of messages delivered by market-driven advertising agencies. The power of the media/market to make meaning in relation to the power of the audience (reader/viewer) or consumer to deal with it has become a fundamental question in studies of consumer culture, as we will see. These critical responses to productionist theories of consumption developed into perspectives focussing more on 'modes of consumption' and 'consuming dreams, images and pleasures' (Featherstone 1991). Reference to alienation and exploitation gave way to ethnographic accounts, on the one hand, and celebrations of consumer culture, on the other. We will briefly outline these two alternative perspectives on consumption.

The 'modes of consumption' approach has studied different social groups in which consumers become active as producers of undesigned or unanticipated uses and meanings of goods and services. Consumption becomes a means of personal empowerment, subversion or resistance, that is, it is mediated by active consumers/audiences. De Certeau (1984) and Fiske (1989, 1993), for example, focussed on the practices of everyday life to maintain, strengthen and challenge social and cultural boundaries associated with class, gender, race and age. For them people use consumption to create identities, social bonds and distinctions or social distance; to display and sustain differences; and to open or close off opportunities for selves and others. This form of social closure is conducted in the pursuit of different sports practices as well as elsewhere according to Pierre Bourdieu (1984/1979). After extensive sociological research in Paris and its neighbouring regions, Bourdieu (1984/1979) showed how taste in cultural goods acts as a marker of class and class fractions (Featherstone 1987, pp. 121ff.). Related to taste is style – foregrounding the importance of the aesthetic or 'the stylisation of life' – as life becomes a project (Featherstone 1991, p. 86). There is a tension between the market dynamic and the agency of consumers that can be seen particularly in research into gender, 'race' and consumption (Gilroy 1987, Lury 1996, pp. 159–182).

The first 'mode of consumption' studies considered that people possessed and displayed goods as a means of demonstrating superiority in a system of social status, and concepts such as 'positional goods', 'emulation' and 'distinction' were widely deployed (Hirsch 1977, Bourdieu 1984/1979). Although this focus on conspicuous consumption was sociology's main contribution to consumption studies, it began to be treated as more complex. The relationship between hierarchical social inequalities – especially class – and consumption behaviour began to be seen as less clear-cut for a number of reasons. *Horizontal* differentiation – within social classes and groups – began to be seen as more significant than *vertical* social divisions – between social classes and groups. It was argued that there was less clear-cut classification of consumption practices. A democratisation of taste was occurring that permitted wider access for most of the population to previously exclusive consumption activities. The proliferation of cultural items in consumer culture made it difficult for most people to recognise and rank all of them, and 'a growth of cultural omnivorous-ness which collapses the separation between high and popular culture' developed (Warde 2002, p. 12). Class was seen as a less important social division. Consumption behaviour was considered to be becoming more *individualised* so that lifestyles could no longer be associated with specific social groups. Except for those on the lowest incomes, most people could participate in a similar way in consumer culture, pursuing their own preferences in a self-conscious and self-regarding way.

The third approach concerning the consumption of 'dreams, images and pleasures' was derived from media and cultural studies in which the utopian/positive moments of consumption had been identified and often celebrated. Some of the inspiration for this approach to consumption was derived from the fragmentary writings of Walter Benjamin on the so-called 'Arcades Project' (Buck-Morss 1991, Benjamin 1999). His writings on the shopping arcades in 19th-century Paris are contemplations on mass culture and commodification (Rojek 1997). Benjamin drew attention to the places and people who occupied them – especially the *flaneur* (literally 'male stroller'), the gambler, the rag picker and the prostitute – and indicated that whilst consumer culture involved manipulation it equally contained the germs of a popular creativity and a new democratic aesthetic. Hence in consumer culture there may be a dialectical relationship – between false consciousness and the sources of collective energy and inspiration to overcome that same false consciousness (Buck-Morss 1991, p. 253). Unlike his contemporary and sometime colleague Adorno, Benjamin resisted a totalising critique of mass culture, looking for the utopian moments locked into commodity relations. He argued instead for a re-enchantment of the world that offered both loss and redemption (Buck-Morss 1991, pp. 253–256). For Benjamin the child rather than the adult can negate the various myths of modernity through play. Play has three dimensions – transgression, mimesis/ imitation and collecting. While each of these has come to be manipulated by advertisers (Buck-Morss 1991, p. 274), writers adopting the consumption of pleasure approach concentrate on the opportunities for inspiration that they provide. The Russian critic Bakhtin (1984) explored similar themes in his concept of the 'carnivalesque'. Many writers draw on his discussions of the pre-industrial carnival and show how certain forms of consumer culture have drawn on this tradition which evokes the pleasures of various forms of excess. The impulse towards play, sensation, immediacy and transgression leads to revelling in disorder, ambiguity, artificiality, the strange, exotic and spectacular. In the second half of the 19th century, the music hall, the market place and the department store incorporated aspects of the carnival. Contemporary media (advertisements, video and cinema) and leisure sites (holiday resorts, theme pubs, video arcades, shopping complexes and sports events) illustrate the persistence of carnival, which can also become sites of 'ordered disorder' (Featherstone 1991, p. 23). However, it is worth noting that most writers in this approach recognise that carnival is only temporary. Hence it can be seen as a socially sanctioned transgression that is ultimately instrumental in compelling conformity with the social status quo.

Several writers that adopt the third approach embrace consumption. For them consumption fosters meaningful, non-alienated, work in non-necessary areas of activity (Finnegan 1989, Moorhouse 1991). It promotes 'serious leisure' (Stebbins 1992). Consumption facilitates rebellion, or at least a channel for 'escape attempts', from everyday life (Hebdige 1978, de Certeau 1984, Cohen and Taylor 1992). Consumption also nurtures possessive individualism (see Saunders 1990). This in turn is welcomed because it encourages hard work and increases economic productivity. Robust demand for consumer goods is a major systemic requirement of capitalist economies and the 'work-and-spend' culture that is a central feature of it (Schor 1992, Cross 1993). The accumulation of property and possessions may be quite harmless and a stimulating source of personal satisfaction. 'Rather than being manipulated pawns of marketers, collectors are proactive de-commodifiers of goods who creatively wrest meaning from the marketplace' (Belk 2001/1995, pp. 157–158). 'Enthusiasms' is the general term that Alan Warde (2002) uses to describe much contemporary leisure time activity. He argues that, unless conducted in total isolation, enthusiasms are generally 'positive both for the individuals concerned and because they involve social participation which builds social capital and sustains relationships of civil society'. Hence taking part in or attending a classic car rally, a football match, a flower show or a sheep-dog trial can all be seen as a 'means of confirming group membership and belonging'. As such, he asks, what is wrong with consumption if it 'can promote comfort, pleasure, self-esteem, escape and decontrol'? (Warde 2002, p. 17).

Criticisms of these two approaches to consumption have focussed on three issues. First, the modes of consumption and pleasures of consumption approaches have tended to research spectacular, rather than mundane, consumption. Most consumption is probably mundane, routine and inconspicuous – made out of habit rather than fully conscious reflection (Warde 2002, p. 19). Yet the processes such as habituation, routinisation, normalisation and appropriation are key bases of the compulsion to consume particular goods and services and worthy of investigation. From where does the need to consume arise? As Barrington Moore Jr (1969, p. 486) once wrote in *Social Origins of Dictatorship and Democracy*, 'To maintain and transmit a value system, human beings are punched, bullied, sent to jail, thrown into concentration camps, cajoled, bribed, made into heroes, encouraged to read newspapers, stood up against a wall and shot, and sometimes even taught sociology.' To this we might add that they are also encouraged to participate in and watch sport and develop consumer values such as judging worth on the basis of personal benefit.

Secondly, there has been a focus on identity and pleasure as opposed to what might be called the 'real world' of consumption – the investigation of consumption as possible defence mechanisms against alienation, anxiety and ontological insecurity. The sociological orthodoxy with respect to consumption used to be one of critique. Consumption and consumer culture were considered to have detrimental effects on personal character, waste, privatism and disregard for the people whose labour was embodied in commodities. Television viewing, for example, can put one in touch with, but also veil, reality. As such consumption can become a strategy of survival. Thirdly, the uncritical populist emphasis on the active and (apparently) powerful consumer ignores the wider structural forces of exploitation and injustice. As Warde (2002, p. 17) also noted, few enthusiasms 'could now operate without either the availability of commercially manufactured equipment or commercially organised events and meetings'. Warde (2002, p. 12) argues that the irony is that 'Sociologists seem to be losing interest in the determining aspects of the system of commodity production and exchange just as it seems set to consolidate further its grip on consumption behaviour'. Advertising spending grows, production increasingly concentrates, globalisation enables the targeting of larger audiences, creating needs is not hidden, and moreover 'commodification is accelerating, with the alternatives to commodity exchange – through state provision, communal reciprocity and household production – consequently in decline' (Warde 2002, p. 12).

Understanding Contemporary Consumer Culture

How are we to make sense of these developments? Again it is important to clarify the meanings of the terms. The economist Juliet Schor (1998, p. 217n) adopts the following definitions in her book *The Overspent American*. For Schor 'consumption' refers to all monetary expenditure, whilst a 'consumer society' is one in which discretionary consumption has become a mass phenom-enon and consumerism has become a way of life. This 'consumerist society' is underpinned by a consumer culture in which 'Nonsatiation becomes the general norm' (p. 217n) and social and political stability become dependent on the delivery of consumer goods. Whilst sociologists might want to expand the definition of consumption, it is clear that sociologist Zygmunt Bauman using slightly different conceptual language makes a similar point about what he calls 'the consumer attitude' and 'the consumerist syndrome' (Bauman and May 2001, Bauman 2004a). In the transition from what he calls 'solid' to 'liquid modernity', he argues that needs have been replaced by desires, wants and even wishes as the main motivators of consumption (Bauman 2004a, p. 297). There is a shift from social order being chiefly secured through normative regulation and policing to it being secured through needs arousal and seduction. To ensure that economic growth is about perpetual acceleration in wants and desires is the job of, amongst other cultural intermediaries, marketing and advertising specialists.

Abercrombie et al. (2000, pp. 71–72) outline key features of consumer society – 'modern societies...increasingly organised around consumption' (p. 71) – that we will encounter in different parts of this book. Consumer society is one in which there is rising affluence, with more money spent on consumer goods and experiential commodities such as holidays, sport and leisure. Declining working hours since the 19th century have provided more time for sport and leisure. In these circumstances consumption and leisure become key sites of personal identity formation – and this creates a consumer culture (or way of life). Some argue that the aestheticisation of everyday life through the consumption of commodities based on desires, not needs, leads to a greater emphasis being placed on the construction of coherent lifestyles. Lifestyles and the consumption of what economists call 'positional goods' act as signs of social position or status distinction. Following this it is suggested that social class, gender and race are (or are being) replaced as the major sources of social division by consumption cleavages – between how different people acquire goods and services. It is also suggested that growing consumer power over the production of goods and services influences production decisions, and the economic power of the consumer increasingly replaces the political rights and duties of the citizen. Finally, Abercrombie et al. note that some view the increased commodification of products and services on a market basis that were previously not accessible in this way as having implications for their format, distribution and accessibility. It also leads to the shopping/consumer experience becoming a leisure activity.

Abercrombie et al. note that it is not clear that these developments all exist with equal prominence, whether they are socially positive or negative and what their significance is – epochal, transitory or superficial amidst continuity? Since class, gender and race divisions remain important sources of social differentiation, only a minority are involved in the aestheticisation of everyday life, and the power of consumers is somewhat overstated, it can be suggested that consumer society masks the extension or expansion of capitalist values to wider aspects of more people's lives. We will consider these arguments as part of three main concerns about contemporary consumer society – growing inequality, increased commodification and globalisation (Holt and Schor 2000).

Inequality in the distribution of wealth and consumer spending in consumer societies continues to grow despite apparent equality on the basis of the ability to pay using credit facilities. Personal borrowing has grown (reaching 1 trillion pounds – 12 noughts! – in July 2004 in the UK alone). There is an assumption of achievement of social position through a meritocracy, but for many of the population of consumer societies the reality is continuing ascription. As Bauman (2004b, p. 39) notes, 'consumers are the prime assets of consumer society, flawed consumers are its most irksome and costly liabilities'. The individualisation of choices and risks is part of this development (Urry 1995, p. 118, Bauman and May 2001, Beck and Beck-Gernsheim 2002). In working life this is experienced as the growth of '*institutionalized precariousness*' (Bourdieu 2003, p. 29) or 'precarization' (Bauman 2004c in Gane 2004).

About the former, Bourdieu (2003, p. 29) states that it is 'a mode of production that entails a mode of domination based on the *institution of insecurity*, domination through precariousness: a deregulated financial market fosters a deregulated labor market and thereby the casualization of labor that cows workers into submission'. By the latter, Bauman refers to 'the deliberate expansion of the element of uncertainty in the existential modality of the dominated' (Bauman 2004c in Gane 2004, p. 251). To write about sport in consumer culture in a world in which relative wealth shares and life chances are more polarised than ever might seem to some like an indulgence and an irrelevance (Smith 2003, Bauman 2004b). For Eco (1986, p. 165) 'sports chatter is the glorification of Waste, and therefore the maximum point of Consumption. On it and in it the consumer civilization man actually consumes himself.' Rather than provide another example of the 'phatic speech' that Umberto Eco has suggested surrounds all 'sports chatter' (Eco 1986, pp. 159–165) however this book seeks to provide a means of understanding the contemporary social significance of sport.

Increased commodification refers to the growth of a market-mediated mode of life and the marketisation of goods and services hitherto mainly available outside the profit nexus (Frank 2000). Marketisation or commodification has grown rapidly in many areas of non-market life in the last two decades of the 20th century (Leys 2001). Concerns expressed about the failings of the market (O'Neill 1998, Smart 2003) raise interesting questions about whether some goods and services should be *hors commerce* ('outside the commercial market'). Should sport be treated in this way? To take one example, the New England Patriots secured their third Super Bowl victory in four years (and record equalling ninth successive post-season win) in February 2005 at *Alltel* Stadium, in Jacksonville, Florida. This raises the issue of the increasing commercialisation of public space. Should sports arenas which were 'previously named for communities' now 'sport corporate logos'? (Holt and Schor 2000,

p. ix). Another issue is the impact of the symbolism and branding of sport and sports celebrities as public channels for creating meanings, and *consumer*, rather than *citizen*, consciousness (Whitson and Gruneau 1997). Sport and sports celebrities can provide an 'international currency' (Jackson et al. 2005) for reimagining the nation via promotional culture (Gruneau and Whitson 1993, Silk et al. 2005). Wernick (1991, p. 106) noted how 'anyone whose name and fame have been built up to the point where reference to them, via mention, mediatised representation or live appearance, can serve as a promotional booster in itself'. Hence sport stars act as intermediaries, but with a dynamic of their own in which celebrity-hood can become 'free floating' (Wernick 1991, p. 109). The use value of celebrities is not their consumption so much as their 'associative power to move other merchandise' (Wernick 1991, p. 109). As Smart (2003, p. 77) notes, celebrity brands promote a way of living, doing something, and being. Bauman (2004a, p. 303) states that 'brands breathe authority'.

In circumstances where there appears to be only *One Market Under God* (Frank 2000) nothing is uncommodifiable. Even forms of resistance can be co-opted as signs of lifestyle creativity. Differences, dissent and opposition have all been used in advertising as commodity signs (Frank 1997, and on consumer culture in the USA in the early 20th century also see Ewen 1976). The deployment of irreverence or 'preemptive irony' in advertising and marketing has not only contributed to the spread of social informalisation since the 1960s but it has also punctured a hole in debates about authenticity.

Globalisation is the third main concern that we shall consider in this book. Capitalist economics and the associated ideology of consumerism has been spreading for decades but since the end of the 1980s and the collapse of the Soviet Union it has taken off globally (Sklair 2002). In this context, Jay Coakley and Peter Donnelly (2004, p. 330) identify two main reasons why commercial sports have also become global in scope. The first is that driven by the profit motive the owners of sport are always looking to expand their markets and increase their profits. The second is that transnational companies, as sponsors, can use sport to promote their goods and services in new markets. That business strategies developed in one society may work well in other parts of the world is an argument that underpins George Ritzer's 'McDonaldization thesis' (Ritzer 1993). Recently, Alan Bryman has suggested that in 21st-century marketing and branding the 'ludic ambience' developed by the Disney Corporation (Bryman 2004) increasingly acts as an ideal template for the spread of contemporary consumer cultures of advanced Post-Fordist capitalism throughout the world. However, efforts to use successful sports clubs to make money may come up against stiff opposition if they conflict with the social and cultural values and meanings associated with the teams. This partly helps to explain the protests staged by fans and the initial reticence of the board of Manchester United to embrace an offer – valuing the club at £787 million – made by Malcolm Glazer, the fish-oil and property tycoon ranked the 278th richest American by

Forbes magazine, in February 2005 (*The Economist* 26 February 2005, p. 72). What worked well in the USA – since Glazer bought the Tampa Bay Buccaneers (American Football) team for US$ 192 million in 1995, it was thought to have grown in value to nearly US$ 800 million in 2005 – was not received in the same way on the other side of the Atlantic Ocean.

And Finally: An Introduction to the Discipline and the Rest of the Book

To engage in sport requires discipline. So too does the attempt to discuss, explain and understand sport in society. This book attempts to do this through an examination of contemporary developments in sport via the literature of social science (primarily sociology) and sport studies. Sociology offers a means of approaching a subject which few other disciplines can match. There are five main features of sociology that make it helpful in making sense of sport in consumer society. First, sociology encourages taking a wide view of issues and problems, seeing them in social and historical context and making connections between different aspects of social life. Secondly, because sociology is interested in more than just the economic, political or business aspects of sport, it requires us to put aside partial perspectives and consider how different academic and theoretical approaches make sense of sport. Sociology is inherently theoretical and comparative – against how other disciplines see the same topic or how different social formations develop. Thirdly, and because of the first two features, sociological insight provides knowledge that is useful to everyone, as consumers or citizens, students or researchers. Fourthly, sociology is a 'critical activity' (Burns 1995, p. 174). The purpose is 'to achieve an understanding of social behaviour and social institutions which is different from that current among the people through whose conduct the institutions exist; an under-standing that is not merely different but new and better' (Burns 1995, p. 174). Fifthly, sociology is an empirical discipline in so far as the different perspectives, theories and critiques are open to assessment and evaluation by reference to research. Pierre Bourdieu once compared sociology with the martial arts: 'I often say sociology is a martial art, a means of self-defense. Basically, you use it to defend yourself, without having the right to use if for unfair attacks' (Pierre Bourdieu in 'La Sociologie est un Sport de Combat', F 2000, directed by Pierre Carles).

There are alternative theoretical approaches in sociology, but it is not our intention to argue for one or other of these here (Giulianotti 2004, 2005). As sports historian Allen Guttmann (1992, p. 158) once observed in relation to the figurational approach (of Dunning and Elias), 'no key turns all locks'. Like Zygmunt Bauman (2004a), on the one hand we believe that it is important to be wary of 'school loyalty' (which can even turn into 'school confinement') since as a rule it signals a drive to promote one theory to the exclusion of others and wind up the argument rather than open it up. The last thing you want from a book is a wind up. On the other hand, we are convinced that there is a need to approach the study of sport in consumer culture with more emphasis placed on the production of consumption than has hitherto been the case. We hope, therefore, that this book opens up arguments and generates ideas about a new research agenda in sociology of sport.

The Structure of the Book

The structure of the book is as follows. There are three parts dealing with each of the major issues identified above. Part I focusses on globalisation, consumerisation and the mass media. Chapter 2 outlines the size, composition and trends in the global sports market. The development of professional sport in the UK and the USA, and the impact of commodification on sports fans, and players are assessed. Chapter 3 deals with the sport–media relationship and the growth of sports coverage in the media. The political economy of the ownership and control of the media and sport is assessed through a case study of Murdochization and the escalation of media rights payments for sports events and leagues. The relationship between sports journalism, fans and audiences is considered as constituting a process of consumerisation.

Part II of the book deals with commodification, regulation and power. Chapter 4 considers the importance of sponsorship and advertising for contemporary sport. Advertising and marketing agencies and organisations acting as cultural intermediaries facilitate the process of commodification. Chapter 5 deals with the politics of sports consumption. In the past twenty years, government sports policy – concerning regulation, consumer protection and sports promotion – has developed in a context of the spread of neo-liberal economic ideology and globalisation. This has produced a change in the relationship between sport and the state. Different states use sport for different non-sports ends. The state constructs what is and what is not legitimate sports practice and in doing so effectively determines what the sports consumers' interest is. Finally Part III (lifestyles, identities and social divisions) contains Chapter 6 which asks how much has leisure and sport specifically become a site for identity formation? What are the coherent lifestyles constructed around sport? How, if at all, as a result of increasing consumerisation, has the role of sport in the construction, maintenance and challenging of lifestyles and identities altered? Chapter 7 examines differences in patterns of involvement and participation in sport by class, gender and 'race' and the consumerisation of sport especially aimed at children. The concluding chapter, Chapter 8, summarises the book and indicates that the research agenda in sociology of sport needs to consider consumer processes and politics more centrally than it has done to date.

Part I

Globalisation, Consumerisation
and the Mass Media

2

Consumer Culture and the Global Sports Market

Introduction

This chapter focusses on the development of institutions and structures that have assisted in the development, ownership and control of sport in consumer culture. It focusses mainly on what sport in consumer culture does to people, rather than what people do with sport in consumer culture. The chapter provides details about the development of consumer culture and the place of sport within it. It examines data about the size, composition, trends and economic significance of the sport goods and services market globally and in the UK. It examines the development of modern professional sport – and finally it considers how fans have responded to commodification and marketisation.

The Development of the Mass Market for Sport in the UK and North America

Hargreaves (1986, pp. 114ff.) outlined five different economic relationships that (theoretically) could obtain between sport and capital. Even though economic and non-economic motivations often overlap in practice, and several of these relationships can be at work simultaneously, it is a useful way in which to comprehend sport as a commercial industry. Some sports are profit maximising. This is most evident in the USA in the approach of professional sports team owners, although few sports have had such aspirations in the UK (for example, professional boxing and horse racing) and most have simply sought to break even. Some sports survive through fund raising, usually conducted by volunteers and supporters. The indirect stimulus to capital accumulation by providing a market for sports-related goods and services has shaped the equipment, clothing and gambling industries. A second form of indirect stimulus is by offering the opportunity for non-sports-related goods and services to advertise and sponsor and thus promote themselves. Finally some investment occurs for non-direct economic reasons – such as prestige, desire for local influence, or the use of sports facilities for corporate entertainment purposes.

Each of these features can be found as modern sport developed at the same time as the emergence of modern consumption practices and the 'mass market' (Fraser 1981). Developments in retailing, department stores and chains of shops, were accompanied by the growth of mass circulation newspapers and magazines. Sport, like advertising, can be seen as both constitutive of meaning in modern everyday life and also part of the 'magic system' that Williams (1980) identified which helps in the promotion and marketing of goods in capitalist economies. Participants in sport lend themselves to becoming agents of the promotion of goods and services ('endorsees') and 'media sport stars' (Whannel 2002a). Sport as a mass-mediated spectacle helps to sell newspapers and other channels of communication whilst at the same time encouraging sports enthusiasm.

Sports historian Tony Mason notes that 'Business and sport have never been entirely unconnected in Britain', although the relationship was not always a straightforward commercial one. One hundred years ago the 'entrepreneur was not attracted to sport for the profit that could be made out of it' (Mason 1988, p. 115). Hence football clubs were limited liability companies with boards of directors and shareholders, but dividends were limited to 5 per cent and directors were not paid. In the USA by comparison, it was the profit maximisers who won the battle between those 'who saw sport as something separate from business and those who saw no reason not to make profit from sport' (Mason 1988, p. 115). A brief consideration of the sports market in the UK and the USA will illustrate the differences.

By 1895 one estimate suggests that British expenditure on sport reached £47 million per year and that investment in sport represented 3 per cent of gross national product (GNP) (Mitchell and Deane 1988, p. 828). By 1912 expenditure on golf alone was £7 million, with £600,000 being spent on 7.2 million golf balls annually. Growth of manufacturing in golf and cycling was also partly responsible for economic recovery in areas affected by economic depression. Whilst in 1892, 915,856 cycles were exported at 'the height of the cycling boom, in 1896, the figure had increased to 1,855,604' (Lowerson 1995, p. 226). Other sports required equipment to be imported but many middle-class people seized the new investment opportunities offered by sport. 'They generated not only income and capital formation but also social prestige and opportunities for local influence, so that expected gains were not always expressed in economic terms' (Lowerson 1995, p. 226). Mason (1980) and Korr (1986) amongst others have shown how businessmen and professionals manipulated local status networks to enable professional football to develop. Boards of football clubs had a minority working-class presence: the dominant groups were wholesalers and retailers (Mason 1980, pp. 33–43).

Benson (1994) summarised changes in the consumer experience of shopping, tourism and sport between 1880 and 1980 in Britain. He posed the question:

how did people's interest in sport influence their behaviour as consumers; as players buying equipment, clothes and footwear; as spectators paying for tickets and entrance fees; as enthusiasts buying books, magazines and newspapers; and as gamblers visiting bookmakers and betting shops? We can also add as entrepreneurs interested in the production of sport as a part of consumer society. Benson argued that there has been: a major increase in the reorientation in the amount of money spent playing sport; increases in the amount spent watching sport; and increases in the amount spent gambling on sport. These changes have been differently experienced according to place of residence, age, social class and gender.

Varda Burstyn (1999) focusses more on class and gender relations in her award-winning study of the development of sport in North America. She argues that at the beginning of the 20th century – the outset of consumer culture in North America – people preferred to trade leisure hours for work hours, instead of working harder in order to buy more consumption goods. In order to stimulate demand a different strategy was adopted. To promote consumption commercial propaganda – advertising – was developed. North American workers had to be persuaded to change their attitude from being investors in the future to being spenders in the present (Ewen 1976). The key was 'the organised creation of dissatisfaction' (Burstyn 1999, p. 109) and this lies at the centre of advertising in consumer culture to this day. Advertising for many consumer goods and services shifted from relying on utilitarian arguments and descriptive information to emotional appeals relating to social status and social differentiation. The source of social status also shifted: from being able to make things, the ability to buy them – wealth – began to count. The 1930s were the years of economic depression but images of wealth and plenty in such popular cultural forms as Hollywood films kept such status dreams alive.

Sport was linked to this in the USA in a number of ways. It could attract large audiences to radio but also could be used to sell other goods. In 1939 Gillette paid $100,000 for exclusive coverage of the baseball World Series. Sales increased by 350 per cent. Baseball teams began to negotiate individual radio contracts. The salaries of players increased. Advertising, increasingly targeted at male sports fans, developed further. Team owners and athletes were more concerned with national media audiences rather than the local game and audience. Burstyn argues that the media moved from covering sport and gaining from it indirectly, to effectively controlling it (Burstyn 1999, p. 112).

The 1950s and 1960s saw the further 'athleticisation' of North American culture, and government legislation (Public Law 87–33) permitted professional sports teams to combine their broadcast rights in order to sell them to the highest bidder (in effect to become monopolies). Sports audiences were thus made and attracted advertisers who wanted to reach the lucrative male market. The 'de facto' power of television over athletes and teams expanded. Corporations were prepared to pay a great deal for exclusive access to the male sports audience. By February 2005 broadcaster Fox could charge $2.4 (£1.3) million for each of the 59 thirty-second advertising slots during the XXXIX NFL Superbowl held in Jacksonville (*The Guardian* 5 February 2005, p. 14).

Consumer magazines have helped to sustain this market. In North America today *Sports Illustrated* is the third highest advertising revenue magazine. Marketing of sport in the media has created a large economy of sport-related products. But this has largely been a male market. As Cohen (2003, p. 505n) remarks, 'The emergence of men's magazines such as *Playboy* (1953) and *Sports Illustrated* (1954) in the postwar era provided an important vehicle for male-oriented advertising.' Sport helps to 'deliver the male' to advertisers (see Davis 1997).

Burstyn argues that desire and anxiety are the two key emotions that have been used to make people buy things in consumer culture – and since the 1970s this has increasingly been done using psycho-demographics and market segmentation techniques. The formula involved in the former is the creation of a brand image that a product can deliver something that a potential consumer will find desirable – a more beautiful body, sexual attractiveness, friendship. Without it an anxiety is created that suggests these things will otherwise be unobtainable. On the other hand, market segmentation is an active process of constructing consumer subjectivity where 'before there had been nothing but inchoate feelings and common responses to pollsters' questions' (Frank 1997, p. 24). Frank cites a business historian, R.S. Tedlow: 'Pepsi and other such companies have been more interested in the term segment as a verb than as a noun. They have segmented markets, rather than merely responded to a market segment that already existed. There was no such thing as the Pepsi Generation until Pepsi invented it' (cited in Frank 1997, p. 24).

The Global Sporting Goods Market

One measure of the contemporary global economic significance of sport is retail sports sales figures. An Euromonitor report in 2001 revealed that the consumption of sport was largely the preserve of the advanced capitalist countries (Euromonitor 2001). The USA, Japan, the UK and Germany lead the world in terms of retail sales and retail outlets for sports goods and apparel. Sports clothing and equipment each account for about 40 per cent of the total sales of sports goods and services. Footwear sales account for the other 20 per cent. The US market for sports clothing was worth an estimated $32 billion, ten times the UK market and nearly half of the entire worldwide market of $70 billion in 1999 (Understanding Global Issues 2000). Within the European Community in 2001 the leading countries by economic turnover of sports goods and equipment were Germany, France, the UK, Italy and Spain. Together these countries represented 35 per cent of global sales of sports clothing and shoes, whilst the USA had 42 per cent, Asia 16 per cent and the rest of the world 7 per cent (Ohl and Tribou 2004, p. 142).

Where did this market come from? How did it emerge? The sports goods industry arguably was 'born in the USA'. The US sporting economy overall was worth US$194 billion in 2001 – ahead of chemicals, electronics and food (Schaaf 2004, pp. 325–326). It amounted to more than one per cent of the value of all goods and services produced in the USA. There are 150 major sports franchises, a dozen professional sports tours (such as the P.G.A.) and hundreds of other commercial sports events (Sage 1998, pp. 129–158). As Sage (1998, p. 131) notes, however, contemporary sport 'needs to be understood as a historical moment: today's highly commercialised sport industry is not a cultural universal'. It has been shaped by cultural, political and especially economic forces operating increasingly on a global scale (Miller et al. 2001).

Miller et al. (2001) suggest that the best way of understanding the growth of the sports industry is by using global political economy. Transnational corporations (TNCs) based in advanced capitalist countries have undergone consolidation through mergers and acquisitions. Global horizontal and vertical integration has occurred. The network approach to production and sub-contracting has lead to the existence of several 'vertically dis-aggregated network organisations' (Dicken 1998, p. 234) in the sports goods industry. There has been a transfer of labour-intensive production to the less developed 'South' or Third World. In some of these, 'export-oriented industrialization' has created a New International Division of Labour (NIDL). Miller et al. (2001) suggest that in sport there is a New International Division of Cultural Labour (NICL). In 2001, for example, Nike products were made in 68 factories worldwide, but 57 of them were in Asian countries and only 8 were in the Americas where the Nike headquarters is. More than half a million people were employed in these factories – although strictly speaking they are not 'Nike employees' because they are not directly employed by Nike – and over half of these people were in China or Indonesia (Smith 2003, p. 100).

Reasons for the NICL include the facts that wages are lower and worker benefits fewer in developing countries. There are also fewer organised (unionised) workforces. Hence there is greater management control over the labour process. In addition there are less stringent or simply poorly enforced health and safety regulations. Finally there are fewer stringent environmental and community health and safety regulations. Here are two further illustrations of the NICL in operation.

George Sage (2000, p. 272) describes the actions of the Rawlings Sporting Goods Co. (originally) of St Louis that supplies baseballs for Major League Baseball (MLB) in North America. In 1953 the firm moved manufacturing from St Louis to Licking, Missouri (a non-union plant). In 1964 it moved to Puerto Rico (exploiting a tax 'holiday' for inward investment). In 1969 it moved to Haiti (the poorest country in the Western Hemisphere, where strikes were illegal). In 1990 Rawlings moved to Costa Rica where the factory sewers stitched 30–35 balls a day for US$5–6 and pieceworkers at home earned 15 cents a ball. Christian Aid, in research carried out in 1995, found that in Nike and Reebok factories in Asia two-thirds of the workers were women under the age of 25. Typical workers in Indonesian plants were paid the equivalent of (US) 19 cents an hour, with 10 and a half-hour days, six days a week, with forced overtime. The monthly wage was 30 per cent less than that required to meet 'minimum physical needs'. Hence a pair of trainers sold for £50 in the UK, was made in a production process involving 40 workers who were paid a total of £1 between them. The Nike Air Pegasus sold for US$ 70 in the USA only incurred labour costs of US$1.66 to make. In 2004 Oxfam produced another report, *Play Fair at the Olympics*, which revealed further details of poor working conditions in factories run by the UK-based sportswear company Umbro, including excessive working hours and poor wages.

As we have noted, most sales of sports goods occur in the developed world, yet the bulk of the manufacturing of them is carried out in the poorer less-developed countries for Nike Inc., and other companies such as Reebok International, Adidas-Salomon, K-Swiss Inc. and the Pentland Group. Researchers have drawn attention to the existence of 'global commodity chains' – or the trans-nationalisation – of sports goods manufacturing (Reich, 1991). The commodity circuitry of the Nike shoe has been illustrated by Goldman and Papson (1998, p. 8). Sports participants in the richer countries rely on the manufacturing, distribution and circulation of goods from a global sports industry whose key characteristics are sweatshops, high profit margins and the exploitation of vulnerable groups of workers. The great excesses of capitalist commodification are just as likely to be found in sports goods manufacture as anywhere else. Hence there has been a backlash against the brands (Klein 2000a, Kingsnorth 2003).

Estimating the Economic Significance of Sport in the UK

For information about the total economic significance of sport in the UK we have to rely upon estimates. Benson (1994) accepted that his figures were based upon insecure foundations. Vamplew (1988), Lowerson (1995) and Gratton and Taylor (2000) make equally cautious comments about the lack of precision in economic data on the sports industry. Allowing for these limitations, Benson made the following points about spending on sports goods and services in Britain during much of the 20th century.

Between 1914 and 1979/1981 there was an overall growth in consumer spending on sport. This was the case despite the fact that the proportion of participants spending appears to decline over the period. Benson argues that this was because of the distortion caused by the very expensive costs of golf and tennis in 1914. At the beginning of the 20th century, for example, it was calculated that the average golf club member spent £25 a year on his hobby – equivalent to three months earnings of a well-established clerical worker. These expensive sports have seen their popularity increase over the period whilst previously inexpensive sports – like football, angling and athletics – have seen their costs rise. Whilst information about spectator spending is equally difficult to provide with absolute precision, it would appear that spending has also grown during the period. In 1979 golf, tennis, football and angling accounted for over one quarter of all expenditure on sport goods and equipment (Benson 1994, p. 112). Other sports-related goods and services – such as books, magazines, toys, models and pictures – have also seen expenditure rises. Gambling remains the largest single identifiable amount of sport-related expenditure, however, or as Benson (1994, p. 117) put it, 'the amount of money spent gambling on sport has always been many times larger than the amount spent playing it and watching it'.

The UK government's official statistical survey of annual expenditure, *Family Spending*, contains more recent information about expenditure on sport. In the report for 2000–2001 it was estimated that every week in Britain each person spent £3.30 on sports admissions and subscriptions to sports clubs and other forms of participant sport. In 2000–2001 over £5.2 billion was spent on sports and camping equipment, whilst nearly £4.3 billion was spent on sports admissions and subscriptions (ONS 2001, pp. 128–129). Another £3.90 per head per week was spent on gambling, about a third of which was related to sport in some form or another – horse or greyhound racing, football pools or sporting results. This estimate portrays the UK as a nation of gamblers – over one-third of the annual expenditure on sport is reported as on some form or other of gambling.

The official account is not the only set of data about sport's contribution to the economy however. The leisure industry as a whole accounts for over a quarter of all consumer spending in the UK and spending on sport has increased considerably in the past twenty years. Between 1985 and 1995 consumer expenditure on sport grew by 30 per cent (Gratton and Taylor 2000). Davies (2002) argues that the official measurement of spending on sport tends towards an underestimate of the real figure. She argues that when 'consumers are specifically asked how much they spend on participating and watching sport ... higher levels of expenditure are revealed than otherwise found using a general household survey' (Davies 2002, p. 101). Hence her conclusion is that planners and policy-makers alike in the public and private sector would benefit from a regular independent survey of consumer spending on sport in the UK. Davies suggests that statistics such as those compiled by economists Chris Gratton and Peter Taylor represent a more accurate picture.

According to Gratton and Taylor (2000, p. 19), consumer expenditure on sport in the UK in 1995 was £10.4 billion or 2.3 per cent of total consumer expenditure. The value added to the UK economy by sport-related economic activity was £9.8 billion or 1.6 per cent of Gross Domestic Product (GDP). In the same year, employment in sport was estimated to be 415,000, compared to 324,470 people in 1985. That is, sport accounted for 1.6 per cent of employment in the UK in 1995 compared with 1.52 per cent ten years earlier. Research conducted by Gratton and Taylor's research units at the Universities of Sheffield and Sheffield Hallam on behalf of **sport**scotland (formerly the Scottish Sports Council) suggests that similar proportions of sport-related economic activity occur in at least one part of the devolved UK. In 1998 £1.08 billion or 2.55 per cent of total consumer spending in Scotland was on sport. Of the spending on sport in Scotland £264 million was on gambling (**sport**scotland 2001). Sport accounted for 38,200 jobs or 1.68 per cent of total employment in Scotland. The value added by sport-related economic activity was £1.04 billion or 1.76 per cent of Scottish GDP (**sport**scotland 2001, downloadable from the 'research' section of the website www.sportscotland. org.uk).

Gratton and Taylor's research units also produce an annually revised publication *Sport Market Forecasts* that draws upon relevant official and independent research sources to compile a snapshot picture of sport-related consumer expenditure. From the report for 2002 the following features were most noteworthy. Spending on sports *goods* amounted to £5.706 billion in 2002. This was just over one-third (34.6 per cent) of the total spent on sport in the UK. Of this clothing and footwear amounted to just under 20 per cent and equipment and boats 11.5 per cent. Walking and hiking clothing and trainers and running shoes accounted for the biggest share of sales of sports apparel and footwear. Golf and fitness equipment accounted for the largest share of sales of sports equipment. Books, magazines and newspapers are included in the category 'publications'. The SIRC report attributes a specific share of total expenditure on newspapers to the sport market 'based on the average share of sport in the total content of newspapers' (SIRC 2003, p. 4).

On sport-related *services* £10.782 billion (or 65.4 per cent of the total) was spent. The largest sector of the sport services market was gambling accounting for 15.8 per cent. Of this, horse racing accounted for 70 per cent of all sports-related gambling. The entry on participation sports included admission fees and subscriptions to voluntary sports clubs and public sector sports centres and swimming pools. 'Health and fitness' includes fees for private health and fitness clubs and this has been the second most rapid growth area since the late 1990s. Together membership fees and subscriptions accounted for 24.3 per cent of service expenditure. Sport-related TV and video expenditure – including subscriptions to satellite, digital and cable TV channels – included an estimate for the sport component of the TV licence fee. This has been the most rapid growth area since the late 1990s. The 'Other' category included food, drink and accommodation associated with participation, spectating and other forms of involvement at sport events. The total figure of £16.488 billion was equivalent to approximately 2 per cent of GDP and 2.5 per cent of total consumer expenditure.

The SIRC report noted that 'Although the media has emphasised the strong growth over the recent past in professional sport, and in particular football, consumer expenditure in the sport market consists in the main of expenditures related to the consumer's own participation in sport rather than to sport spectating' (SIRC 2003, p. 4). This conclusion is consistent with other attempts by Gratton to chart the economic significance of sport (see for example Gratton 1998). One indicator of this is the increase in gym membership. In the past ten years private companies such as Cannons, David Lloyd, Fitness First, Holmes Place, LA Fitness and New Generation have developed their market. There are around 2600 private clubs in addition to the public sector leisure centres. Despite warnings that some health and fitness clubs were locking their members into long contracts with large cancellation penalties some 18.6 per cent of the UK population (8.6 million people) have joined. Turnover for private health clubs reached £1.85 billion in 2003, from £1.23 billion in 1999 according to Mintel (Jefferies 2004).

Professional Sport, Commercialisation and Consumer Culture

Under what conditions do commercial sports emerge and prosper? Jay Coakley (2003, pp. 364–366) suggests that the formation of commercial sport relied on specific circumstances that could be found in certain countries especially in North America and Western Europe approximately 100 years ago. First, the existence of market economies in which athletes, team owners, event sponsors and spectators were able to develop. Secondly, large, predominantly urban populations, with time, money and freedom of movement were also required. Thirdly, capital investment of both a public, municipal and governmental, and private kind was necessary. In these ways he suggests that consumer capitalism helped stimulate sport. An urbanised industrial society with relatively efficient transportation and communication systems combined with a standard of living that allowed people the time and money to play and watch sports was the ideal environment for the emergence of commercial sport (Coakley 2003, pp. 364–365). Social class and gender relations were also involved – certain groups being more likely to spectate at certain sports. Spectator interest then developed out of a combination of the 'quest for excitement' (Elias and Dunning 1986), ideologies of hard work and achievement, and programmes of youth sport and media coverage that introduced people to sports and its rules (Coakley 2003, pp. 366–368).

The relationship of sport to commodification and commercialisation has been a constituent feature of debates about modern professional sport since its inception at the end of the 19th century and the beginning of the 20th century. Money especially has been seen as a problem since the outset of modern sport for several reasons (Eitzen 2001, pp. 236–264). Money leads to problems of excess for a variety of reasons. It can impact on athlete's motivations and impact on the outcomes of sports events and fixtures. Some concern has been raised about the profit motive stimulating the desire to obtain monopolies over sporting success (for example, in Formula One motor racing, see Turner 2005). Others note the potential for the undermining of the 'uncertainty of outcome' in sport if leagues and other competitions become unfairly balanced (Michie and Oughton 2004). A favourite of the newspaper press is to highlight the differential rewards for 'star' players as opposed to only 'average' players. Recently the source of the money from sponsors or patrons of sport and the nature of the industries that finance sport have also been questioned (for example enabling Chelsea Football Club to purchase very expensive players, see Scott 2005). The costs of being a spectator or a fan of leading professional sports have been rising much faster than the rate of inflation. In addition, reservations are being increasingly expressed about the opportunity costs, as well as benefits, of being a location for a major team or club, and the opportunity costs and benefits of hosting sports 'mega-events', such as the Olympic Games or the Fédération Internationale de Football Association (FIFA) football World Cup (Horne and Manzenreiter 2004).

At the same time it is important to note that the relationship of sport to commercialism has taken on different forms in different sports in different societies at different times. These differences reflect the balance between sport as a form of entertainment and sport as essentially an aspect of education (or a public good). National and international institutions and structures that govern sport have influenced this balance in turn. The two main models of the financing of professional sport are essentially the European and the North American. In Europe the main tradition has been for leagues to be open – entry being on the basis of ability and promotion/relegation between different divisions being decided by overall performance throughout a season. This partly relates to their relationship with educational institutions and principles. In North America, however, the leagues have tended to be closed – open to a certain number of franchises only. Entry (and exit) has been regulated more by the ability of teams to attract sufficient local support and hence finance. Here the model is more influenced by the principles of the commercial entertainment industry.

Globally since the 1960s there has been a slow but steadily increasing shift from European model ascendancy to the North American model. In part Donnelly (1996) describes this as a shift from 'amateur' Olympism to 'Prolympism'. This new articulation of sport with commerce stems also from 'the absence of a sufficient level of philanthropic support and state aid' (Hargreaves 1987, p. 149). Hargreaves continues: 'organized sport has come to rely increasingly on capital and on modern capitalist management and marketing techniques... sport now functions increasingly as a specialized branch of the entertainment industry'. There have been three crucial stages along the way. First, the International Olympic Committee (IOC) and then other formerly amateur organisations (for example the International Rugby Union) have changed their regulations with respect to professionalism. Secondly, international and national sports organisations have increasingly sought to maximise revenues through commercial sponsorship agreements and enhanced broadcasting rights contracts (for example, FIFA). Thirdly, explicitly commercial sports leagues – such as MLB, the National Basketball Association (NBA) and the National Football League (NFL) – have aggressively attempted, with varying degrees of success, to market their operations on a global scale. We will consider these developments by first looking at professional North American sport (the 'majors') and then association football in the UK.

Making the Majors

According to Leifer (1995) in the 1960s national exposure of selected NFL (American football) games on US TV built up general (not just local) identification with the league, the sport and teams. 'What had previously assumed to exist only for championships – interest not rooted in locale – was here extended into the regular season. Fans were being lured into following not just "their" team but other teams as well' (Leifer 1995, p. 132). Interestingly MLB baseball continued to televise mainly local games (except for the World Series, the overall North American championship decider played between the winners of the two Major League divisions) and revenues from advertising declined below football.

The NHL (ice hockey) tended towards the MLB model – being most enjoyed in Canada rather than the USA – while the NBA (basketball) gained revenue through TV as well as through corporate marketing and merchandising. The key trend has been towards the '"delocalisation" of sporting tastes and loyalties' (Whitson 1998b, p. 65). 'Fans for any team can turn up anywhere' (Leifer 1995, p. 134). Whitson argues that the opening up of new revenue streams (from merchandise such as team gear and other items bearing logos) marked 'the gradual detachment of professional sports from loyalties and meanings based in place, and a normalisation of the discourses of personal and consumer choice' (Whitson 1998b, p. 66). The marketing of sports stars also created 'an unprecedented series of black American celebrities' (Whitson 1998b, p. 66), which in turn promoted the league, the game and teams. The 'circuit of promotion' (Wernick 1991) acted as a vehicle for the promotion of more than one product at a time. At the same time less central control (that is, by the league) over broadcasting rights leads to an enlargement of the revenue gap between larger and smaller market teams. The collapse of negotiations over player salaries in the NHL in February 2005 meant that ice hockey became the first professional sport in North America to miss an entire season due to a labour dispute. The concern for hockey fans was that the knock-on effect might be 'to relegate ice hockey to the ranks of minority sports' – at least in the USA (Hannigan 2005).

Leifer (1995) argued that the commodification of sport requires the continual search for new audiences, including a global audience. Leifer (1995, pp. 295–300) showed that North American professional sports faced limits to the extent they could interest audiences outside of the playoffs and had to consider global strategies. Hence NFL football was televised in 182 countries in 1999, NBA basketball was televised in 205 countries in 2000 and related merchandising was sold. Leifer (1995, pp. 295–300) argued that the idea that sports teams should represent geographic communities, whilst essential at the outset of professional spectator sport and TV, began to act as a barrier to the development of larger (global) audiences. Hence he suggested that global sports teams should represent global corporations and compete on world circuits like tennis and motor racing.

Whitson (1998b, p. 70) argued that European and Commonwealth sports (association football, rugby – both codes – and cricket) have been intensively commodified since the 1990s 'pursuing revenue streams that developed over a longer period in America'. So the present developments lead not to a global (American) sports monoculture but more commodified sport. He argued that one of the costs associated with the development of global promotion of certain sports is the privileging of the highly professional/slickly packaged over local sports. In addition it adds to the presence of the language and imagery of consumerism in public space and discourse. Finally Whitson (1998b) suggested that these developments erode differences between making market choices and social choices amongst consumers, audiences and sports fans. He notes however that 'the ultimate outcome of globalization is less likely to be the hegemony of American sports than the intensive commodification of any sport that will retain a place in a mediated global culture' (Whitson 1998b, p. 70).

Market Football: A Case Study

Any assessment of the recent development of association football in the UK, and especially in England, has to attend to what has been called 'the new business of football' (Morrow 1999, Szymanski and Kuypers 1999, Garland et al. 2000, Finn and Giulianotti 2000, Wagg 2004). These authors suggest that professional football in England and more generally in Europe has been undergoing a fundamental transformation as it finds 'new economic and new cultural locations within advanced capitalism' (Moorhouse 1998, p. 227). They highlight the manner in which the economics of football financing has been transformed by 'mediatization' (Bourdieu 1999b, p. 18) and the way that traditional football authorities and associations in several European countries face the greatest challenge to their legitimacy since their foundation at the end of the 19th century.

The 'new business' of football did have its pioneers. In the mid-1930s for example Herbert Chapman was succeeded as manager of Arsenal by 'George "By Jove!" Allison', a former British Broadcasting Corporation (BBC) radio commentator. His style of commentating had 'brought the game to firesides of thousands who never went near a football ground' (Birley 1995, p. 229).

Allison continued to align his football team with the entertainment industry: in 1939 he allowed the team 'to make a film called "The Arsenal Stadium Mystery" and encouraged players to market themselves' (Birley 1995, p. 308). The latest phase in the history of football in England, however, has been marked by a number of fundamental changes with respect to the game, including its relationship with the media. First, in the 1990s there has been a reshaping of the physical environment of the sport through a mass programme of building modernised all-seater stadia, often in out of town locations. Secondly, the formation of breakaway Premier leagues – in Scotland, as well as England – has increased the division between professional clubs in the top and lower leagues. Thirdly, exclusive live match broadcasting rights agreements made with Rupert Murdoch's Sky satellite television network have brought greater economic rewards to the Premiership teams. These changes have also been accompanied in the 1990s by controversies, as leading players admitted to gambling, alcohol and other addictions, managers were investigated for accepting secret gifts and payments ('bungs') as part of transfer negotiations, and other instances of sporting misconduct, both on and off the field of play, have been reported. The breakaway leagues have not only revitalised the economic fortunes of the top clubs, but also led many commentators to warn about the threat they pose to the fabric of the game (Deloitte and Touche 2000).

Similar to the major American sports team, British football has increasingly required commercial sponsorship, merchandising and broadcasting revenues as replacements for the relative decline in gate money. Compared with North America, however, there are fewer restrictions on output, the greater attachment of communities to clubs makes relocation difficult, and there are fewer restrictions on competition – with fairly limited revenue sharing, no reverse order draft – where the worst team gets the first chance to sign the year's crop of rookie players – or, as yet, salary capping.

Anthony King's *The End of the Terraces* (1998) analysed the 'new business' orientation of football using a critical theoretical framework derived from the Gramscian-influenced neo-Marxist analysis of the development of capitalism. King (1998, p. 39) identified two key factors which have affected the economics of professional football in England: the long-term decline in attendances (and therefore income) from the post-war peak in 1948 through to the 1980s and the impact of the abolition of the maximum wage on clubs' ability to finance their squads. In the 1970s this was compounded as sponsorship, in combination with television interests, began to develop as alternative sources of income for those 'bigger clubs' which enjoyed national, and in some cases international, supporting publics – Arsenal, Everton, Liverpool, Manchester United and Tottenham Hotspur. Alongside commercial and juridical responses to the football crises of 1985 and 1989, in the shape of official enquiries, media negotiations over televising rights, and government efforts to impose a membership scheme on football supporters, King shows how these developments laid the basis for the creation of the English Premier League in 1992.

Rather than view these developments as inevitable, King considered that different actors were involved in contestation over the 'new consumption of football'. On the one hand, there were the new powerful forces of terrestrial and satellite television companies and football club directors of leading clubs who were apparently driving the changes in football finance. On the other hand were traditional football supporters, those who have contributed to football literature and fanzines largely critical of the new economics of the sport, and a group King (1998) referred to as 'the new consumer fans'. King suggested that these latter three groups of people could be seen as representatives of negotiation, resistance and compliance to the new economic order in football.

He argued that as Fordism was replaced by post-Fordism, and the Keynesian orthodoxy collapsed under criticism from the New Right in the 1970s, a new occupational and class structure developed in England. In this era of post-Fordism a new style of consumption of football was stimulated. There has been a shift from football *fandom* to football *consumption* as increasingly fans have been encouraged to become customers of the sport. King concluded that 'Football fandom constitutes a central mechanism of the emerging class compromise developing under the interpretative framework of a Thatcherite hegemony which informs Britain's Post-Fordist transformation' (King 1998, p. 203).

King's thesis was an interesting attempt to elaborate the view that sports develop through processes of social struggle, rather than straightforward diffusion and emulation. A full appreciation of the social significance of football requires both a study of the relations of consumption of this media-saturated product and also a wider analysis of different dimensions of the sport itself (Giulianotti 1999, Williams 1999). Undoubtedly television became a, if not the, main economic driver in 'the new business of football', and the top level of the professional game has largely become 'a television-content business' (Boyle and Haynes 2004, *The Economist* 11 December 1999, p. 100). We consider the importance of the media for English football in the next chapter.

New breeds of entrepreneurs have moved into football to make money from shares and property deals involving the top clubs. These now include the UK's richest resident, Roman Abramovich, as owner of Chelsea F.C. in London. Clubs have become public limited companies and the football business has expanded to meet the needs of shareholders and accountants as much as fans, members and administrators. Premiership football now embodies 'the central features of a modern, high profile sport, as much a mediated spectacle and vehicle for insatiable consumerism as a forum for physical pleasures, cultural affiliation and playful creativity' (Horne et al. 1999, p. 52). As the people's (or peoples') game has become a lucrative global commodity at world level (see Sugden and Tomlinson 1998a) domestic football leagues in Europe have also been transformed by this new constellation of interests. Foremost among them in Britain has been Rupert Murdoch's News International

Corporation (see Chapter 3 for an account of 'Murdochization'). Although gate receipts form the largest part of turnover for even the biggest football club in the UK, efforts have expanded to increase the revenues from other 'experiential commodities' associated with the sport.

The city of Manchester, for example, now boasts two football club museums and 'experiences'. 'The Manchester City Experience' provides insights into football 'the Mancunian way' and a tour of the City of Manchester stadium. Across the town there is the longer established 'Old Trafford Experience', sponsored by Fuji Film. As the world's largest sports brand it is not surprising that Manchester United's operation is much more commercially driven. The current manager, Sir Alex Ferguson, welcomes visitors in his notes to the tour brochure with the words 'Welcome to the Theatre of Dreams from Manchester United and Fuji Film, our official imaging partner'. In addition to the display of footballing achievements, the Old Trafford museum illustrates that football is no longer just a game. Tomato ketchup, champagne, wine, lager, beer, cola and toothpaste are just a few of the consumer products available with the Manchester United brand and logo. In addition, 'MU Finance' offers several opportunities to support the team through acquiring insurance, savings accounts and credit cards. A thirteen-year partnership agreement began in August 2002 with Nike who run Manchester United's worldwide merchandising operation (www.manutd.com) and several mega stores in Singapore, Bangkok, Tokyo as well as in Old Trafford stadium. Pierre Bourdieu has remarked upon how sport has been transformed from being a practice to being a spectacle, from being a form of play to being a form of industry. He argues that television is largely responsible for the trend towards commercialisation in football, and other sports. He describes TV as the 'Trojan Horse for the entry of commercial logic into sport' (Bourdieu 1999b, p. 16).

In England (and to a much lesser extent Scotland) elite clubs have been gaining greater rewards and the gap between the Premier League(s) and the rest of the league has expanded. The distribution of TV revenues for the Premier League clubs since its formation shows that the leading five clubs in the 1990s – Manchester United, Liverpool, Arsenal, Chelsea and Leeds – accounted on average for over 30 per cent of the total TV payments in the period (Gratton 2000, p. 22). In England divisions have opened up not only between the 20 clubs in the Premier League and the 72 clubs in the other three professional divisions of the Football League, but also within the Premier league itself between the top teams, the middle-of-the-table teams and the strugglers (Gratton 2000).

The massive increase in revenue from broadcasting rights to the Premiership has been the single largest factor affecting the economics of Premiership clubs. Whereas Premiership clubs received approximately £8 million per season from TV revenue in 1999, each First division club received just £0.5 million. All these developments have had an impact on players' salaries, creating widening gulfs between Premiership players and the rest. A survey conducted by the

Professional Football Association in 2000 revealed that the average annual wage in the English Premiership was £409,000 (100 players earned at least £1 million per year and 36 per cent earned more than half a million pounds). Players in the English First, Second and Third Divisions earned £128,000, £52,000 and £37,000 per year respectively (reported in *The Guardian* 19 April 2000/1, p. 32). Throughout Europe elite clubs have owners with wider sports, leisure and media interests, and, being dominated by wealthy individuals, can afford to spend large amounts on star players. Hence David Beckham's transfer in 2003 to Real Madrid followed in the wake of the other 'galacticos' Ronaldo and Zidane. With sales of his number 23 shirt accounting for 50 per cent of Real Madrid merchandise income in the 2003/2004 season, Beckham's transfer fee of nearly £25 million was easily recovered (*The Economist* 13 March 2004, p. 87).

There is more money in British football than ever before (from the relatively new television and merchandising income streams especially). A sign of this was the appearance of 10 British clubs in the annual top-20 worldwide 'rich-list' compiled according to income (Scott 2005). In 2003–2004 season Manchester United were once again the top earners with £171.5 million, but Chelsea (4th place with £143.7 million), Arsenal (6th with £115 million) and Liverpool (10th with £92.3 million) were also in the top ten. That the Scottish city of Glasgow had as many representatives in the list as Spain, Germany and France testified to the economic importance of the 'Auld Firm' of Rangers and Celtic. Yet football is also facing financial crisis with more clubs in economic difficulties than ever before. Failure to achieve success – and especially long-term involvement in the lucrative European Champions League – cost Leeds United dearly in 2004. As fans relationship to the game becomes increasingly mediated, and the monetary rewards and investments in it grow, debates about the balance between economic values and sports values have occurred. Ideas developed during the campaign against the take-over of Manchester United by News Corporation in 1999 were exercised again in 2005, as another potential owner (Malcolm Glazer) attempted to buy the world's most famous football club. Associated concerns with the increasing emphasis on club-related merchandise – shoes, shirts and other football star – endorsed products – and debates over different methods of ownership and control of football clubs have also been stimulated (Morrow 1999).

Investigating Fans and the Sport Consumer

This chapter's focus on the global sports market and commercial sport places emphasis on the economic and material dimensions of sport. In order to understand the meaning of sport as practice (including the consumption of spectacles and participation in sport) it is also necessary to conduct studies of the lived experience of consumption. Some researchers have begun to investigate contestation over the consumption of sport from fans, participants and viewers in sport (Crabbe and Brown 2004 in Wagg 2004, Wheaton 2004).

Recent sociological analyses of sports fans themselves have tended to focus on fans' involvement in the game, their self-reflective behaviour, as well as the variations between them (Giulianotti 2002, King 2002/1998, Sandvoss 2003, Crawford 2004). Explorations of fandom have explored 'the informal membership of the cultural world of the fan or supporter to the social experience of being a part of a group of fans' (Whannel 2004, p. 481). As we have seen, King suggested that three kinds of football fans emerged in the 1990s – the traditional, the new writers and the new consumer fans. Giulianotti (2002), influenced more by postmodern social theory, considers football fans as involved in producing a carnival. More recently Sandvoss (2003) has suggested that there are two groups of football fans – some are consumer victims and some newer fans are fashion followers. Crawford (2004) focussed on fandom more generally. We will briefly discuss these two recent studies.

Sandvoss (2003) was interested in the relationship between spectators, football, the mass media and industrial modernity. He argued that football fandom could be viewed as an act of consumption in the light of Bourdieu's analysis of distinction. Football support can be seen as a space of projection and self-reflection. Sandvoss argues that the cultural proliferation of football – brought about heightened media interest in it – adds to the structural transformation of the public sphere. The 'changing regimes of rationalized production' and through television, especially the distribution of football, create football as a postmodern cultural form (Sandvoss 2003, p. 10). He argues that football has no pre-given meaning as vision and information are privileged over participation and experience (Sandvoss 2003, p. 166). Football is McDonaldised (rationalised) and clubs become 'contentless' as fandom is altered if not entirely undermined. Hence placelessness, resulting from de-localisation, produces fans as consumer victims according to Sandvoss.

Garry Crawford argues that there is a need to consider the 'meanings, experiences and consumer patterns of contemporary sports fans' (Crawford 2004, p. 3). Although sport has always involved different forms of consumption, changes in the relationship between sport, media, sponsorship and tourism in the past twenty years have lead '*male* mass spectator sport' (Crawford 2004, p. x) to become more of a means of entertainment and a hyper-commodified spectacle than ever before. But unlike some responses to this, Crawford does not seek to counter-pose the 'authentic' fan against the 'new consumer' fan. Rather he argues that it is a matter of theoretical weakness that fans have not been understood within a wider context of 'consumer culture and consumer practices' (Crawford 2004, p. 11). Rather than create what he calls 'rigid dichotomies' between authentic and inauthentic fans, or true/real and false ones, Crawford argues that a better way forward is to consider fans as consumers and for fan culture to be seen 'primarily as a consumer culture' (Crawford 2004, p. 34). In this respect he extends the idea that consumer culture is a part of material culture (a person–thing relationship), but instead can include person–person relationships, such as consuming the (sporting) performances of others as well as other experiential commodities.

In terms of images of consumers, it is possible to organise the studies of fans using a typology derived from Aldridge (2003, pp. 15–23). He argued that it is possible to understand the figure of the consumer in social thought along two dimensions: an objective power orientation – the consumer as dominated or dominant – and a subjective orientation – the consumer as instrumental – seeking the most rational means to an end – or expressive – fantasising and dreaming. Thus four different images of the consumer are apparent in reformist, economist, Marxist and sociological approaches: the consumer as victim, the consumer as rational actor, the consumer as dupe and the consumer as communicator. Placing the four studies of fans into these categories provides the following classification:

Victims	*Rational actors*
Sandvoss 2003	Crawford 2004
Dupes	*Communicators*
King 2002/1998	Giulianotti 2002

These attempts to understand fans are consistent with other cultural studies analyses of sport but they also share many of the features of research conducted on behalf of the advertising and marketing industry. As an industry, sport seeks to get an idea about who the sports consumer is in order that it can control and at least attempt to influence consumption. A survey of football fans conducted by the English Football Association (FA) and market research company MORI between February and May 2002 provides an example. It found that whilst choice and quality of club facilities and merchandise were generally perceived to be good (lower division clubs being more poorly rated than the Premiership teams), value for money (VFM) for facilities and merchandise was rated higher for clubs in the lower divisions (FA/MORI 2002, pp. 50–53). As Mark Cuban, owner of the Dallas Mavericks in the USA, explained, 'Everyone has thousands of entertainment choices and we don't want to create any excuses for them to go and spend their money somewhere else' (quoted in AT Kearney 2003).

Marketing Strategies in Sport

Using psychographic segmentation analysis, Chicago-based market research company, AT Kearney, have developed six categories of sports consumers. They divide sports fans into six types: Sports Fanatics, Club and Team Loyalists, Star-struck Spectators, Social Viewers, Opportunistic Viewers and the Sports

Indifferent (AT Kearney 2003, p. 3). Using these kinds of categories, sports organisations, leagues and teams can develop strategies to develop their brand awareness. As David Gill, Chief Executive of Manchester United, told *The Guardian* newspaper, 'The new post of commercial director is critical to our ability to deliver this company's key strategic aim of converting more fans to consumers and leveraging the club's brand through our global commercial activities' (quoted in *The Guardian* 2003, p. 14).

In order to examine the sports consumer it is not enough to focus on fans' agency, but crucial questions about the activity of institutions and structures have to be considered. More needs to be said about the structural mechanisms by which, and the context within which, the contemporary culture of sports consumption is being produced. The active consumer is a product of changes in marketing and advertising strategy. Recent arguments, such as that of Alan Bryman (2004) about Disney-*ization* – that the Disney Corporation has created a template for the satisfaction of consumers which is increasingly being globalised – provide an understanding of the new strategies for selling in Post-Fordist times. It helps explain why Disney does not just serve as a model for theme parks and tourism, but other social spaces and sites such as shopping malls and sports stadia. No wonder that it was a former Disney executive that Manchester United F.C. appointed as its first commercial director in 2004 (*The Guardian* 23 December 2003, p. 14).

Bryman's definition of 'Disneyization' – 'the process by which the principles of the Disney theme parks are coming to dominate more and more sectors of American society as well as the rest of the world' (p. 1) – deliberately alludes to the parallel process first announced by George Ritzer over a decade ago. For George Ritzer (1993, p. 1)

> McDonald's is treated here as the major example, the 'paradigm case', of a wide-ranging process I call McDonaldization, that is: the process by which the principles of the fast-food restaurant are coming to dominate more and more sectors of American society as well as of the rest of the world.

A long quotation from Ritzer on the front cover of the paperback edition of Bryman's book dispels any idea that this should be regarded as a competitor concept.

For Bryman both the notions of Disneyization and McDonaldization 'provide viable accounts of some of the changes occurring in modern society' (p. 13), especially with respect to the increasing importance of consumption and globalisation. The principles of Disney offer choice, difference and the spectacular, whereas McDonaldization offered homogeneity. Disneyization is to Post-Fordism, what McDonaldization is to Fordism. Bryman's book consists largely of chapters outlining the four central principles of Disneyization. These are: *theming*, now also widespread in bars, pubs, clubs and so on; *hybrid consumption* (referred to in earlier versions of his argument as *de-differentiation*), or the blurring of conventional boundaries of retailing; *merchandising*, with multiple opportunities to purchase goods bearing corporate logos and signs; and *performative* (formerly called *emotional*) *labour*, in which Disney workers are expected to display emotions through 'deep acting'.

Bryman carefully distinguishes Disney-*ization* from Disney-*fication*. He regards the latter (and possibly more widespread) notion as mainly a derogatory reference to trite Disney 'treatments' of historical events or the content of its theme parks, films and so on. Instead he argues that Disney Corporation has also created a template or format for the satisfaction of consumers which is increasingly being globalised. Bryman suggests that Disneyization is taking up where McDonaldization left off. Disneyization offers a new strategy for selling in Post-Fordist times. It offers 'a framework for making goods, and in particular services, desirable and therefore more likely to be bought' (p. 175). Disneyization is a relatively new mode of delivery and strategy, via 'ludic ambience' (Bryman 2004, p. 160), for manipulating consumers. He therefore also draws attention to the techniques of surveillance and control (of both workforces and consumers) that underpin it. Hence Disney serves as a model not just for theme parks and tourism, but also for other social institutions and *leisure* spaces and sites.

Alan Aldridge (2003) has suggested that with McDonaldization the emphasis was on quantity and there was only an illusion of choice. With Disneyization the emphasis is on quality and choice is more a reality. Consumers of the former are treated more like dupes, whereas with the latter consumers are encouraged to be (knowingly) involved in play-like fantasies. But as Bryman points out, both processes involve strategies of control and manipulation, and like Ritzer, he concludes that there are irrationalities produced by the appliance of rational business strategies. Do we need another process named after a leading multinational corporation to help us understand contemporary global consumer capitalism? Do we gain from this addition to the stockpile of concepts applicable to leisure and popular culture? I think so. Bryman's argument complies with the requirement that any new (and old) theoretical concepts should be empirically testable and open to being re-tested.

Conclusion

In keeping with the emphasis of this book we have concluded this chapter on the theme of the production of sport as consumption. The chapter considered the growth of a global goods and services industry in sport as well as the distinctive nature of professional sport in different societies. Research into sports fans shares features of research carried out by marketing and advertising agencies. There has been a shift from viewing fans as passive to active and inter-active agents (Ross and Nightingale 2003). We have noted how marketing and advertising strategies in sport have been focussed on discovering more about fans and attempts to produce a new consumer fandom have been made (King 2002/1998). More generally, however, we have argued that the consumerisation of sport is a product of heightened commodification and marketisation in society. Despite this, as Whitson et al. (2000, p. 146) observe, 'As an industry, professional sport is actually much smaller than its cultural visibility (and its own publicity) would suggest, making up a statistically tiny part of any metropolitan economy.' The following chapter will look in detail at the most significant influence on the promotion of sports image and which has also helped to stimulate many of the new opportunities for advertising and sponsorship in contemporary sport – the mass media.

3

Sport, Consumerisation and the Mass Media

Introduction

Neil Blain (2002), as we have seen in Chapter 1, makes the case for maintaining a distinction between the media and sport as a form of cultural life outside of its purely symbolic representation. Sport is both modern, as practice, and postmodern, as part of media culture. As Raymond Williams (1990, p. 67) also noted 'the extraordinary development of the many kinds of professional spectator sports in the twentieth century antedates broadcasting. Radio and television came to satisfy and extend an already developed cultural habit.' Williams (1990) also provides an important reminder that the media, and especially television, are the product of technologically sophisticated societies. Technologies have been implemented for a reason. The main ones being commercial and the national interest, as defined by different governments. What is especially marked in the past fifteen years in the UK and throughout the advanced capitalist economies is the enormous increase in the amount of sport on television and covered in the press, radio and other forms of media. David Rowe (2004a, pp. 1–4) provides a cameo of one 'day in the life of the media sports consumer' living in advanced capitalist society. He suggests that sport today 'is increasingly indistinguishable from the *sports media*'. That this has coincided with a period of neo-liberal inspired government de-regulation is not a mere coincidence.

The Sport–Media Relationship

The relationship between the mass media and sport has always been an important one (Whannel 1992, Horne et al. 1999, Ch. 6). The media have helped to construct what is meant by sport. In the early part of the 19th century 'sport' was a word restricted to describing field sport (hunting, shooting and fishing) and what have later become known as 'cruel' sports, such as bull and bear baiting and cock fighting. At the end of the 19th century the newly forming modern press assisted in boundary marking and boundary shifting of what was defined as sport and even what a champion was. Derek Birley (2000, pp. 140, 144) and Christopher Brookes (1978, pp. 120–137), for example, have both noted that it was only after the press began publishing ' "league tables" and talking of a "championship" ' that a sub-committee of leading county sides established the County Cricket Council and the MCC (Marylebone Cricket Club) established an organised competition in English cricket in 1894.

In the mid- to late-19th century popular culture in Britain was increasingly shaped by the two forces of the state (public and municipal bodies, including the education system) and the capitalist market (private and commercial leisure enterprises, including music hall/entertainment, holidays, mass spectator sport and the printed mass media of newspapers and magazines). In the 20th century these influences on popular culture continued. The state has shaped popular culture in many ways through prohibition, regulation and promotion. In the UK through government regulation of broadcasting the British Broadcasting Corporation (Company until 1926) had a monopoly (from 1922 until 1954) in radio and then television, which helped it to construct popular culture, including what came to be understood as national sporting occasions. These included such events as the FA Cup Finals, Cricket Test Matches, the Derby and Grand National horse race meetings and, revealing the exclusive social background of many of the 'cultural intermediaries' in the BBC, the annual boat race between Oxford and Cambridge university students. Commercial leisure expanded in many ways, but the mass media have been central to the formation of popular culture, especially the cinema in the pre- and immediately post-Second World War period, commercial terrestrial television from the mid-1950s onwards and satellite television since the 1990s.

Burstyn (1999) demonstrates the centrality of the media for the development of sport as spectacle in North America. The foundations of the sport–media complex were laid in the 1890s when a new urban culture of entertainment, which included the sports press, magazines and journals, was formed. Sport sold newspapers and newspapers sold sport. Newspaper owners often invested in athletes, teams, stadia and advertising. The professionalisation of core sports occurred because of this. Professional teams attracted larger audiences for commercial products and increased the readership of newspapers. The improved dramatic performances increased the number of paying spectators. Such performances required a higher standard of skill than was possible on a part-time ('amateur') basis. Hence 'professionalisation was both a precondition and a beneficiary of the turn-of-the-century sports press' (Burstyn 1999, p. 106). Some sports retained an 'amateur' status and hence the rhythm and pacing of commercialisation varied between sports. But standards and conventions of play and training in the local and participatory levels of sport were affected by professionalisation/commercialisation elsewhere.

Upper-class magazines decried commercialisation – expressing concern about the impact on sport's character-building qualities and potential.

Working-class (male) fans enjoyed the promotion of working-class heroes through sport – another opportunity to assert masculinity and provide a forum for symbolic equality, or even gain revenge on the upper classes (Burstyn 1999, p. 107). That this was mainly symbolic was emphasised especially after 1922 when baseball team owners were given legal protection from anti-trust legislation, tipping the balance in the favour of owners rather than players and spectators. How sport has evolved from a local, active and participatory experience to an abstract, passive and spectatorial one has been considered from different theoretical perspectives. Burstyn (1999, pp. 133–135) adopts a feminist approach influenced by Marxism. She equates participation in sport as about play, pleasure and social bonding – and therefore freedom. Sport as spectacle is connected to commercialised, commodified and controlled behaviour.

The philosophical question, what is, and what is not, sport has been decided pragmatically by what appears in the sport sections of newspapers or in radio or television broadcasts. Hence the press and magazines, then cinema newsreels, radio and television, have been active in the process by which dominant, residual and emergent sports practices have been defined as such (Williams 1977, pp. 121–127). Hence competitive team and individual sports (the dominant), and hang gliding, wind surfing and jet skiing (the emergent) are more likely to appear in contemporary sports pages and sports reports than cruel sports and field sports (the residual).

Mediated sport has also played a role in the structuring of space and time. Television, for example, has moved from being an item of communal consumption fifty years ago (when people used to pay a small sum of money to watch television on tiny screens in booths set up in railway stations and other public places) to being a major feature of the domestic sphere. Since the 1980s, sports bars have developed which have recaptured sports media consumption as a communal event, but for most people in advanced capitalist countries the television set remains a, if not the, primary piece of domestic leisure technology. The media transform sports consumption practices and also people's sense of geographical space. Media sport focusses attention on the similar sportscapes of modernity – the stadium, the pitch, the court or the course. Media sport provides a structure to people's everyday lives as they tune to regular broadcast times and schedules. Sport also establishes people's sense of calendar time as an annual round of mediated sports events is produced.

The relationship between sport and the media has been described as a symbiotic one (Coakley 2003, p. 402). Why is that? What do the media and sport gain from each other? Sport, on the one hand, is primarily interested in the media because of the need for exposure. Exposure for a sport attracts new recruits. It attracts fans, consumers and spectators. In the past forty years media exposure has also boosted the chances of gaining, if not guaranteeing, sponsorship. The media, on the other hand, are interested in sport, first, because intrinsic aspects of sport form the basis for an ideal news story. All sports offer a predictable occurrence with an unpredictable outcome and the ideal news story is exactly that. Second, with a few exceptions, sport attracts a predominantly male audience which most commercially driven media organisations otherwise find difficult to reach. Thirdly, sports provide moments of immense public interest, via the possibility of identification with an absorbing universe of condensed simplicity, which attracts large audiences, boosts reading, listening and viewing figures and can be relied on to produce regular consumers.

In the 1960s, media sociologists Galtung and Ruge (1981/1965) argued that above all else a news story must fit with three requirements of the media organisations that report them. What became news depended on three factors. First, news *organisation*, or periodicity, meant that stories had to fit in with planned categories and thus be predictable. Key categories of news coverage include home, international, crime and sport. Secondly, Galtung and Ruge identified news *selection* as important. This referred to aspects of stories such as negativity, their dramatic or unpredictable nature, continuity and tradition, or, if they involved high status people, celebrities or stars. Hence 'a predictable event with an uncertain outcome is the perfect news story'. Sport obviously figures strongly in such a definition of a good news story. Thirdly, news *presentation* was also important. Stories about subjects that were unambiguous could be personalised, and had meaningfulness to the reader (that is, had many points of identification) and were more likely to be reported than others that did not share these characteristics (such as an account of long-term economic or social trends). In sum, former journalist Leonard Koppett (1994, pp. 17ff.) outlined seven characteristics of sport that make it particularly attractive to the media: its comprehensibility, continuity, readability, coherence, hazard, low cost and opportunity for vicarious experience (of violence, triumph, second-guessing and patriotism).

The Growth of Sports Coverage in the Contemporary Mass Media

Recent developments in the expansion of sport in the media, especially television schedules, illustrate the attraction of sport well. At the end of the 1990s a survey by market research agency Mintel in the UK found the following. Between 1996 and 1999, coverage of sport on terrestrial TV stations (BBC1 and BBC2, Independent Television (ITV), Channel 4 (C4) and Channel 5 (C5)) increased by 56.9 per cent to 4302 hours. On satellite (which in the UK essentially means News Corporation's Sky TV) and cable TV the percentage increase over the same period was less (46.6 per cent) but amounted to 26,453 hours of broadcasting (Mintel 2000, p. 50). According to minutes of coverage, football (soccer) was the most widely covered sport on TV followed by 'general sports' (magazine-type sports programmes), golf, motor sports, cricket, tennis, motorcycling, horse racing, boxing and rugby union (Mintel 2000, p. 51). In 1999 football accounted for over one quarter of BBC1's sports coverage and tennis for over one fifth of BBC2's output, closely followed by snooker at 19 per cent of output. Football accounted for 46 per cent of sport on ITV, horse racing for 30.9 per cent of sport on C4 and general sports for 22.5 per cent of sport on C5. Football accounted for 20.4 per cent of sport on C5. The TV stations C5 and C4 provided a much higher coverage of sport than ITV (80,045 minutes and 51,985 minutes respectively as opposed to 36,835 on ITV. Both C5 and C4 provided more coverage of minority sports – baseball, American football and snowboarding, for example. Of Sky's sport broadcasts 19.4 per cent was football, compared with 13.1 per cent of Eurosport's, whilst 15.2 per cent was tennis.

The pre-eminence of football is not just peculiar to the UK market. In 2000 – not a World Cup year – football comprised 58 per cent of total worldwide sports coverage on TV. It was a long way ahead of the Sydney Olympics (10 per cent), boxing and basketball (5 per cent), Formula 1 motor racing (4 per cent) and baseball (3 per cent) (*SportsBusiness* No. 58, June 2001, p. 54). As Brian Barwick, former Controller of Sport for ITV and currently the Chief Executive of the English FA, told an international television and sport convention in 2001, 'In the U.K. like in the majority of European countries, football is king. They [*sic*] are basically two types of sports rights negotiations in the U.K.: football and then every other sport' (cited in SPORTEL 2001, p. 9).

What explains the growth of sport in the media? What caused the increased media interest in sports programming? It certainly was not simply due to either greater free time or more widespread interest in sport on the part of television audiences and consumers. Partly it can also be explained by the growing commercialisation of TV. With the start of satellite and cable broadcasting there are clearly more commercially driven television companies around than ever before. A second feature is the fact that the cost benefits of televising sport, vis-à-vis other TV shows – drama, documentaries and so on – remain high. That is, because there are very few 'origination costs' (sport is going to take place any way without media networks constructing stadia, inventing competitions or hiring athletes, officials and so on) sport is relatively cheap TV. The cost per hour of sport on BBC TV increased during the 1990s – from £39,000 per hour in 1990 to £102,000 per hour in 2000. Compared with several other TV programme genres, however (features and documentaries, light entertainment, music and art and costume drama), it remained cheap television (*The Guardian* 19 and 20 November 2001, pp. 7 and 5). This suits commercial media organisations operating on 'mini-max' principles (minimal outlay for maximum return) as well as those operating with a public service remit. Total annual BBC TV output of sport programmes thus grew from 375 hours in 1970 to 1450 hours in 2000, by then a much more competitive market (*The Guardian* 19 and 20 November 2001, pp. 7 and 5). Thirdly, the advent and introduction of the so-called 'new media' – video, cable, satellite, digital, the Internet, mobile phones – have all required content and sport is available to fill that gap. Fourthly, the new television broadcasters have seen gaining access to sports exclusives as a strategic means of attracting subscribers and purchasers of the new technology needed to access sport.

To examine these developments in more detail we shall explore the production, construction and consumption of sport in the media. The chapter next looks at the contemporary political economy of media sport, including ownership and control, the politics of the press and the regulation of the media. Then it considers global media conglomerates, global media sport and the emergence of the 'unholy alliance' during late 20th-century transformations in what a number of authors have referred to as the 'sports/media complex'. Attention is then given to the role of journalism in the social construction of sport and the impact on its audience. Finally media sport audiences – consumers of media sport – are discussed in relation to their reception practices, the format of sport and their access to sport in the light of the impact of new media technologies.

Producing Sport for the Media

The classic definition of the study of the mass media of communications (expressed by Harold Lasswell in the 1950s) was that it was the study of WHO says WHAT to WHOM through WHICH channel (or HOW) and with WHAT effect? Despite some variations the study of the media has followed these principles. Researchers have been interested in the communication circuit, the production, texts and appropriation of the media and so on. There have been two main research 'camps'.

On the one hand there are those who have focussed on debates about ownership and control in the media. Researchers have been interested in how production factors (institutions and organisations, technology, government regulations and commercial influences) have influenced both the output of the media (the texts, symbols and signs) and its reception by audiences and consumers. Following Raymond Williams' (1990, p. 120) amendment to Lasswell's formula, many have been interested in posing an additional question – 'for what purpose?' Two main suggestions are that in market economies commercial media have sought to assist in the creation of profits and more broadly promote ideologies consistent with corporate capitalist interests. Researchers associated with the critical political economy of the media place questions of ownership and control at the centre of their enquiries.

On the other hand some researchers have been more interested in the response of audiences to the messages produced by the media, their impact and their effects. Some of these researchers have concentrated on the study of how active audience members can be, the reception of and work of interpretation required to 'read' the media (Nightingale and Ross 2003, Ross and Nightingale 2003). Others have been interested in the creation of ideas and ideologies in the media. Those that have focussed on the audience as active have tended to be more interested in the media's role in the construction of everyday lives and personal identities. Those interested in ideas and ideologies have tended to be more critical of the media's role, seeing it as manipulative. So research into the media and sport parallels approaches to consumption and consumer culture more widely (Rowe 2004a,b). Consistent with the approach in this book we will primarily emphasise the production of consumption of sport – how the separate cultural domains of the mass media and sport combine as part of the modern mechanisms of circulation and consumption.

Ownership and Control in Media and Sport

Power has increasingly been concentrated into the hands of a few large media conglomerates (Law et al. 2002). De- (or as some prefer to call it re-) regulation of the media by government has benefited these conglomerates. For example, in December 2003 a new Communications Act became law in the UK. It established an office of communications (known as Ofcom) to regulate the big three companies in 'telephony' – the new word used to describe the potential for merging TV, radio, the Internet and telephone communications. In Britain the big three companies are the BBC, the telecommunications company BT (formerly British Telecommunications) and the British-based broadcasting company owned by the multinational media group News Corporation, Sky TV.

Since December 2003 Ofcom has had responsibility for five aspects of media regulation previously dealt with by separate organisations. Ofcom thus deals with regulating mergers, for example approving the merger of the two largest UK commercial terrestrial TV companies Carlton and Granada into 'ITV plc' in 2004, content, that is maintaining standards of taste and decency, ownership, adjudicating over non-EU ownership of British media and rules governing overlapping press and commercial TV ownership and radio.

Yet globally power in mass communications has increasingly become more concentrated into the hands of a few very large multinational media conglomerates. Whilst the existence of six or seven conglomerates – including Time Warner, Disney, Viacom, Vivendi, Bertelsmann, News Corporation and Sony – suggests that there is the possibility of competition, in fact there are many interconnections between them (Law et al. 2002, p. 298). The massive media conglomerates are mostly American-owned. General Electric, one of the five biggest American corporations, owns NBC and CNBC and MSNBC cable channels. Walt Disney Corporation owns ABC and Viacom owns CBS (Sage 2002, p. 213). De-regulation of the media by governments influenced by new right agendas since the 1980s has actually benefited these media conglomerates. The media have become increasingly commercialised and thus more reliant on advertising and revenue streams other than public licence fees. What Leys (2001) calls 'market-driven politics' has lead to more consumer-driven politics and created the conditions for 'consumerisation'.

Advertising (including sponsorship) is the (not so well) hidden subsidiser of the mass media. With respect to the print media, the cover price of newspapers and magazines is related to type and quantity of readership and advertising revenue. With TV there are three main forms: public service (such as the BBC in the UK) paid for by some form of licence fee, terrestrial commercial (in the UK ITV, C4 and C5) paid for by revenues collected from companies wishing to advertise their products in allocated time slots, and subscription and cable television (in the UK, Sky TV, ntl and so on). New technologies have developed and continue to develop to enable consumers to access television in different ways (digital decoders, personal video recorders). In 2005 access to public service TV in the UK (the BBC and other terrestrial channels) cost licence fee payers £121 per year. Terrestrial commercial TV companies (ITV, C4 and C5) received 53 per cent, 20 per cent and 8 per cent of television advertising spend respectively. Subscription TV (Sky, ntl and other cable operators) shared the rest (19 per cent). But these figures are changing as the UK develops into a multi-channel television nation.

Television offers sport a form of economic subsidy and this has had implications for the format of sport. With a greater focus on media values – entertainment and advertising – sport has thus become a more central part of consumer capitalism. Increasingly commercialised TV seeks cheap products/content filler according to the 'mini/max' principle and sport is ideal. Commercial sponsors pay money, not for the good of the game, but for the good of their companies' profit. Sponsors (and advertisers) buy audiences, not sports. The real product of media sport can be said to be the television 'commodity audience' (Ross and Nightingale 2003). Elsewhere we have noted that the statements that 'television companies sell us to advertisers' (Horne et al. 1999, p. 276) and 'we pay for televised sports' (Cashmore 2000a, p. 284) are useful reminders of the economic relationships involved. However, it is also worth noting, as Law et al. (2002, p. 297) remind us, that 'while sport is arguably the most important content for some (media) structures, it does not necessarily hold dominant place in all'. The media are always on the look out for alternative means of attracting audiences, especially ones with money or that are usually difficult to reach. As Richard Royds, the Merrill Lynch Investment Management marketing director responsible for the company's £1.3 million a year sponsorship of the Chelsea Flower Show, told one journalist, 'There will be 10 hours of BBC1 programming during the week. Last year it generated a bigger TV audience of ABC1s [that is, higher income earners] than the FA Cup final' (Collinson 2004).

The Contemporary Politics and Economics of Media Ownership and Control

Curran and Seaton (2003, p. 391) have noted that there are many inconsistencies in UK media policy. Television and radio, but not the press, are required to be impartial in news reporting. The partisanship of the press regarding sports teams has been analysed by many writers. The media of any one country tend to support their own athletes (Blain et al. 1993). Where there exist substantial ethnic or regional differences the media will reflect this in their coverage of sports news. Regional or city-based newspapers will tend to reflect on the fortunes of their home teams more than others. Apart from anything else it makes sound economic sense to do so.

Leading television organisations in the UK (BBC TV, ITV and C4), on the other hand, must strive to achieve a threshold of quality programming and content and impartiality, whilst newspapers, C5 and satellite TV broadcasters need not. A public corporation (the BBC) and a state-appointed public trust (C4) are deemed to enhance the quality of broadcasting, whilst similar organisations are considered unthinkable for the press. Curran and Seaton (2003, p. 391) conclude that at the heart of UK media policy lies the contradiction that 'public service broadcasting is defended but no equivalent defence is offered for a free market approach to the press. The latter is just assumed to be right, without any argument being given.'

Who are the agencies that own, sponsor and promote sports and what are their interests? To answer this question it is necessary to briefly consider the relationship between sport and political economic processes at local and global levels. This includes the role of transnational companies, including the media, in the production of sport and the sports industries. As we noted in the previous chapter, Andreff and Staudohar (2000) have identified a shift in the financing of sport. They argue that the 'Amateur Sports Model', in which the main sources of finance were subscriptions and private cash donations, had the primary aims of generating members interested in the practice of the sport, maintaining the activity as a form of recreation and the development of young (new) players. Professional sports models of finance are different and come in two forms according to Andreff and Staudohar. The 'Traditional' (more European) model sought gate receipts as the main income source. They called it the SSSL model ('Spectators-Subsidies-Sponsors-Local'). The main aim was to break even, cover costs or, in economists' language, aim at 'utility maximisation'. In contemporary professional sport Andreff and Staudohar argue that the main source of revenue is television. This MCMMG model – standing for 'Media-Corporations-Merchandising-Marketing-Global' – derived from North America, aims at the production of economic surpluses and 'profit maximisation'.

The impact of the new model on sport in Europe has been to see greater acceptance of a more North American system of professional sport (ownership of leagues, team relocations, permitted league failures and mergers – see Harvey et al. (2001) on the North American experience). It has raised various issues including the use of sport as a media content business strategy – referred to as 'Murdochization' by Cashmore (2000b) and 'Foxification' by Andrews (2004). We will briefly turn to a consideration of the economic processes that underpin these developments.

'Murdochization': A Media–Sport Business Strategy

Cashmore has noted that Murdoch's company News Corporation has been undertaking strategies of consolidation, integration and diversification in different parts of the world where it operates. Cashmore (2000b, pp. 292–293) defined 'Murdochization' as 'a process by which corporations primarily involved in mass media of communications appropriate and integrate into their own organizations sports clubs. In doing so, the media groups gain access to and control of the competitive activities of the clubs, which they can distribute through their networks.'

Consolidation is the acquisition of an interest, preferably exclusive, in several elements or sub-units of a market sector – for example, a sports clubs, stadia or events. Conglomeration, which is a version of this, has been occurring in the media industry for several decades. In the UK, for example, the three biggest corporations controlled 62 per cent of national daily and 60 per cent of national Sunday newspaper circulation two years after the end of the Second World War (1947). By 2002 the percentages increased to 70 per cent and 79 per cent respectively. The three leading newspaper corporations – including News International (part of News Corporation), Trinity Mirror plc and the Daily Mail and General Trust plc – also have interests in other media and non-media companies and industries (Curran and Seaton 2003, pp. 76–79). Although the Government usually regulates ownership – for example, in the UK ownership of assets over £70 million are referred to the Office of Fair Trading and the Competition Commission – it is still possible for acquisitions to put conglomerates in influential positions.

In 1997 News Corporation controlled 780 enterprises worldwide. Net assets in June 30 1997 amounted to Australian $12.4 billion, with a net operating profit of Aus.$41 million. Filmed entertainment accounted for 29 per cent of revenue, TV accounted for 25 per cent, whilst 22 per cent came from newspapers, 11 per cent from magazines, 7 per cent from books and 6 per cent from other sources (Cowe and Buckingham 1998). In the UK, News Corporation controlled 37 per cent of daily and 39 per cent of Sunday national newspaper sales in 1995. News Corporation also owned HarperCollins publisher and weeklies such as *The Times Education Supplement* and *The Times Higher Education Supplement*. News Corporation had a 35 per cent interest in satellite television via BSkyB (Williams 1995). In Britain no commercial broadcaster can control more than a 15 per cent audience share, and no company with more than 20 per cent of newspaper circulation can own a terrestrial TV company. Thus News Corporation, which owns the daily national newspapers *The Sun* and *The Times*, cannot currently own a terrestrial TV station, but that does not stop its newspapers promoting its satellite broadcaster, Sky TV, or being critical of public service broadcasting.

Consolidation can take place via vertical or horizontal integration. Vertical integration can be both backward ('upstream') or downward ('downstream') and involves undertaking a number of stages in the supply of a product, for example owning a flour mill, the bakery and the shops from which to sell the bread and cakes made. In sport, owning a football club, a media corporation, subsidiaries and distribution networks offers another illustration. Horizontal integration refers to the specialising in a particular level of a product rather than different stages of it. In the UK mergers of firms making the same or similar products leading to a 25 per cent share of the total market for that product face an enquiry from the Office of Fair Trading and the Competition Commission. Finally diversification is the strategy of supplying a range of different products and therefore operating in a number of different markets in order to 'spread the risk', for example film, TV, books, magazines, newspapers and the Internet.

The significant feature of News Corporation's activities is that Murdoch has used sport as part of a global corporate expansion strategy more than any other media corporation. In 1996 addressing the AGM of News Corporation, Murdoch announced that '"We will be doing in Asia what we intend to do elsewhere in the world – that is, use sports as a battering ram and a lead offering in all our pay television operations"' (quoted in Cashmore 2002, p. 64). Murdoch called sport a 'battering ram' for developing the market for satellite TV subscriptions in Britain and elsewhere (Andrews 2004, p. 105). In North America Murdoch owns the Fox TV network. In 1994 Fox paid US$1.58 billion to the NFL and US$155 to the NHL for exclusive coverage of the sports for the rest of the decade (Coakley and Donnelly 2004, p. 383). He purchased the Los Angeles Dodgers baseball team for a then record payment of US$311 million in 1998 and tried to do the same with Manchester United – then valued at about US$1 billion (£625 million). This latter bid was not allowed to proceed because the UK government argued that it would give News Corporation an unfair position in the football industry. In 1997 Fox TV paid US$17.6 billion for the rights to televise NFL games until 2005. In the UK, News Corporation's Sky TV won an exclusive deal worth £304 million with the English Premier Football League in May 1992. By 1996 it controlled 90 per cent of the revenues generated by subscription TV. It then secured a new five-year deal with the Premier League worth £670 million and gained exclusive coverage of English Rugby internationals played at Twickenham for £87.5 million. Murdoch's company has continued to acquire sports exclusives since then. These developments lead some to argue that Rupert Murdoch was 'the most powerful person in sport' at the start of the 21st century (Cashmore 2002, p. 63). Undoubtedly he operates one of the 'most powerful media organizations in the world' (Coakley and Donnelly 2004, p. 383).

Whilst this might appear convincing it is also worth noting two things. First, the commercial world of the media is constantly changing. Conglomerates merge and de-merge, acquire new partners and dispose of old ones. Hence, unfortunately, much of the information in this book and most of the published articles about the political economy of the media will be out of date by the time that they are published – for example, AOL Time Warner sold their music division in 2003 and Bertelsmann sold its BMG music group to Sony in 2004. But do not despair, as long as you know where to go to ask the right questions it is not difficult to find out who currently owns who! Secondly, as Law et al. (2002, p. 298) point out, 'while there is substance to the claim that the sport media complex is a "globalized" and "globalizing" phenomena, its structure is quite uneven and reasonably decentralised'. What they are alluding to here is that technological and political developments, such as the Internet and supranational and national media regulation policies, can 'further fragment distribution origins and destinations' (see also Harvey and Law 2005). The impact of the new media in the battle for control over sport between consumers and producers is set to become an increasingly important topic of debate (Stoddart 1997, see Boyle and Haynes 2002, 2004). At the start of 2005 in the UK the TV sport 'pie' was divided between satellite and terrestrial TV. On the one hand, Sky TV had secured exclusive live coverage of Premier League football, England's Test Matches and one-day series (cricket), and many leading rugby union, rugby league, tennis, golf and boxing events in the UK. On the other hand, terrestrial television stations (the BBC, ITV, C4 and C5 which was still free-to-air) covered the English FA Cup, the FIFA World Cup, Union of European Football Association (UEFA) European Championship (football), the IRU World Cup and Six Nations Championship (rugby union), the Open golf championship and the US Masters, Wimbledon tennis, as well as horse racing, Formula 1 motor racing and some boxing and athletics tournaments. In addition in the future the European Commission has signalled that it is unlikely to allow Sky to retain its virtual monopoly over football rights.

The Escalation of Sports Media Rights

The escalating media rights costs for both domestic leagues and competitions and global sports mega events illustrates both that the race to gain sports exclusives between media organisations is highly competitive and, moreover, that the corporations chasing the events believe they can nonetheless make even more money out of them. Television has helped to transform the nature, scale and interest in major sport event cycles such as the Olympic Games and the Football World Cup (Roche 2000, pp. 159ff.).

Since the 1960s, US broadcasting networks have substantially competed to 'buy' the Olympic Games. Next in order of magnitude of rights payments is the consortium representing the interests and financial power of Europe's public broadcasters, known as the European Broadcasting Union (EBU) that buy the rights to transmission in Europe. In addition media rights fees are paid by the Asian broadcasters (including Japan and South Korea) and national media organisations, such as CBC and CTV in Canada. So in addition to the US$300 million paid by the US corporation NBC to the IOC in 1988 (Seoul Summer Olympics), the EBU paid just over US$30 million and Canada paid just over US$4 million for media broadcasting rights. By 2008 (Beijing Summer Olympics) NBC will pay US$894 million, the EBU will pay over US$443 million and Canadian broadcasters will pay US$45 million just for the rights to transmit pictures of the action (Table 3.1) (Westerbeek and Smith 2003, p. 91, Coakley and Donnelly 2004, p. 382).

Similarly to the Olympic Games since the 1980s the FIFA World Cup has attracted substantial media interest and commercial partners. Sugden and Tomlinson (1998a) argue that the IOC and FIFA are part of the 'apex of a multi billion dollar global political economy'. The sport–media–business triangle transformed sport in the late 20th century through the idea of packaging, via the tri-partite business model of sponsorship rights, exclusive broadcasting rights and merchandising. The Football World Cup is a huge media event. The resources made available for the communications systems, the enormous media centres and the amounts paid by national broadcasting systems to televise the event provide ample evidence for this. At the Football World Cup Finals co-hosted by South Korea and Japan in 2002, for example, each Local Organising Committee (LOC) was responsible for arranging its own media facilities, infrastructure and services (Horne and Manzenreiter 2002b). In order to reach the global television audience the World Cup was serviced by two International Media Centres (IMCs), one in Korea and one in Japan. The Korean IMC was in the COEX exhibition centre in Seoul, which at 37,000 square metres actually offered a larger area than the IMC in Paris for the whole of the previous World Cup in 1998. The Japanese IMC was in the Pacifico Yokohama Exhibition Hall and was a little over half the area (20,000 square metres). In addition at each of the 10 stadiums in the two countries there were Stadium Media Centres.

In the case of the Olympic Games, TV rights account for approximately one-third of the total income, followed by sponsorship, ticketing and merchandising in that order of magnitude (Roche 2000, p. 168). In the case of the 1990 Football World Cup, sales of television rights were estimated to amount to US$65.7 million (41 per cent), sales of tickets to US$54.8 million (34 per cent) and sales of advertising rights to US$40.2 million (25 per cent). Twelve years later the world TV rights (this time excluding the US) for the 2002 and 2006 Football World Cup Finals were sold for US$1.97 billion. This was a six-fold increase on the US$310 million paid by the EBU for the three tournaments held in the 1990s.

Coakley and Donnelly (2004, p. 381) note how the broadcasting rights fees paid by US corporations for the four major North American men's professional leagues have grown since the mid-1980s. The NFL received US$400 million per year in 1986. In 2005 it received US$2.2 billion. Second in 2005 in terms of remuneration for broadcasting rights was the NBA (US$767 million) whereas in 1986 professional basketball had received only US$30 million.

Table 3.1 *US broadcasting network payments for Olympic television rights (US$ million) 1960–2012*

Year	Summer Games			Winter Games		
	Place	Network	Amount	Place	Network	Amount
1960	Rome	CBS	0.39	Squaw Valley	CBS	0.05
1964	Tokyo	NBC	1.5	Innsbruck	ABC	0.59
1968	Mexico City	ABC	4.5	Grenoble	ABC	2.5
1972	Munich	ABC	7.5	Sapporo	NBC	6.4
1976	Montreal	ABC	25.0	Innsbruck	ABC	10.0
1980	Moscow	NBC	87.0	Lake Placid	ABC	15.5
1984	Los Angeles	ABC	225.0	Sarajevo	ABC	91.5
1988	Seoul	NBC	300.0	Calgary	ABC	309.0
1992	Barcelona	NBC	420.0	Albertville	CBS	240.0
1994				Lillehammer	CBS	295.0*
1996	Atlanta	NBC	456.0			
1998				Nagano	CBS	375.0
2000	Sydney	NBC	705			
2002				Salt Lake City	NBC	545.0
2004	Athens	NBC	793†			
2006				Turin	NBC	614
2008	Beijing	NBC	894			
2010				Vancouver	NBC	820‡
2012	London	NBC	1.181 billion			

* From 1994 Summer and Winter Games have been staged in different years, allowing US TV to spread the burden of raising advertising revenue over two years.
† NBC paid $2.3 billion for rights to the 2004, 2006 and 2008 Games after the merger of ABC & CBS in 1995.
‡ NBC agreed to pay just over $2 billion for the rights to 2010 and 2012.
Sources: Whannel 1992, Toohey and Veal 2000; www.olympicmarketing.com – accessed 6 June 2003.

Baseball (MLB) was third, when local television and radio broadcasting rights fees were not included (US$558 million in 2005). Finally came (ice) hockey and the NHL. Since the 1980s the NHL has always received the lowest rights settlement of the four main North American sports, and after the decision to cancel the 2004–2005 season owing to a dispute over player salaries it is likely to continue in this way. In 2005 the NHL had been scheduled to receive US$120 million, plus C$60 million from CBC (all figures from Coakley and Donnelly 2004, p. 381).

Outside of North America, as we have noted, it is association football that receives the largest media attention. Gratton (2000) has shown how the costs of broadcasting live football in the top division in England (called Division 1 until 1992 and then the Premiership) have grown since the 1980s (Table 3.2). The fee per live game grew from £260,000 in 1983 (10 live matches a season) to £5,610,000 (66 live matches) in 2001.

Pierre Bourdieu suggests that football has been increasingly 'commercialised in the form of televised spectacle, a commercial product which is especially profitable because football is very widely practised' (Bourdieu 1999b, p. 16). He argued that the result of these developments was the 'extension to sport of the rules of neo-liberal economics' (Bourdieu 1999b, p. 17). He also argued that 'through the intervention of television' into global sports events (like the Football World Cup and the Olympic Games) the 'ritual celebration of universal values has become a medium for nationalism' (Bourdieu 1999b, p. 17). For Bourdieu, 'spectacularization' turns sport into an important issue for nation-states, including concern over training methods and performance-enhancing drug taking as a structural feature of elite performance sport. In what he calls the *champ sportif* ('artistic field') of sport, Bourdieu lists the various actors who compete over the commercial stakes. First are the athletes, the objects of the spectacle. Next, sports industry event managers of TV and sponsorship rights. Then come TV channel managers in competition for coverage rights. Finally are the bosses of major corporations with an interest in sport as a marketing vehicle. Bourdieu argues that 'Mediatization' has the following effects. It increases the number of matches (via the growth of European and international matches and tournaments). It increases the number of matches televised and creates a trend for subscription and pay-TV channels to get exclusive rights to certain events. It also leads to TV increasingly dictating the timing and scheduling of events, changing the structure of competitions and stimulating corruption scandals. Finally it creates opportunities for globe-trotting by increasingly cosmopolitan players, which affects the relationship between supporters and players and the clubs (Bourdieu 1999b, p. 18). Whilst mediatisation also produced stylistic innovations in TV production and commentary, Bourdieu asked, at what price?

Television rights are at the centre of the new political economy of world sport (Sugden and Tomlinson 1998a, pp. 83–97). In 1996 FIFA sold the world television rights (except for the USA) for the World Cups in 2002 and

Table 3.2 *The cost of the rights to broadcast live football league matches from the top division in England: 1983–2001*

	Start year of the contract						
	1983	*1985*	*1986*	*1988*	*1992*	*1997*	*2001*
Length of contract (years)	2	0.5	2	4	5	4	3*
Broadcaster	BBC/ ITV	BBC	BBC/ ITV	ITV	BSkyB	BSkyB	Sky
Rights fee (£million)[†]	5.2	1.3	6.2	44	191.5	670	1,110
Annual rights fee (£million)	2.6	2.6	3.1	11	38.3	167.5	370
Number of live matches per season	10	6	14	18	60	60	66
Fees per live match (£million)	0.26	0.43	0.22	0.61	0.64	2.79	5.61

* In addition Sky agreed to pay £22.5 million for interactive services and ITV agreed to pay £183 million for highlights. NTL initially secured an additional 40 PPV (pay per view) games for £328 million, but withdrew owing to financial difficulties. OnDigital (later renamed ITVDigital) stepped in but partway through the first season also ran into financial difficulties, largely due to the costs of football rights, and went into receivership.
[†] Approximate figure based on the rights fee divided by the number of years in the contract.
Source: Adapted from Gratton 2000, p. 21.
N.B. In 2000/2001 (final year of the old agreement) Premier League Domestic TV Payments were divided according to the formula: 50% total money shared on an equal basis to all 20 clubs (£6,297,250 each) and relegated teams to receive approximately 50% of the equal share – £3,070,500 – for two seasons following relegation ('parachute payments'); 25% paid as facility fee (TV appearance – £523,014 BSkyB/live, £53,290 BBC1/highlights); and 25% paid on merit (final league position, e.g. Manchester United received £6,728,440, Arsenal £6,392,018, Liverpool £6,055,596 etc.).

2006 to the International Sport and Leisure Marketing company (ISL) and KirchMedia, acting jointly. ISL/KirchMedia were therefore set the task of handling rights and securing arrangements with all the broadcasters in the rest of the world for the televising of the 2002 and 2006 World Cups. The price paid was US$2.2 billion (or £1.45 billion: £650 million for 2002 and £800 million for 2006) and was six times more than for all three World Cups in the 1990s (Herman and McChesney 1997, p. 77). In 1987 a consortium of European broadcasters had secured the rights for the 1990, 1994 and 1998 World Cups for a total of £141 million. This meant, for example, that BBC and ITV, the two main terrestrial channels in Britain, paid about £5 million for the right to televise the 1998 World Cup, whilst French TV paid approximately 50 million francs. With the ISL/Kirch deal, and other changes in the financing of professional football, some business commentators felt that the influx of 'corporate cash' meant that European soccer changed more in the year 1996 'than in the previous hundred' (*Business Week* 23 September 1996, p. 66).

As we have noted eight or so vertically integrated media conglomerates dominate the global media market. KirchMedia, run by Leo Kirch, was a second-tier media firm behind the likes of the major players – News Corporation, Time Warner, Viacom, Sony and Bertelsmann – but it had equity joint ventures, equity interests and long-term exclusive strategic alliances with most of them (Herman and McChesney 1997, pp. 70–105). The company sought to capitalise on commercial and pay TV and fill regional or niche markets. For example, while Rupert Murdoch's News Corporation had a minority stake in Premiere, one of Kirch's Pay TV channels, with two million subscribers in Germany, Kirch had a majority stake in SLEC, a company which owned the rights to televising Formula One motor racing for the next 100 years. Kirch also launched DFL, Germany's first digital satellite service, and signed exclusive deals with all the major Hollywood film studios in 1996. Securing the non-USA rights to the two World Cups in the same year fitted well with this strategy. It led several commentators however to warn that France 98 might be the last free-to-air World Cup, since Kirch would need to recoup the vast sums of money paid in securing the rights. In 2000 it became increasingly clear that Kirch was holding out for a much larger sum from British broadcasters than ever before. A stand off in negotiations – in which Kirch was reported to have asked for £170 million for 2002 only and the BBC and ITV were only prepared to offer £55 million – was announced early in 2001. Then the news about the financial collapse of International Sports Media and Marketing (ISMM)/ISL began to change the situation.

The idea of selling exclusivity of marketing rights to a limited number of partners began in Britain in the 1970s with Patrick Nally and his associate, Peter West, as the media agency WestNally. In the early 1980s the idea was taken up by Horst Dassler, son of the founder of Adidas, and at the time chief executive of the company. With the blessing of the then FIFA President Joao Havelange, Dassler established the agency ISL in 1982. ISL was 51 per cent owned by Adidas (Dassler) and 49 per cent owned by the largest Japanese advertising agency, Dentsu. It was clearly a means of maintaining Adidas's position as the leader in the sportswear market. Klaus Hempel was appointed as the ISL President. Later in the 1980s ISL linked up with the IOC, presided over by Juan Antonio Samaranch. It was ISL that established TOP, or 'The Olympic Programme', in which a few select corporations were able to claim official Olympic partner status. In 1987 Dassler died and the influence of Adidas in the world sportswear market declined as Nike, Reebok, Umbro and other companies challenged on a number of fronts. In 1991 Hempel and Jurgen Lenz left ISL to establish a rival marketing agency called TEAM (initially 'The Event and Marketing' AG, then 'Television Event and Media Marketing' AG). Whilst TEAM has provided services for the UEFA in establishing sponsors for the European Club Championship (or 'European Cup') and then the expanded UEFA Champions League, ISL has acted for FIFA and UEFA during Euro 96 held in England. The problem for ISL was that its parent company ISMM had begun to lose influence in football and sought to act for other sports. Different reports suggest it paid either £160 million or £800 million to the ATP tennis tour for a ten-year deal. ISMM also signed a deal with CART motor racing in the USA, the International Amateur Athletics Federation and the International Basketball Federation. It increasingly became over stretched and in April 2001 filed for bankruptcy in Switzerland with debts of £350 million (US$500). Further discussion of the problematic nature of the relationship between FIFA and UEFA – the leading organisations in world and European football – is dealt with in more detail in Sugden and Tomlinson (1998a).

The new political economy of world sport now includes television, sponsors and marketing agencies, in addition to the international associations and federations of sport, as parties in a 'golden triangle' or as McCormack once famously put it, an 'unholy alliance' (see Whannel 1986). In Britain, with the 1996 Broadcasting Act requiring that all World Cup matches should be available on terrestrial television, the two major free-to-air broadcasters eventually agreed to sign their largest sports rights agreement ever. The BBC and ITV agreed to pay £160 million in October 2001. However, both parties claimed the deal a success. The sum agreed was very close to that originally asked for by Kirch. Yet the agreement covered both television and radio transmissions for two World Cups (2002 and 2006). Although the timing of events for Western European audiences was not good in 2002 – matches kicked off at 7 am, 9 am, and 12 noon in Britain, for example – the 2006 finals that start in Munich in June 2006 are perfect for European television. So although the two broadcasters have paid nearly 40 times more than previously for a World Cup in television cost terms the deal is not unreasonable. The companies have bought 128 football matches, at approximately £1.25 million for two hours of programming. Compared with the costs in Britain for costume drama (£1 million per hour) and detective series (£600,000–700,000 per hour), the price is not excessive when the low origination costs of football tournaments are taken into account.

Just as modern competitive sport and large-scale sport events were developed in line with the logic of modernity, sports mega events and global sport culture are central to late modern societies. As media events, the Football World Cup provides cultural resources for reflecting upon identity and enacting agency, and more 'generally, for constructing a meaningful social life in relation to a changing societal environment that has the potential to destabilise and threaten these things' (Roche 2000, p. 225). Sport 'mega-events' – 'large-scale cultural (including commercial and sporting) events

which have a dramatic character, mass popular appeal and international significance' (Roche 2000, p. 1) – are important elements in the orientation of
nations to international or global society. We will return to these in Chapter 5.

Constructing Sport: Sports Journalism

It is important to consider the substance of the media gloss on sport if we are
to see how influential it is in attracting and creating the sports consumer. For
that reason, in the next sections, we will look at the role of sports journalism
and studies of the media audience. What ideas and themes are portrayed in the
images and messages of sport in the media and what is the impact on viewers'/
consumers' behaviour?

Koppett (1994) articulates a forceful argument for the importance of the
sports journalist in creating sport as a product to be consumed. He argues that
people's preconceptions about sport are largely shaped by what newspapers,
radio and television tell them, in 'great quantity from an early age' (Koppett
1994, p. xiii). He suggests that it is only through the mass media that
consumers – 'the spectators – get the information they need to make the
entertainment entertaining' (Koppett 1994, p. 4).

Sports journalists work with and on sport, Koppett (1994, p. 12) argues, to
help to construct the essential nature of the commodity a sports promoter has
to sell. This is 'the illusion that the result of a game matters'. The consumer
needs this illusion, he (1994, p. 15) suggests, because 'the entertainment
value of sports lies not in the physical actions observed but in the feelings
aroused in those who interpret the meaning of those actions'. Caring about
the outcomes of sporting events '*is* the entertainment' (Koppett 1994, p. 15). It
is generally 18–49-years-old, middle-class (ABC1) men who are preferred
when the audience is treated in this way 'as a commodity' (Lowes 1999).
Hence it is little wonder that Maria Burton Nelson could state 'The sports
pages have consistently told me that the sports I participate in don't count...
and the sports I like to watch don't count....Editors, writers, producers and
advertisers are primarily white, wealthy men. Sports coverage reflects their interests and their attachment to the status quo' (Burton Nelson 1996, pp. 200, 219).

Koppett (1994, p. 13) argues that people's voluntary emotional commitment
is to the sports illusion and 'the sports business consists of finding ways to
create and maintain this illusion'. In television sport has been presented
through its personalities, as much as the drama that they create. Sometimes,
however, this is not enough, as sports journalist Gene Collier (2000) wrote in
the *Columbia Journalism Review* after deciding to leave his profession: 'I
hated sports and I hated writing about them, and as I was aware those were
not the things people are looking for in a 44-year-old sports columnist....Sports
journalism in America remains the culture's omnipotent Department of Hero
Maintenance and Disposal'.

The manufacture of sport news is the product of news work (Lowes 1999). Journalists act as selectors, formulators and authors, and not simply reflectors of sports news. But they do this in the context of three main influences: institutional and market pressures; sports news values; and existing models of sports news writing ranging from what Rowe (1992) has called 'hard news', 'soft news', 'orthodox rhetoric' and 'reflexive analysis'. The basic unit of organisation of team games is the league and of individual sports is the tournament (Koppett 1994, pp. 32–33). Sports reporters cover these by following work routines. Like all journalists, sports reporters have to work within the confines of limited space, quotas and deadlines. Lowes (1999, pp. 33–47) states that the 'institutionalised work routines' of sports journalists are well recognised and widely accepted ways of doing things. These include 'working the sports beat' or following 'the routine round of institutions and persons to be contacted at scheduled intervals for knowledge of events'. For the journalist, sports publicity is treated as news.

There are two main, routine, that is, old and predictable, sources of sports news (Lowes 1999). First, professional sports organisations actively service the media. They have increasingly appointed media relations staff who produce press releases and hold news conferences. Secondly, journalists cultivate personal contacts 'on the beat' – athletes, coaches, trainers, agents, league and team executives. We observed earlier that the argument in much media analysis since the 1960s has been that news stories often present the 'predictably unusual' and unexpected. The media adopt a gatekeeping, or news filtering, role. In this way the media play a part in agenda setting. That is, not necessarily telling the reader or listener what to think, but what to *think about*. Since these arguments were first put forward, however, it can be seen that print journalism has begun to change, as have the conditions within which the media operate in general.

Changes in the news media in the UK since the 1960s include the following (Whannel 2003). There has been a rise in human-interest content (a secular change begun as long ago as the 1930s) – and it would appear that readers tend to read these sections of newspapers more than the serious news. Tabloidisation – in many respects stimulated by Rupert Murdoch's purchase of the *The Sun*, the move of his newspapers from Fleet Street to offices in Wapping and the defeat of the print unions, and technological developments in the production of newspapers – has left many British newspapers consisting of little more than a collage of images in which the meaning of a story can be seen at a glance (rather than traditional text-based columns). In terms of content there has been erosion of the public–private distinction – and the rise of sensation, scandal and gossip news has continued to grow. There has been a breakdown of the categories 'news' and 'entertainment' – leading to what Kellner (2003) calls the 'infotainment society'. Television – the pre-eminent mass medium of the past thirty years – creates intimacy and people on TV are seen as more familiar than big screen stars (Langer 1981). At the same time the rise of celebrity culture has been stimulated by the press and magazines (the top six celebrity magazines in 2004 in the UK were *Now, Heat, OK!*, *Hello, New* and *Closer* with weekly circulations ranging from 590,000 to 334,500). Large sections of the media have become increasingly commercialised and reliant on advertising revenue – as already noted commercial media seeking cheap content according to the 'mini-max' principle find sport is ideal. Finally TV now offers certain sports economic subsidies through exclusivity deals and rights agreements, with an impact on both the format and the appearance of sport and access to televised sport.

Burstyn (1999, p. 136) and Sage (2002, p. 219) note how in North American sport since the 1970s there have been several changes to enhance viewer appeal and the needs of TV schedules. These include the rescheduling of NFL football games, including the Super Bowl to night time, time outs at the discretion of television officials (football), the abolition of zone defences, and the introduction of the 3 point shot, slam dunk and the 24 second clock (basketball), more night games, the enlargement of the strike zone and the boundary fences moved closer in baseball, and the expansion of the NHL and rescheduling of the Stanley Cup final in professional ice hockey. Primarily these changes have come about because the media (television especially) favours a 'visible, star-studded personality driven form of sport' because this kind of sport 'best organises and exploits their audience' (Gruneau, quoted in Burstyn 1999, p. 136). The result has been the growth of officials and entrepreneurs at the expense of those who play the sport. Similar changes have been occurring in European competitions, as Bourdieu suggested earlier.

In the contemporary media landscape an event happens and now official and unofficial reactions to it alike can be almost immediate. Whannel (2002a, p. 206) suggests that the concept of 'vortextuality' is a useful way of describing these contemporary conditions. Vortextuality is a metaphor for the whirlpool-like process wherein it becomes impossible for the media to talk about anything else, but some 'super-major events' or celebrities, that come to dominate the headlines for a few days or weeks (Whannel 2002a, p. 206). Hence the vortex effect can be seen in the coverage of the death of Princess Diana, the marriage of David Beckham and Victoria Adams in 1999 and even the reporting of Beckham's supposed infidelity in 2004. The implications of this media context are that Beckham's wedding in 1999 and events like the death of Princess Diana in 1997 both acquired a greater intensity of focus. This has also increased the centrality of sport in the media, although many sports and localities are not part of the vortex. In a 'winner takes all' culture those who appear to have it all become great figures of fascination. Sports stars are also central figures in the social construction of contemporary ideals of public morality, gender and celebrity (Whannel 2001, 2002a, Cashmore and Parker 2003). At the same time, Whannel (2002a) argues that vortextuality alters the circulation and definition of issues. Moral panics – episodes of widespread fear and anxiety triggered by trivial events – can occur more frequently and just as easily disappear more rapidly. Concerns about the impact of commercialisation on sport and the behaviour of sports stars are just two such moral panics in contemporary society.

Consuming Sport: The Audience for Media Sport

It is possible to imagine the media in the shape of a circuit. Sometimes this is called the production–text–audience (PTA) model, with each part reflecting a stage in the circuit of communication. Under each stage specific aspects of the operation of the media have been studied. Researchers, such as Lowes (1999), who focus on the sender or production stage are likely to investigate production practices, professional ideologies and the nature of news values that assist journalists in the construction of their reports. Others, for example Whannel (1992), are interested in the messages being sent and aim to deconstruct or analyse texts, either through content analysis or semiology – literally 'the study of signs' – or a combination of these methods with other techniques drawn from literary studies. They investigate the production of spectacle, dramatisation and personalisation. Less frequently in the academic study of sport and the media, researchers have investigated the third stage – what does the media messages mean to audiences – the readers, viewers, listeners – of sport. What the audience do and what they make of sport in the media are, however, of fundamental interest to those who treat viewers as consumers. It is to some of this research that we will now turn.

Audience ratings research – via television set top recorders, surveys and focus groups – delivers commercially sensitive information of great value to commercial and public media organisations. This information is valuable since 'the real product of sport is the television audience, which is produced by televised sport performance, and the consumer, who is paying for it is the sponsor. In other words, television companies sell us to advertisers' (Horne et al. 1999, p. 276). It is not surprising therefore to find the close fit between the most watched sports on television and most read about sports in the newspapers and those that receive the most sponsorship. Clarke (2003, p. 46) confirms that football is 'king' (in the UK at least). Of the adults 29.5 per cent watched football on television and 18.5 per cent read about it in the newspapers in 2001. No other sport was read about by more than 9.2 per cent of the population. Only snooker (22 per cent), Motor racing (20.7 per cent) and Track and Field Athletics (20.4 per cent) obtained more than 20 per cent televising viewing.

Research into the influence of the media on the audience has a long history, attracting many different approaches and traditions. They can be broadly grouped around two emphases: What the media do to people and what people do with the media. The history of effects research over the past sixty or seventy years involves various swings in and out of favour for one or other of these broad approaches. The 'hypodermic syringe' or 'magic bullet' tradition (from 1900 to the 1940s) conceived of the media message as 'a one step flow', with the media treated as all-powerful, and the audience as composed of passive individuals. The 'two step flow' approach (from the 1940s onwards) recognised that media messages are often interpreted for others by 'opinion leaders', significant people in a community. This remains an important element in contemporary advertising strategies (Frank 1997). What people *do with* the media became popular after the development of the 'uses and gratifications' approach (also from the 1940s onwards) – in which people's needs, expectations, selective exposure to the media and gratifications – ranging from diversion, personal relations, personal identity, to surveillance or news gathering – are taken into account.

In the 1970s the Birmingham University Centre for Contemporary Cultural Studies (CCCS) developed what Abercrombie and Longhurst (1998) call an Incorporation/Resistance approach derived from the 'Encoding/Decoding' model of Stuart Hall (1973). He argued that 'preferred', 'negotiated' and 'oppositional' readings of media messages were made by socially structured individuals on the basis of their class, gender or racial social position. The origin of the notion of these three readings actually derived from work by the Weberian political sociologist Frank Parkin (1973) into the sources of social stability in society. During the late 1970s and early 1980s attention switched to the mass media as domestic leisure technology and the focus was placed on the social context of the consumption of the mass media rather than the messages' impact (for example, Morley 1986). At about the same time audiences started to be treated as fans who often interacted with the material they viewed, read and listened to. Studies of the pleasures of the text and viewers and readers as fans began to develop (for example, of soap operas, Hobson 1982, Ang 1985, see Ross and Nightingale 2003). Finally the Glasgow University Media Group (GUMG) began in the 1970s to analyse the media as 'agenda setting' organisations – guiding audiences not what to *think*, but what to *think about* (for example, Eldridge, 1993).

Each of these models are still utilised by different researchers. Like most social theories, they do not get replaced simply when a new one comes along. It is not appropriate to think that the latest is necessarily the best or provides all the answers. How useful are these models to think about media sport audiences? What do they tell us about the relationship between audiences for sport and the media? These are the sort of questions that ought to be asked of them.

In studying sports fans as consumers, Garry Crawford draws on the arguments of Abercrombie and Longhurst (1998) to question the incorporation/resistance paradigm (IRP) of audience research, in favour of one stressing spectacle and performance (the spectacle/performance paradigm, or SPP). Broadly speaking, this theory of audiences extends the critique of the dominant ideology thesis first articulated by Abercrombie et al. (1980). Crawford argues that too many studies of sports fans have looked for signs of either incorporation or resistance to a dominant ideology. Instead he wants to draw attention to the many other permutations of behaviour available to sports fans, whilst also portraying such activities in less romantic or judgemental terms. Rather than focus on the exceptional fans – such as football hooligans or members of the 'Tartan' or 'Barmy' Army, for instance – Crawford argues for attention to be paid to the ' "ordinary" everyday practices that patterns of sport related consumption and fan culture' are located in (Crawford 2004, p. 158). His argument is that contemporary society provides members with opportunities to shape and develop their identities by drawing upon 'cultural texts', and sport is a principal forum whereby and within which audience members can also become performers. Where Crawford departs company slightly from Abercrombie and Longhurst is in arguing for the continuing importance of what he calls 'social power'. In this respect he finds the post-structural arguments of Maffesoli (1996) about 'neo-tribes' persuasive.

Crawford argues that audience members use consumer goods and the mass media as 'resources' (Crawford 2004, p. 160). Their position in a fan group or audience is contingent and dynamic rather than fixed. Hence Crawford is also critical of those studies of sports fans that have attempted to locate audience members as belonging to a particular category (Wann et al. 2001). Instead he argues, drawing on Chicago sociological theory, that fans can best be considered as pursuing a (moral) 'career trajectory'. People change their location in the career progression as a result of life course changes but also 'several times each day' (Crawford 2004, p. 50). But Crawford also leaves himself open to a critique regarding the SPP he adopts. Is it such a satisfactory theoretical advance on other models?

In its original version (Abercrombie and Longhurst 1998) and with Crawford, the idea of the SPP model implies a teleology. People have moved from being isolates to being part of the masses and now comprise more ' "diffused" ' members of audiences, whereby 'we become both audience members and performers in our everyday lives' (Crawford 2004, p. 50). This is a model of audiences for postmodern times in which narcissism and the pursuit of life projects are considered the dominant cultural condition. It is also remarkably similar to the marketing and advertising view of audiences having moved from being 'passive saps' to active agents and now 'interactive players' (Ross and Nightingale 2003, p. 146). Without the re-insertion of a dominant ideology thesis, any sociological theory of fandom surely has also to ask whence did the propensity to narcissism, to performance or, for that matter, to consume sport arise?

Therefore it is important to reflect on the ways that different forms of the mass media create different ways of being a sports consumer. Readers of sport in the newspaper press and magazines tend to be men. In the UK they often read the newspaper back to front – starting at the sport sections – and this section of the paper is a great opportunity for advertisers to reach them. Magazines have been central to 'delivering the male' for at least the past fifty years. Listeners (to radio) have increasingly been given the opportunity to interact via radio phone-in programmes. But commentators often address their audience as if it were predominantly male, laddish and holding reactionary values. Viewers (of television and Internet images) largely, but not completely, watch sport in domestic settings. With multi-channel television it is now possible for audiences to become connoisseurs, even selecting the type of commentary they get. Finally Internet surfers may be seen as in the position to disrupt old patterns and producers are increasingly trying to outthink them. We consider new media and sport in the next and final section.

Sport and the New Media

Brian Stoddart (1997) argued that the mass media's role in the globalisation of sport could not only affect how people consume sport, 'but also the forms of revenue raising in which sports themselves are involved, ranging across merchandising, sponsorship, viewing, fan idolatry and news dissemination' (Stoddart 1997, p. 94). He argued that because of new media convergence consumers might also be able to challenge the alliance of sport and TV. Convergence involves the merger of TV, computer and telephone services to provide a wider range of delivery and merchandising services. From the point of view of the producer/provider this is a more targeted form of communication, but from that of the consumer it offers the possibility of greater control over selection. In Britain the announcement of a £30 million shirt sponsorship deal, the largest in the sport's history, between Manchester United and telecommunications giant Vodafone, was one indication of the direction that the growing convergence of the new media with sport might take. Fans of Manchester United and other top Premier League clubs can access information and live transmissions of matches via their mobile telephones. Yet Stoddart argued that the new online sports data services also create the possibility for a new subculture of sports fans. They could engage in 'a postmodern version of spectatorship and fan affiliation . . . which offers a curious form of resistance to the mediated forms of information and attitudes fed to fans by mainline information sources' (Stoddart 1997, p. 96). He suggested that sport consumers might be caught between twin processes of Murdochization and Microsoft-isation (Stoddart 1997, p. 101). Alternatively the Internet might 'provide a redress in balance in favour of the fan?' He outlined the following contrasting scenarios:

BI (Before Internet)
sports consumers are trapped by producers (unknowingly for the most part) by sports/ cultural intermediaries – for example, Mark McCormack and the corporation IMG's involvement in golf and tennis: own players, organise tournaments, and own TV rights.

AI (After Internet)
many sports consumers have the potential to go to other sources of information; some major 'old media' corporations attempt to connect to the on-line development, but so too do the new media, especially telephone companies. (adapted from Stoddart 1997, pp. 99–100)

In the first scenario the sports consumer/viewer can only access a tightly controlled product and, in the example, IMG recoups money at all stages of the sporting event. Stoddart (1997, p. 100) argues that in the second scenario 'the Net offers the potential for an alternative sports communication system'. How far this second scenario is likely to emerge is debatable, however, given the power of global corporations and the development of convergence. Even where active and interactive fans appear to be at the forefront of breaking down the distinction between production and consumption (Jenkins 2003), the 'media industries have sought to reintroduce the distinction' (Nightingale and Ross 2003, p. 217). Disputes over the online sharing of music, film and other forms of electronic intellectual and artistic property 'demonstrate the countervailing force' of the industry as opposed to the fan or consumer (Nightingale and Ross 2003, p. 217).

Conclusion

Television offers sport a form of economic subsidy through exclusivity deals with two main implications for the format of sport. First, a greater focus on media values, entertainment and advertising, and secondly, the issue of access for consumers to sport. The format of sport has changed alongside a narrowing of the range of sponsored/televised sports available on the main terrestrial channels (football plus a few others). Multi-channel television means that there are some minority sports networks, but these are only available to the subscriber. At the same time elite performance sport becomes a more significant part of consumer capitalism – sports adopt marketing and promotional strategies suited to the media ('branding') and become more 'spectacular', personality- and star-driven. Access to televised sport has altered since the 1950s in the UK. Between the 1950s and the 1980s there was competition for live sports coverage between the terrestrial broadcasting duopoly of the BBC and ITV. From the mid-1950s they had agreed not to compete for certain listed events: the FA and Scottish FA Cup Finals, the Wimbledon tennis championships, All Test Matches in cricket, the Derby and the Grand National horse races, the Oxford and Cambridge Boat Race, and the Olympic and Commonwealth Games. In the early 1980s the FIFA World Cup Finals were also added to this list.

With de-regulation of the media in the late 1980s and the 1990 Broad-casting Act, restrictions on bidding for exclusivity were lifted and the new satellite companies benefited – signing deals to broadcast live football, golf, cricket, snooker, darts, rugby league and some rugby union internationals. Since the late 1990s ITV has vigorously attempted to gain sports exclusives (including English Premier League football highlights, the Rugby Union World Cup and the annual Oxford and Cambridge Boat Race). Whilst the UK government still appears ready to maintain certain sports events as shared cultural experiences – hence regulation of the media and sport continues – the number of these becomes fewer and fewer.

Herman and McChesney (1997, p. 75) noted that ' "the sure fire winners" in global television are news, animation, and sports'. They also noted that turmoil in the global communications market was stimulated in the 1990s by the digital revolution, which eliminates the technological barriers that have divided media from telecommunications and both from computers and information. The ultimate shape of the global media is associated with the fate of global telecommunications and computers. As we have seen, Brian Stoddart (1997) argues that because of convergence consumers may also challenge the alliance of sport and TV. Sports viewers in the UK, for example, are concerned about the drawbacks of sponsorship – the majority in one survey felt that it made some events (and TV programmes) too commercial and gave sponsors too much power over events (Mintel 2000, p. 170). But the power to do something about it is outside the grasp of consumers alone.

As Toby Miller (1999) suggests, it is important to understand the connections between TV and sport in the broader context of the spread of neo-liberal economic policies since the 1980s. These have cut cross-media ownership regulations, reduced public sector broadcasting budgets, opened up terrestrial TV to international capital, and attacked public service broadcasting as elitist and inefficient (Miller 1999, p. 123). Sport has played a significant role in these developments since it provides relatively cheap content for filling the hours of TV and is attractive enough to some viewers to entice them to new technologies, like digital TV. As Miller (1999, p. 123) suggests, 'showing favoured sports only on digital systems is the favoured tactic for the millennium'. Miller argues, 'the television/sport/nation nexus is in turmoil' as we see the 'televisualization of sport and the sportification of television' (Miller 1999, p. 124). In sum, audi-ences originally created by public institutions are turned into consumers for the output of private capital as new technology, which is otherwise not attractive, is linked to the 'sports habit' (Miller 1999, p. 124). The media interest in audience behaviour, as consumers, certainly shows no sign of declining. New technologies and opportunities for advertising, such as virtual imaging projected onto the televised sports event or in the press, continue to be explored (PVI Europe n.d.; Newspaper Marketing Agency 2004). Rather than simply focus on national marketing strategies, however, now a lot more money is going into global events aimed at global markets. We shall consider some of these developments in the next chapter.

Part II

Commodification, Regulation and Power

4

Advertising, Sponsorship and the Commodification of Sport

Introduction

Karl Marx began his famous study of capitalism, *Das Kapital (Capital)* with the sentence, 'The wealth of societies in which the capitalist mode of production prevails appears as an immense collection of commodities' (Marx 1976/ 1867). A commodity, George Sage notes in his study *Power and Ideology in American Sport*, 'is something whose value is defined in monetary terms; commodity production is one in which goods and services are produced to be sold' (Sage 1998, p. 129). The authors of *Globalization and Sport* define the process of commodification as 'the making into a commodity for sale on the marketplace of items or services which were previously not part of market logic' (Miller et al. 2001, p. 130). We consider in this chapter the central role of advertising and sponsorship in the growth of consumer culture and the commodification of sport. First, we outline the emergence of consumer culture in distinct phases, with particular focus on the most recent third phase. Next we discuss advertising and the production of consumption through sport, especially the importance of brands. As an example of branding, we will consider the development of the sports celebrity endorsement culture. Finally we will assess the growth of the commercial sponsorship of sport.

The Formation of Consumer Culture

According to Nick Abercrombie and Alan Warde (2000, pp. 349–355), talk of consumer society implies that consuming things, usually buying them, including leisure goods, services and experiences, has become a central life interest and shopping a major preoccupation. It also suggests that consumption has become a key source of personal identity – both material and symbolic, that is it meets needs and it expresses a person's place in the world. When people live their lives in relation to the consumer objects around them

71

there is a consumer culture, or way of life. Alternatively, Mike Featherstone (1991, p. 114) argues that consumer culture refers to the social environment where advertising, the media and other meaning-making (semiotic) practices have become central and these practices and institutions remake the meaning of goods (and services) in order to sell them. In these circumstances, print, broadcasting and new media (information and computer) dramatically expand the reach and power of the commodity form.

Social scientists, as well as ordinary members of society, are highly ambivalent towards the advantages of consumer society or culture. It provides freedom and choice (if you have the ability to purchase goods and services) but contrasts with a time when purchases were deemed more secure and authentic. People at different stages of the life course and different generations therefore respond differently to consumer culture. Younger people find pleasure in acquiring objects, and more readily accept debt as a contemporary condition, while older people have a more moralistic attitude towards it and are more suspicious of borrowing too much. Writers evaluate the appearance of consumer society and commercialisation of leisure in different ways. Some see the changes as destructive – consumers are fed ready-made leisure, at a price and making a profit for others, which serves to distract attention away from important social problems, while providing pleasures often right inside the home. This is what Raymond Williams (1985, pp. 188–189) once referred to as 'mobile privatisation', where '...people are increasingly living as private small-family units...(or)...private and deliberately self-enclosed individuals...(whilst there is)...a quite unprecedented mobility of such restricted privacies'. Others argue that consumer society offers unprecedented freedom and opportunities to choose and shape identities and lifestyles.

Much of the debate about the emergence of consumer culture is related to definition. If consumer culture is the culture of 'consumer society' (Featherstone 1991, p. 113), then there is a need to shift investigations from the mechanisms of production to those of selling and the creation of wants and desires. Different accounts of consumer culture note its emergence at different times in different countries and for different social classes. Featherstone refers to historians who have suggested that the middle classes enjoyed a consumer culture in Britain from the 18th century. Ewen (1976) views it as a product of the 1920s in the USA, associated with the rise of advertising, fashion and cosmetic industries, and mass circulation newspapers and magazines. Some claim it began in the 19th century for the working class in Britain, France and the USA 'with the advent of advertising, departmental stores, holidays, restaurants, mass entertainment and leisure' (Featherstone 1991, pp. 113–114). Others note the connections between the expansion of consumer societies and the rise of neo-liberal economics and the so-called 'post modern' sensibilities (Dodd 1999, p. 136). For our purposes, it is possible to identify three phases of consumer culture.

The First Phase of Consumer Culture

The first phase of consumer culture relates to the production, promotion and consumption practices derived from industrialisation, advertising and the print media in the 19th century. This saw the development of mass-produced goods and markets on a national scale and the proliferation of consumer sites, sights and experiences. During this phase we see the emergence of modern features of retail consumerism – fixed prices, packaged as opposed to bulk goods, shop windows, gas lighting – and the emergence of the department store and other modern forms of retailing. By the end of the 19th century newspapers and magazines were also major sites of advertising. Richards (1991, p. 268) calls this the era of 'commodity culture'. Later, radio, the print media and advertising helped to create the consumer, and the associated ideology of 'consumerism'. Department stores held a critical place in this phase of the formation of consumer culture – such as the dream worlds of the Paris Bon Marché, Harrods in London and Jenners in Edinburgh – places where merchandise was transformed into a spectacle. Along with this went the apparent democratisation of luxury, via the creation of these new public spaces especially for middle-class women, and the reshaping of cities from being mainly places of production towards places of consumption.

To understand the economics of consumer culture, it is necessary to appreciate two aspects of Karl Marx's critique of capitalism as a way of organising production. On the one hand his admiration for its revolutionary productivity and on the other hand his recognition that this very success would create crises of over production. As Urry (1995, p. 118) notes, modern capitalist society was the first known one 'in which the dominant class has a vested interest in change, transformation, and in dissolving economic and social relations as fast as they come to be established'. As Marx and his collaborator Frederick Engels wrote in *The Communist Manifesto*, 'The bourgeoisie cannot exist without constantly revolutionising the instruments of production, and thereby the relations of production' (Marx and Engels 1973/1848, p. 45). Capitalism offers a life of permanent revolution – live over four or five decades and all will be revealed!

The Second and Third Phases of Consumer Culture

Marx also argued that capitalist success in maximising production would create problems. People (consumers) would have enough, as their needs would be met. The means to overcome this was to stimulate more consumer demand in some way. Various solutions to the problem of capitalist overproduction (Fordism, Keynesianism and the New Deal in the USA, for example) were developed in the 1920s and 1930s and the policies of the post-World War

Two Labour Government (1945–1950) sought to stimulate demand and create mass consumption. A second phase of consumer culture can therefore be associated with Fordism and Keynesianism in the 1920s and 1940s whilst a third phase developed with post-industrialisation and post-Fordism from the 1970s onwards. These phases saw, first, the growth of the mass production and circulation of goods and secondly, the growth of markets for them on a global scale. In what follows we focus on the period since the 1970s.

Following twenty-five years of relative economic stability and growth, the economic downturn of the 1970s – involving the oil crisis provoked by the oil producing and exporting countries (OPEC) seeking better returns for their product, and resultant impacts on the national economy, such as in the UK the 'three-day week' introduced to save fuel – led to new measures being introduced to deal with the volatility of capitalism. Monetarist economic policies, sometimes referred to as 'Reaganomics' and 'Thatcherism' after the former President of the USA, Ronald Reagan, and former UK Prime Minister, Margaret Thatcher, were seen as the new solution to the instability of capitalism. These economic policies, introduced in the 1980s, involved the privatisation of public services and utilities (that is selling public assets to private shareholders), the de-regulation or, as some would see it, re-regulation of industry (to provide it with more favourable conditions for profitability) and the cutting back on public welfare provision. Late 20th-century capitalism broke with Fordist and Keynesian principles on production, the organisation of work and consumption. A key feature of Post-Fordism was the introduction of new patterns of consumption (Urry 1995).

Post-Fordism refers to an unevenly emerging movement from the mass manufacturing base and assembly line practices of the Fordist era to 'flexible' and de-industrialised patterns of employment brought about by the implementation of technological change. This 'flexible accumulation' strategy includes the contracting out of functions and services, greater emphasis on choice and product differentiation, on marketing, packaging and design, and the targeting of consumers by lifestyle, taste and culture (Hall 1989, p. 118). Associated with it are changes in the international economy. The growth of world trading blocs and transnational companies, the internationalisation of labour and money markets, and the rapid growth and extensive application of new information and communication technology bring about the experience of 'time-space compression' in the 'condition of postmodernity' (Harvey 1989).

Lee (1993, p. 135) suggests that the importance of cultural and service markets in what we are calling the third phase of consumer culture represented a de-materialisation of the commodity form and the growth of 'experiential commodities' including cultural events, heritage attractions, theme parks, commercialised sport and other public spectacles. Echoing Harvey (1989), Lee concludes that the rapid growth of these experiential commodities represents a 'push to accelerate commodity values and turnovers'

(Lee 1993, p. 20) and 'make more flexible and fluid the various opportunities and moments of consumption' (Lee 1993, p. 137). Hence the last two decades of the 20th century saw the restless search for novel ways to expand markets in the advanced capitalist economies and develop new ones elsewhere. Lee (1993, p. 131) suggests that this explains the spread of consumerism to the rest of the world, the development of a vast children's market and 'the deeper commercial penetration and commodification of the body, self and identity'.

New production, circulation and retailing practices have assisted in the process of market expansion. These practices have included, *firstly*, obsolescence, product senility and the declining life span of goods on the one hand, and aesthetic obsolescence, involving the rapid turnover of style and fashion on the other. It is doubtful if any of the readers of this book know anyone who still ventures on to court with a wooden tennis racquet. Even more rapid is the turnover in sports footwear and apparel. *Secondly*, as Lee (1993, p. 133) suggests, another change has been the 'liberation of consumption' from restrictions of time and space – goods can be used and carried in a variety of locations and timeframes thanks to the application of micro-technologies. Miniaturisation means that there is always room for other goods for people on the move – whether portable digital music players and recording devices, cameras, telephones or computers. *Thirdly*, retailing has been reorganised and shopping is no longer limited by time and space either – 24-hour opening, home delivery and online shopping and banking mean that consumption opportunities are an ever present reality. *Fourthly* and finally, methods of communicating with consumers have developed alongside methods of facilitating consumption. In the 1980s the former included targeted mail-shots, teleshopping and mail-order retailing. In the 1990s marketing developed new audience and consumer research methodologies, including 'customer relationship marketing', based upon statistical analysis of the choices made by consumers via their credit cards (Ross and Nightingale 2003, pp. 42–71). At the same time, in-store credit facilities and credit cards (and more than 1500 different credit cards are currently available in the UK) along with opportunities to take out personal loans have fuelled consumer debt. According to the Office for National Statistics, debt in the UK reached 'historically unprecedented levels' in 2003 (cited in Walker 2003). By the end of 2003 it was estimated that consumer debt had reached £109 billion, or nearly £6000 each on credit cards, loans and overdrafts for over 18 million people. By the middle of 2004 newspapers carried stories with headlines such as 'Britons rack up £1m debt every four minutes' (*The Guardian* 3 June 2004). In short, promotion, selling and shopping have altered and assisted the growth of the third phase of consumer culture.

These changes in consumption have been referred to as leading to the 'aestheticisation of everyday life' (Featherstone 1991) in the midst of 'sign-saturated landscapes' (Lash and Urry 1994). Shopping complexes, malls, strips and retail parks shape the character and function of urban landscapes. Public space has been colonised by commercial interests. These changes are not isolated in one leading nation, but a global phenomenon. With only a few minor modifications for local language and target markets, one can see the same advertisements for clothes, sportswear and computers in the public places and transportation systems of Tokyo, New York and London. Klein (2000a, p. 117) calls this 'mono-multiculturalism'. In addition there has been a growing emphasis on product design and image. As Haug (1986, p. 50) noted a commodity's 'second skin' appears often much better than the first. The surface appearance does the work of seductive selling in promotional consumer culture. We will next consider how sport is implicated in this (Jhally 1987).

Advertising and the Production of Consumption through Sport

Advertising – the means by which goods and services are promoted and marketed in consumer culture – is the 'hidden hand in the story of the media' and equally the story of contemporary sport (Whannel 2002a, p. 36). Advertising has been central to change in the media – in battles between rival newspapers, the formation of commercial broadcasting, and the launch and development of satellite and cable television. It is also increasingly influential on the World Wide Web. In the form of sponsorship, product endorsement and corporate hospitality, it has also played a major role in the transformation and commodification of sport. In 1998, worldwide advertising expenditure was estimated to be US$435 billion and likely to grow faster than ' "the world economy by one-third" ' over the next two decades (Klein 2000a, pp. 8–9). Although it experienced a recession in the early 2000s, worldwide advertising was expected to reach US$363 million again in 2005 – and over 40 per cent of it was TV advertising (*The Guardian* 2 March 2005, p. 23). Advertising can therefore be seen as at the centre of the formation of consumer culture or 'promotional culture' as Wernick (1991, pp. 92–121) calls it.

Much advertising is entirely uncontroversial (for example, the classified advertisements for jobs or used goods in a local newspaper). Debates about advertising are mainly concerned with manufacturers' consumer advertising – the selling of mass-produced goods like cars, clothes, electrical goods, drink and household items – through television, radio, press, magazine and poster advertising. Raymond Williams (1980, pp. 178–179) explained that modern advertising developed in '...the half-century between 1880 and 1930,...as part of the modern distributive system in conditions of large-scale capitalism'. In particular the retailing boom and the emergence of the modern mass media at the end of the 19th century helped to produce the advertising industry. It was also at this time that a growth in sport participation boosted the early development of the sports goods and clothes industry.

Williams (1980, p. 189) once described advertising as a system of magic that manufactures desires and anxieties, 'You do not only buy this object: you buy social respect, discrimination, health, beauty, success, and power to control your environment.' Although Williams originally wrote his critique of advertising in the 1960s, it is still possible to find examples of the *magic system* in action today. Over a period of two to three weeks collect advertisements for sports goods (shoes, clothes and equipment) and sports services (events, health club memberships and so on) from newspapers, magazines, the radio and TV. Here are some questions to think about. Who is the advertisement aimed at? What is being sold in addition to the product/experience? How are the commodities (material or experiential) associated with cherished values and relationships – such as social status, taste and discrimination, health, beauty and so on? In what ways do contemporary advertisements suggest that the products they sell can provide answers to 'problems of death, loneliness, frustration, the need for identity and respect'? (Williams 1980, p. 190). What do you consider will be the impact of the advertisements? Discuss your findings with others in a seminar, a class paper or via a poster presentation.

For Leiss et al. (1986, p. 11), the consumption of goods and services, in which advertising plays a leading role, has come to take on the function of providing people with guideposts for personal and social identity, 'telling one "who one is" or "where one belongs" or "what one might become" in life'. Williams (1980) concluded that advertisements act as social narratives or fictional tales about identities and social relationships. When advertising has such a central role in society and generates people with consumer values geared towards personal consumption, consumerism literally becomes a way of life – a consumer culture (Miles 1997). Some have argued that the emphasis on images, rather than text, in contemporary advertising has also contributed to the formation of a specifically postmodern culture based more on visual stimuli rather than the written word.

Critical accounts of advertising have focussed on three main dimensions: economic – it is costly and wasteful; cultural – it stimulates consumerism and materialism; and social – it expresses conformist and often reactionary values. At the root of the criticisms is the view that advertising stimulates desires for products that consumers do not need. As Lee (1993, pp. xi, 18) notes, advertisers – the cultural intermediaries (Featherstone 1987) – know what they are doing. As we have seen, Burstyn (1999) argues that advertising was developed in the USA to promote consumption and persuade North American workers to change their attitude from being investors in the future to being spenders in the present. The key was 'the organised creation of dissatisfaction' (Burstyn 1999, p. 109) and this lies at the centre of advertising in consumer culture to this day. However, advertisements are judged by consumers according to their relevance, rather than the fulfilment of the promises made in them. Neither advertising nor consumption are just about manipulation, deception or irrationality. They offer and invoke a degree of creativity – choice within constraint. It is in this way that commercial and corporate interests play a major role in shaping personal and social meaning and identity.

Alongside the shift in consumption from Fordism to Post-Fordism (as outlined in Chapter 2), it has been argued that the consumer has become more 'unmanageable' (Gabriel and Lang 1995). This is where advertising remains important. Defenders of advertising suggest that the power of advertising is not so great. It aims to inform consumers about new products or maintain brand awareness, rather than manipulate them. Critics respond that so much money is spent on advertising and it is so pervasive that advertising must be cost effective. Since the Labour Party's first election victory under the leadership of Tony Blair in 1997, the UK government's Central Office of Information (COI) has become one of the biggest spenders on advertising in Britain. In 2001 the COI actually headed the table of the top 20 advertisers in Britain listed in the *Advertising Statistics Yearbook* (AA 2002, pp. 228–229) with total spending of £142.5 million (an increase of 38.5 per cent on 2000). The other 19 included more predictable consumer conglomerates such as Procter and Gamble (£114 million), DFS (£50.6 million), Sainsbury's (£46 million), Kellogg's (£41.9 million), Unilever (£39 million) and Mars (£36.9 million), telecommunications companies such as British Telecom (£91.7 million) and Orange, and car manufacturers such as Ford (£82.1 million), Peugeot (£45.6 million), Renault (£64.3 million), Vauxhall (£55.5 million), Volkswagen (£41.1 million) and Toyota (£36.8 million). Although there was an advertising recession in Europe in the early years of the 2000s, by 2004, with the combination of the UEFA European Football Championships in Portugal and the Summer Olympic Games in Athens, alongside the US presidential election, an upturn in advertising spending was predicted by industry analysts (*The Guardian* 10 March 2004, p. 23). The expansion of advertising also follows the growth of the amount of goods and services available to be purchased. In the UK in 2005, for example, there were over 800 different consumer markets, 2300 models of motor car (all with different engine size, colour, trim and so on), and supermarkets offered more than 150 varieties of lager and beer and nearly as many different types of breakfast cereal (Fletcher 2005). In the midst of all this choice, advertisers claim that advertising assists consumers to decide on what to buy. Whatever the view, however, it is clear that sport and sports 'mega-events' have been increasingly incorporated into the business cycles of multinational conglomerates, media corporations and advertising companies. As Silk and Andrews (2001) noted during these events, sport has also been used 'as a de facto cultural shorthand' in the advertising campaigns of TNCs to signify particular representations of national distinctiveness (also see various contributions to Silk et al. 2005).

Global Sports Goods and Brands

From an economists' viewpoint a brand is simply 'the name, term or symbol given to a product by a supplier in order to distinguish his offering from similar products supplied by competitors' (Pass et al. 2000, p. 44). As Coakley and Donnelly (2004, p. 333) note, however, ranchers 'sear their logos (brands) onto the hide of the animals, so there is no doubt about ownership or control. Corporations have done the same things with sport.' In 2000 a major exhibition at the Victoria and Albert Museum in London examined consumer culture and the proliferation of brand identities at the beginning of the 21st century (Pavitt 2000, Williams 2000). Sports stars and sports brands were a significant part of the exhibits on display. One of the co-curators of the Victoria and Albert Museum noted that 'Brands also have a cerebral dimension, which is the reputation they enjoy in the minds of consumers' (Williams 2000, p. 7). He argued that a brand is 'a sign loaded with meaning that we choose to consume because we feel we relate to it' (Williams 2000, p. 7). As Smart (2003, p. 77) notes, 'whereas advertising hawks the product, branding promotes a way of living, a way of doing something, a way of being'. In this respect, brands and branding can be seen as more insidious than simple advertising. How does this occur?

One development remarked upon by those who describe contemporary culture as postmodern is the ambiguity of so much consumer advertising. The reader or viewer increasingly has to produce meaning from an advertisement. This creates a sense of freedom, choice and creativity on the part of the (would-be) consumer (Kellner 1992, pp. 170–171). Kellner argues that there is no single culturally dominant message in much contemporary consumer advertising. Advertisements are aimed at diverse audiences according to assumed market segments. This illustrates for Kellner (1992, p. 172) that 'wherever one observes phenomena of postmodern culture one can detect the logic of capital behind them'. Additionally Buxton (1990, p. 429) noted with respect to rock music stars' involvement in the development of consumerism that commodities absorb signifiers and thus gain 'enhanced use value'. Advertising assists this absorption, generalising the commodity to mass status by loading it with symbolic value. This has been done successfully for electrical goods – such as the Sony Walkman and Apple iPod – as well as sportswear – such as Nike sport shoes (Du Gay et al. 1997, Goldman and Papson 1998). The product (commodity) – be it a CD or tape player, recording device or sports shoe – transcends its immediate functional use to become a symbol of a whole 'lifestyle'. Equally the star (of stage, screen, music or sport) becomes known not for what they did (performing extraordinary deeds) but who they were, and what they were 'like'.

In order to make the association with the branding of sports stars clearer, we can consider a number of ways in which different kinds of brands are constructed. 'Real things' make claims to authenticity (being 'the real thing' or 'the genuine article'). Examples include older brands such as Coca-Cola, Levi-Strauss and, in sport, the English FA Cup. 'The appliance of science' involves claims to trust (via the use in advertising of people – usually men – 'in white coats'). Examples include researched and tested brands, such as various items of sportswear, equipment and footwear. 'Excessories' are the opposite of necessities and relate to the 'conspicuous consumption' of objects, for example luxuries and indulgences, including premium sports events tickets and tourism. 'Get on and get up' brands make claims to empowerment (such as Nike's 'Just do it' slogan) and have involved information technology, mobile phones as well as other sportswear brands. 'Irreverent and independent' involves mocking the promises of branding (for example, Diesel versus Levi's jeans and several sportswear companies but especially Nike). 'Wonderlands' are places where the brand is available undiluted – for example, Disney World, Manchester United's Old Trafford stadium – referred to as the 'theatre of dreams' – and other sports stadia that base their appeal on heritage and nostalgia (Ritzer and Stillman 2001). 'Fun and friendly' brands offer promises of a good time. Examples include McDonald's, the use of animals to sell products, and advertisements for live events as spectacles. 'Guilt and anxiety' make appeals to people's conscience and responsibilities, for example, on the basis of ecological and social (especially parental) responsibilities. Finally 'Globally local' claims are made by international brands about their local meaningfulness, for example portraying American brands as welcome worldwide ('On planet Reebok there are no boundaries', Barber 1995, p. 24). The apparent universality of sports performance has meant that leading the way in much contemporary transnational advertising have been a few selected sports stars.

Michael Jordan, Beckham-Mania and the Sport Celebrity Endorsement Culture

Why has sport moved from the periphery to the centre of popular culture? One explanation is the increasing commercialisation and commodification of sport (Hoch 1972). The media, sponsors and marketing agencies are merely exploiting a growing interest in sport, which has been created by increasing media coverage of sport. A second explanation refers to increasing concerns about embodiment and the care of the body in somatic society (Turner 1992, 1996). Sport displays and tests the health of the body and is increasingly attractive because of that. A third approach considers the focus on celebrity as a symbol of the growth of achieved celebrity over ascribed celebrity, which in turn is part of a broader socio-cultural shift to an achievement-based or meritocratic culture (Rojek 2001). Celebrity culture appears to be a product of what Douglas Kellner (2003) calls an increasingly 'infotainment society'. Such new compound words (others include 'advertorials', 'infomercials') are a product of the collapsing of public and private discourses and a sign of the commercialisation of more and more features of social life. This is the general social climate within which consumer culture and the sport celebrity endorsement culture can be seen as 'two sides of the same coin' (Blackshaw and Crabbe 2004, p. 75).

Michael Jordan retired in April 2003 for the third time. During his career he helped fuel the 'trainer wars' between Nike, Adidas and Reebok. There was an advertising war wherein different companies tried to tag the personality of a brand across to the consumer. Important here was the use of slogans and strap lines such as 'There is no finish line' and 'Irreverence justified' (Nike) and 'The Edge' (Reebok). 'Spikey and Mikey' advertisements, featuring Michael Jordan and produced by Spike Lee, were met by negative advertising from other companies. In 1992 Jordan earned US$20 million for endorsing Nike shoes, more than the company paid their entire 30,000 strong Indonesian workforce (see www.nosweat.org.uk). In 1998 a *Fortune* magazine journalist estimated that the 'Jordan effect' on the global economy – including sales of drinks, cereals, tickets and sports shoes – was US$10 billion. By 2003 the same journalist estimated Jordan's impact had grown to US$13 billion, despite the fact that his best playing days were behind him.

Three factors explain the celebrity of Michel Jordan. First, Michael Jordan was an exceptional athlete. Jordan helped his team – the Chicago Bulls – to win consecutive NBA championships twice – in 1991, 1992 and 1993 *and* 1996, 1997 and 1998. Secondly, he arrived on the basketball scene at the same time as the NBA launched itself as a globally mediated commodity sport. In 1979 the NBA cable TV contract was worth US$ 500,000, by 2003 it was worth US$223 million annually. NBA, cable company ESPN and Nike all grew with Jordan. Jordan-branded Nike products alone realised US$340 million in 2003. Thirdly, Jordan emerged as black American culture became increasingly commodified. He became part of American 'soft power', and part of the spread of global capitalism (LaFeber 1999). Andy Milligan (2004) has subjected the career of David Beckham to a similar analysis. He argues that Beckham has also been managed as a brand – systematically using all the same techniques that have been developed to brand other commodities. It is no surprise that Beckham appointed Simon Fuller (the creator of the Spice Girls) in 2003 to help develop his image.

Cashmore (2002, Cashmore and Parker 2003) and Whannel (2001, 2002a,b) have studied David Beckham as an example of contemporary sports media celebrity. Like Whannel, Cashmore (2002, p. 2) asks, why is Beckham's every move – from tattoo, to clothes, to hairstyle (from 'soft Mohican' to 'corn row' to 'crop' style) so closely monitored and minutely dissected by the media? Cashmore argues that Beckham has become 'a product that we all consume' because his life is desirable (Cashmore 2002, p. 5). Somewhat over stating the case he writes: 'We're part of a generation of emotionally repressive, self-aware, brand-conscious, label-observant, New-Man attentive, gossip-hungry, celebrity worshippers' (Cashmore 2002, p. 5). For Cashmore, the Beckhams have become 'living advertisements, commodities in their own right' demonstrating and exhibiting 'a vision of the good life to which others aspire' (Cashmore 2002, p. 6).

Playing for Manchester United – one of the world's most well known sports teams – enabled Beckham to become associated with a global brand (see Andrews 2004). The involvement of Rupert Murdoch, Sky TV and the commercialisation of the English Premier Football League helped promote Beckham (signed in 1992, coming to prominence in 1995) as football became spectacularised. Football players began to enjoy a similar status to pop and film stars – and heap similar rewards through endorsement deals. Hence 'Beckham' as image received the same treatment as Michael Jordan as a global sport icon. Beckham has emerged in the era of celebrity culture. Cashmore (2002, p. 14) argues that 'The engine behind all these changes is known as commodification – the seemingly irresistible process in which everything is subject to being turned into an article of trade that can be bought and sold in any market place in the world.'

Klein (2000a, p. 57) cites American basketball player Denis Rodman as an example of the cross-promotion potential of superstar athletes, and Beckham is in the same mould. British sport has become part of 'the media entertainment industry' (Boyle and Haynes 2000, p. 103). Of course, Michael Jordan is the prime example of the sport endorsement culture and the production of a global sports superstar (Klein 2000a, p. 52). Adidas hope to do with Beckham what Nike did with (to and for) Jordan. For Beckham the image has been a composite of family, adherence to the good life and his achievements in sport (Cashmore 2002, p. 138). Pepsi-Cola advertisements play on the greatness and humility (in gladiatorial costume or in a sumo match). Police eyewear advertisements – their sales figures doubled after he modelled them (Cashmore 2002, p. 140) – utilise his image as a member of an elite. Advertisements for Meiji chocolate in Japan promote 'Life is Sweet' Beckham T-shirts. Beckham left Manchester United for Real Madrid in June 2003. A year later, and despite an indifferent and in many ways disappointing season, most of Beckham's £25 million transfer fee had been recouped from sales of his number 23 shirt.

Most analysts agree that Beckham has become a *polysemic* figure in the mass media – 'fans can read into Beckham whatever they want' (Cashmore 2002, p. 157, Blain 2002). This position is struggled over –'compound publicity' occurs when 'stories about stories' appear (for example, about the wedding, the names of his three children, the hairstyles, the rejection from The

Simpsons and so on). Ultimately for Cashmore (2002, p. 165) 'the fans and consumers who comprise his audience,... are active constructors of the Beckham phenomenon'.

Athletes used to be heroes rather than stars – known for their actions rather than their looks (Cashmore 2002, p. 173). Today celebrities are a product of television and rely 'less on doing, more on being noticed' (Cashmore 2002, pp. 178–179). Andrews and Jackson (2001, p. 4) note how the 'celebrity industry has evolved into a multifaceted, integrated, and highly rationalized phenomenon'. But what for? Cashmore argues that in consumer culture celebrities can be lived through – they assuage a sense of ontological insecurity (Cashmore 2002, p. 182) and negate a sense of powerlessness in other aspects of people's lives (Cashmore 2002, pp. 182–187). They offer another means of living with contemporary conditions of globalisation, risk and uncertainty. Hence Beckham fits the contemporary culture perfectly. Branding, marketing and celebrity endorsement have become central to both professional sport and contemporary consumer culture (Whannel and Philips 2000).

Sport and Commercial Sponsorship

Sport is often assumed to be autonomous from the wider political, economic and social environment. Yet it is faced with the problems of autonomy and dependence common to other forms of culture. Sport requires patrons or sponsors. Patrons have been the wealthy, the state (for example, indirectly via public broadcasters for much of the 20th century), educational institutions (both private and state-financed) and clubs (involving members acting in an unpaid voluntary capacity to support sport as a leisure activity or in accordance with amateur principles in the case of Olympic sports). Sponsorships have come from manufacturing capital, media/symbolic capital and more recently from financial capital. As Harvey (1989) and Zukin (1991) have demonstrated, capital investment moves to where the best returns can be made. The 'condition of postmodernity' speeds up the circulation of capital via developments in transportation and media of communication. Discourses about sport, industry and business become increasingly entwined through circuits of mutual promotion – commodification, spectacle, competition, performance, professionalism, globalisation, market logic and 'market populism' lead to the beatification of corporate culture (Wernick 1991, Frank 2000). Birkinshaw and Crainer (2004) and Bolchover and Brady (2004) provide recent examples of the tendency to forge relationships between sports management and managers of sports teams and management styles and techniques more generally. The growth and impact of commercial sponsorship on a select number of sports is, however, the most tangible feature of the relationship between sport and business corporations and is discussed in the next part of this chapter.

The Growth of Commercial Sponsorship

The Third Edition of *The Shorter Oxford English Dictionary* defines a patron as a 'person of distinction who protected a client in return for certain services', and 'one who supports a practice, a form of sport, an institution, etc.'. Patronage is defined as 'the action of a patron in supporting, encouraging or countenancing a person, institution, work, act, etc.' (*The Shorter Oxford English Dictionary* 1987, p. 1529). It is an act of altruism carried out with no expectation of return. The same source defines sponsorship as meaning (since 1931) 'A business firm or person who pays for a broadcast programme which introduces advertisements of a commercial product.' The individual or organisation concerned provides financial or material resources in return for some (not necessarily specified) commercial benefits such as publicity for the sponsor. Sponsorship derives from the same root as 'spouse'. The relatively recent growth of sponsorship as a crucial source of income for professional (and recreational competitive) sport can be seen as a form of 'marriage' between commercial corporations, including TV, and sport. The question many people have asked however is, is it a marriage between equals?

The Howell Committee, established by the Central Council for Physical Recreation (CCPR) defined sponsorship as 'the support of sport . . . by an outside body or person for the mutual benefit of both parties' (CCPR 1983). More recently Sleight's (1989) definition is cited by market intelligence company Mintel: 'Sponsorship is a business relationship between a provider of funds, resources or services and an individual, event or organisation, which offers in return rights and associations that may be used for commercial advantage' (Sleight in Mintel 2000, p. 8). Finally Kolah (1999, p. 1) noted that sponsorship is 'an investment in cash or in kind activity, in return for access to the exploitable commercial potential associated with that activity'. He continues that 'Those capable of being sponsored are . . . known as "properties".' Whatever definition is used it is undoubtedly the case that sponsorship – of not only sport but also the arts and other public events and occasions – has grown considerably in the past twenty years.

The actual amount of sponsorship in circulation is based on estimates; there is no definitive figure. Reports by the CCPR (1983), Kolah (1999), the market research company Ipsos-RSL and the account in Gratton and Taylor (2000) provide the basis for the following figures. It is worth noting that they may both over- and underestimate the extent of sponsorship. The overestimate may be a reflection of the desire to exaggerate the involvement of private businesses in public life. The underestimate may be a product of the methodology used to collect the figures. The estimates suggest that sports sponsorship in the UK grew from about £2.5 million per year in 1971, to £46 million in 1979, £100.2 million in 1983, and by 1998 it had reached at least £350 million. In 2002 sports sponsorship in the UK was estimated by the company Ipsos-RSL (2003) to be worth £442 million. As this figure was based only on rights fees released into the public domain and did not include personal endorsements, kit deals, one-off international events (such as the Commonwealth Games held in Manchester in 2002), activation costs or any other 'hidden extras', the actual figure is likely be at least 10 per cent higher. Worldwide Kolah (1999, p. 1) estimated that expenditure on sports sponsorship had risen in the 1990s from US$7.7 billion in 1990 to US$19.5 billion in 1998. He argued that commercial sponsorship was 'no longer just beneficial to sport – it is fundamental to its future'. We will look at some of the reasons why the commercial sponsorship of sport has developed in this way.

As we noted in the previous chapter, two global sports mega events – the Olympic Games and the Football World Cup – have lead the way since the 1970s in developing a transnational sport–media–business alliance worth considerable millions of dollars. Sugden and Tomlinson (1998a) argue that the IOC and the FIFA are part of the 'apex of a multi billion dollar global political economy' (Sugden and Tomlinson 1998a, pp. 83–94). The sport–media–business triangle transformed sport in the late 20th century through the idea of packaging, via the tri-partite model of sponsorship rights, exclusive broadcasting rights and merchandising. Sponsors of both events (Tables 4.1 and 4.2) have been attracted by the association with the sports and the vast exposure that the events achieve.

As Sugden and Tomlinson (1998, p. 93) summarise, 'Fast foods and snacks, soft and alcoholic drinks, cars, batteries, photographic equipment and electronic media, credit sources – these are the items around which the global sponsorship of football has been based, with their classic evocation of a predominantly masculinist realm of consumption: drinking, snacking, shaving, driving.' Despite attempts at so-called 'ambush marketing' (saturation advertising in locations and sites of the event without actually being the official sponsor) – in the case of both mega events, for example, by Nike whilst Adidas pays several millions of dollars to be a legitimate sponsor – the marketing of products of global corporations throughout the world via the vast television audiences attracted has been successful. In fact even Adidas have been subject to criticism as their 'three stripes' logo is such an integral part of their sportswear that they circumvent the IOC regulation forbidding advertising in the Olympic stadium.

At the national level, three main factors can be identified to explain the growth of the sponsorship of sport in the UK in the past forty years. They are financial crises in sport, technological developments and the expansion of television, and the banning of tobacco advertising in 1965. In discussing the growth of sponsorship of British sport in this period, it is impossible to ignore the importance of the government ban on tobacco advertising on television in the mid-1960s. As Makins (1972, p. 969), writing a few years after it came into force, remarked, 'Thrown out of the front door the tobacco companies nipped sharply in again at the back, by way of sport.' There were fewer

Table 4.1 *TOP sponsors (The Olympic Programme/Partner Programme) 1988–2004*

TOP-1 1988 Seoul	TOP-2 1992 Barcelona	TOP-3 1996 Atlanta	TOP-4 2000 Sydney	TOP-5 2004 Athens	Commercial sector
Coca-Cola	Coca-Cola	Coca-Cola	Coca-Cola	Coca-Cola	Soft drinks
Kodak	Kodak	Kodak	Kodak	Kodak	Photography
Sports Illustrated/Time	Sports Illustrated/Time	Time Inc.	Time Inc.	Time Inc.	Media
VISA	VISA	VISA	VISA	VISA	Credit cards
Bausch & Lomb	Bausch & Lomb	Bausch & Lomb			Optical, dental
		Xerox	Xerox	Xerox	Photocopying
Brother	Brother				Typewriters
Philips	Philips				Audio and TV
3M	3M				Magnetic tapes
Federal Express	United States Postal Service (USPS)	United Parcel Service	United Parcel Service		Couriers
Matsushita Electric (Panasonic)	Matsushita (Panasonic)	Matsushita (Panasonic)	Matsushita (Panasonic)	Panasonic	Video
	Ricoh				Fax
	Mars				Food
		IBM	IBM		Data processing
		John Hancock	John Hancock	John Hancock	Insurance
			Samsung	Samsung	Communications
			McDonald's	McDonald's	Fast-food restaurants
				Swatch	Watches
				Atos Origin	IT services

Sources: de Moragas Spa et al. (1995) *Television in the Olympics*. London: John Libbey, p. 29; Kristine Toohey and Tony Veal (2000) *The Olympic Games: A Social Science Perspective*. Oxford: CABI, p. 108; www.olympic.org (accessed 5 July 2004).

Table 4.2 *FIFA World Cup partners 1990–2006*

1990 Italy (9)	1994 USA (11)	1998 France (12)	2002 Korea/Japan (15)	2006 Germany (15)	Commercial sector
Coca-Cola	Coca-Cola	Coca-Cola	Coca-Cola	Coca-Cola	Soft drinks
Gillette	Gillette	Gillette	Gillette	Gillette	Men's toiletries
Fuji	Fuji	Fuji	Fuji Film/Fuji Xerox	Fuji Film	Photographic
Philips	Philips	Philips	Philips	Philips	Audio and television
JVC	JVC	JVC	JVC		Audio and television
Canon	Canon	Canon			Photography
Mars	Snickers	Mars			Food
Vini Italia					Wine
Anheuser-Busch		Casio*	Budweiser	Budweiser	Beer/calculators
	MasterCard	MasterCard	MasterCard	MasterCard	Credit cards
	McDonald's	McDonald's	McDonald's	McDonald's	Fast-food restaurants
	Energizer				Batteries
	General Motors	General Motors			Automobiles
		Adidas	Adidas	Adidas	Sports wear
			KT/NTT		Telecommunications
			Hyundai	Hyundai	Automobiles
			Toshiba	Toshiba	Electrical goods
			Avaya	Avaya	Communications
			Yahoo!	Yahoo!	Internet services
				Continental	Car tyres
				DeutscheTelekom	Telecommunications
				Fly Emirates	Airline

* French legislation placed restrictions on alcohol advertising and Budweiser sold their rights to Casio.
Sources: John Sugden and Alan Tomlinson (1998a) *FIFA and the Contest for World Football* (Cambridge: Polity), pp. 92–93; http://fifaworldcup.yahoo.com (17/01/02, 10:05 pm); *FIFA Magazine*, May 2004, Number 5, p. 82.

loopholes when the UK Tobacco Sponsorship and Advertising Act, together with a European Commission directive, came into force on 1 August 2005. One of the most affected sports was Formula 1 motor racing. Since the mid-1970s, many Formula 1 teams have become synonymous with tobacco companies and raced under their colours. The British American Racing (BAR) team was actually established as a subsidiary of British American Tobacco and raced under the 'Lucky Strike' colours (Kelso 2005). More recently Ferrari ('Marlboro'), Renault ('Mild Seven') and McLaren Mercedes ('West') have all retained sponsorship deals with tobacco companies. The issue that the European ban on tobacco advertising raised (and was still being debated at the time of writing) was whether races staged outside of the European Union (EU) but broadcast within it also had to cover up the (mobile) advertisements.

Several authors, but most notably Whannel (1992), identified the root causes of the financial crises in British sport in the 1960s and 1970s as the product of four factors. First, the social and cultural background and related 'gentleman-amateur' ideology of sports administrators. Secondly, the artificial depression of costs of sport. Thirdly, the reducing flow of income from spectator sports. Fourthly, the ability of sport to dictate terms to the media (especially television). The first factor meant that, in the UK at least, there was a cultural aversion to running sport as a business. Sport was conceived of as a game and a pastime and not as an industry. Sports administrators were not expected to adopt management practices or adhere to commercial business ideologies. Partly this was because so much of top sports talent came either from the deferential working-class or middle-class amateurs. Neither group were paid a 'market rate' for their employment, and in the case of the latter nothing at all. During the 1950s the post-war boom impacted on sport by creating a wider variety of attractions on which people could spend discretionary leisure income. There was a resulting decline in live sports attendances and hence gate receipts. Whilst loyal followers did keep returning there were marked declines in all major gate-money sports. Finally sport dictated to the media and kept it (especially the then relatively new technology of TV) at arms length. Hence if money was made out of sport it was made around it, rather than in it (Hargreaves 1986).

These conditions changed in the 1960s and 1970s and in the development of the sport 'media sponsorship–advertising axis' or 'Unholy Alliance' (Whannel 1986). First, the artificial controls over professional athletes' wages were contested in the courts. The professionals won (in the case of football players, for example, when the maximum wages regulation was overturned). Secondly, traditional governing elites found their competence stretched and more professional administrators were employed. Thirdly, the mass audiences for sports events continued to drift away and created more of urgency in finding alternative income streams. Fourthly, attitudes towards generating money from the media and sponsors changed dramatically. TV and sponsorship became crucial sources of funding for sport. Sport acquired the commercial media's focus on two key aspects in this triangular relationship – entertainment and advertising. Hence it was, as Hargreaves (1986) wrote, these circumstances that 'rendered sports vulnerable to market forces and subject increasingly to a capitalist pattern of rationalization'. Sport started to revolve more 'around the media sponsorship–advertising axis' (Critcher 1987) and became incorporated into contemporary consumer culture. As we have seen in Chapter 3, for media executives certain sports (especially association football in the UK and most of the world outside of the USA), and sports mega events (such as the Summer Olympic Games and the Football World Cup), could provide 'killer content' to attract audiences to advertisers, new channels and new technologies, which in turn provided new means of consuming the spectacle.

Developments in Sports Sponsorship in the UK

As we have noted, the model for financing professional sport has changed according to Andreff and Staudohar (2000) from 'SSSL' to 'MCMMG'. By 1999, commercial sponsorship of sport amounted to 48 per cent of total sponsorship money in the UK (the rest was divided between the arts, community and broadcasting). This was equivalent to 9 per cent of all companies' marketing budgets.

In the summer of 2004, apart from the Olympic Games in Athens, the following sponsorship deals were on offer for sport in Europe and the UK especially (Collinson 2004). In football – Euro 2004 (Portugal) – eight sponsors (Canon, Carlsberg, Hyundai, JVC, MasterCard, McDonald's, T-Mobile and Coca-Cola) paid an estimated £120 million to the organisers UEFA. In tennis, Wimbledon's official suppliers included IBM, Rolex, Coca-Cola, Hertz and Slazenger. Motor Racing and the Formula 1 British Grand Prix at Silverstone had a minimum sponsorship price of £10 million per team. In total, though, Ferrari, for example, had a total sponsorship budget of US$250 million, including US$72 million from Marlboro, US$45 million from Vodafone and US$33 million from Shell. In the more exclusive Polo Gold Cup the sponsor was Veuve Cliquot. In Cricket Npower sponsored the Lord's Test Match (England versus West Indies) for £7 million. In Yachting, Cowes Week was sponsored by Skandia for £1 million.

There are many different types of sports sponsorship – a few examples of the main ones will suffice to demonstrate its scope. Airline companies in North America and the UK have sponsored sports venues (the Air Canada Centre in Toronto, the United Center in Chicago, and from 2006/2007 Arsenal FC in North London will play at the newly built Emirates Stadium). Most surfaces associated with sport are open to branding, hence Brentford FC, whose stadium is under the flight path of Heathrow Airport, agreed a £500,000, three-year deal with Qatar Airways to put their name on the roof of the stand. It has been estimated that 130 million people could see it. Communications and Finance and Insurance companies have also sponsored venues, including the Brit-Oval cricket ground in London. Sponsors of competitions include banks such as the Royal Bank of Scotland (RBS) Six Nations Rugby Union Championship, the NatWest One-day International cricket series and the Barclays Premiership Football League. Coca-Cola took over the sponsorship of the English First, Second and Third Divisions in 2004–2005 and transformed them into the Championship, League One and League Two respectively. Major events can be sponsored but usually not by one corporation. The NFL's Super Bowl is as well known for the hugely expensive television commercials that underwrite the event as for the game, and people outside the USA can see them via the website www.superbowl-ads.com.

Many different teams, sports and individual athletes are capable of being sponsored. In May 2002 *The Daily Telegraph* (29 May 2002) reported a sponsorship deal with the headline 'PERSIL sponsors kit for naked petanque team'. The company Lever Faberge that makes Persil were providing sweat bands, socks, baseball caps and towels for the British Naturist Petanque Team to use at the international championships to be held in Rotterdam in August 2002. They also met travel costs for the ten competing couples. There were reported to be only about 25,000 naturists in Britain and about 170 clubs, but the opportunity to gain newspaper coverage outside of traditional advertising space was probably enough to recoup the cost. Individual athletes have also been prepared to change their names for sponsorship. Thus Garry Hocking, captain of the Geelong Cats Australian Rules Football team, 'became Garry Whiskas to promote the cat food brand and raise AU$120,000 for his club' and snooker player Jimmy White became 'James Brown' by deed poll as a means of securing sponsorship from a sauce manufacturer during the Masters tournament held in Wembley in February 2005 (*The Guardian* 'Sport', 14 February 2005, p. 27).

In the UK Finance/Insurance, Sports Goods and Hotel/Travel/Leisure industry companies constituted 35 per cent of all sports sponsoring companies in 2002 (*Sportscan Monthly*, January 2003). Between 1994 and 1999, football and motor racing saw the highest growth in income from commercial sponsorship, had the biggest media coverage and produced the highest paid stars. Rugby union, following professionalisation in 1995, saw the greatest percentage increase in sponsorship – from £10 million in 1994 to £22 million in 1998 (a rise of 120 per cent). The distribution of sports sponsorship in the UK remains highly skewed however. In 2002, for example, football, rugby union, golf, cricket, athletics, rugby league, tennis and motor sport secured 85 per cent of the sponsoring companies and 87 per cent of the deals (*Sportscan Monthly*, January 2003). The singular attraction of football sponsorship in the UK is also clear – football attracted 28 per cent of all sponsors and 33 per cent of all deals. Whilst football enjoys the largest slice of the sponsorship deals, the income is not distributed equally around the sport. Small town football teams and those with little media exposure gain least. Even within the English Premier League, shirt sponsorship deals reveal the difference between those sides that dominate newspaper coverage, are regularly broadcast on Sky TV and are involved in European competitions – that is, that offer sponsors maximum exposure across all media. Thus according to *Sportscan Monthly* (July 2004) at the start of the 2004–2005 season Manchester United received £9 million per year from their shirt sponsor, and Chelsea (£6 million), Liverpool and Arsenal (£5 million) had other lucrative deals. This compared with Crystal Palace (£300,000), Portsmouth (£330,000) and West Bromwich Albion (£500,000) that fared less well.

The types of companies sponsoring sports in the UK have altered in the past ten years. Clarke (2003, p. 51) shows that sports goods and telecommunications have grown mostly since 1994, the latter undoubtedly comprising many of the mobile phone companies seeking international events, such as Euro 2004 (T-Mobile) and Formula 1 (Vodafone), to match their global networks. Clarke (2003, p. 52) suggests that six industries are likely to continue to dominate European sports sponsorship during the first decade of the 21st century – telecommunications, automobiles, finance and credit cards, beer, soft drinks and sports goods.

There are five typical objectives of the sponsors of sports (Clarke 2003, p. 46). First, to gain access to a specific target population on which the sponsor wishes to focus and create awareness or a predisposition to buy products in the future. Secondly, to gain association with a prestigious team, achievement or event. Thirdly, to gain increased television exposure for an intensified period of time with a guaranteed audience of loyal fans who are all submerged in the excitement of the sport. Fourthly, to develop corporate entertainment opportunities with new or existing clients. Fifthly, to launch a new product, create brand awareness or micro-market test products. According to responses to a survey reported by Clarke (2003, p. 49), the main reasons that companies gave for choosing to sponsor sports in the UK were to enhance their image (64.8 per cent), maximise awareness at national level through the media (42.5 per cent), gain access to specific target audiences or new markets (40.7 per cent), maximise awareness locally through regional media (38.9 per cent), develop relationships with customers (35.2 per cent), take advantage of corporate hospitality opportunities (29.6 per cent) and support new product launches (13 per cent). Less than 10 per cent suggested that it was for philanthropic reasons (9.3 per cent).

Problems with Sponsorship

If sport has been speeded up, has had changes in scoring introduced to create excitement and has more breaks introduced to allow for advertising (or a word from the sponsor), some might say what is the problem? Alternatively if you take a look in the media for examples of sport and sponsorship, ask yourself, which sports get sponsorship? Which sports get little? As we have seen, the distribution of sponsorship revenue is skewed towards a small number of sports – the big four in the USA, the top eight in the UK, rugby (both codes) and cricket in Australia and New Zealand. In 1985 Gratton and Taylor (1985, p. 64) assessed some of the arguments about sport sponsorship. They considered that sponsorship could be seen positively to expand the 'demand for both product and sport', generate income, provide a private market subsidy to sport and give it additional publicity. On the negative side, they considered the potential for loss of control over sport, the possibility of greater conflicts of interest between the sponsors and the governing bodies and the focus of most sponsorship on a few sports. More generally problematic according to Whannel and Philips (2000, p. 46) is the way in which sport has been established as the paradigm for the commercial funding of public activity. They (Whannel and Philips 2000, pp. 53–57) identify six concerns with commercial sponsorship, which we can add to Gratton and Taylor's to make the following list of problems with sponsorship.

First, sponsorship is unstable and unregulated – available more at the sponsor's whim rather than the sponsored sport's need. Secondly, sponsorship masks public funding – compared to the vast amounts of money spent by central and local government annually on sport and physical recreation through leisure services, public space, schools and universities (that is, the sports infrastructure), private sponsorship still remains a very small sum. Thirdly, sponsorship promotes self-censorship – that is, less risk-taking with events and competitions. Fourthly, sponsorship promotes commercially influenced judgements and compromises moral stances – that is, it can potentially conflict with the integrity of sport (for example, Cadbury's chocolate sponsorship of sports equipment for schools in 2003 – subsequently withdrawn – at a time when there was a moral panic about obesity). Fifthly, sponsorship is advertising disguised as benevolence – sponsorship is often viewed as philanthropic generosity but we have seen that this is not why many companies do it. The UK Inland Revenue certainly sees sponsorship through less rose tinted spectacles as it regards sponsorship as advertising for taxation purposes. Sixthly, there is an uneasy tension between sponsorship, citizenship and democracy – increasing reliance on commercial sponsorship can be seen as leading to the replacement of publicly accountable funding decisions by those of non-elected private interests. Seventhly, sponsorship tends to favour an elite group of sports – predominantly male, team, and of course televisual, sports. Finally, eighthly, sponsorship creates the possibility of conflict between governing bodies, clubs and athletes, for example where the athlete has individual sponsorship contracts different from those of his or her club or governing body, and a sport and its consumers, for example by changing its format to suit television which in turn attracts sponsorship.

Whannel and Philips (2000, p. 58) conclude that the perception that commercial sponsorship is a form of 'benevolent patronage' may be another legacy of the Thatcher years (1979–1990). As we have already outlined earlier, patronage and sponsorship should not be confused, and sponsors always enter into an agreement motivated by some commercial interest. Sponsorship is generally treated as a good thing and yet, in Britain at least, it cannot replace public subsidy which is several times greater than sponsorship. There is a need for greater monitoring and regulation of commercial sponsors.

Conclusion

Jackson and Andrews (2005, p. 4) suggest that by the year 2020, global advertising spending could be in the order of US$2 trillion and they argue, as we have also done in this chapter, that sport is now centrally involved in the media–advertising–business relationship. Venues, spaces, events, bodies and equipment are just a few of the places where corporate logos can be found in sport. In many cases public space has effectively been colonised for private interests. Rather than challenging social arrangements, contributors to the Jackson and Andrews collection conclude that sports advertisements mainly sustain and reproduce hierarchies based on 'race', gender, sexuality, disability and national identities. Today 'relationship marketing' and 'viral marketing' are the techniques thought most appropriate to sell goods in an interactive environment. Viral marketing, for example, involves marketers creating content 'that consumers want to actively circulate among friends. Even unauthorized and vaguely subversive appropriations can spread advertising messages' (Jenkins 2003, p. 290). As Dewhirst and Sparks (2003, p. 373) note in their discussion of the brand narratives used by three Canadian tobacco companies,

> Sponsorship messages comprise a system of commercialized metanarratives about the relationships between people, products and ways of living in a consumer culture. This system helps to normalize the integration of brands and brand promotions into people's daily lives as a status attribute of celebrities and a social marker for consumers.

Part of the problem for the critic of these developments is what Umberto Eco (1986, pp. 148–150), with his characteristic invention, referred to as 'the multiplication of the media'. What he wrote is worth considering at length:

> (L)et's try to imagine a not imaginary situation. A firm produces polo shirts with an alligator on them and it advertises them (a traditional phenomenon). A generation begins to wear the polo shirts. Each consumer of the polo shirt advertises, via the alligator on his chest, this brand of polo shirt (just as every owner of Toyota is an

advertiser, unpaid or paying, of the Toyota line and the model he drives). A TV broadcast, to be faithful to reality, shows some young people wearing the alligator polo shirt. The young (and the old) see the TV broadcast and buy more alligator polo shirts because they have 'the young look'.

Eco then posed questions – 'Where is the mass medium? Is it the newspaper advertisement, is it the TV broadcast, is it the polo shirt?' In fact there has been a 'multiplication of the media' in which some act as media of media. What is worse for the cultural critic is that it is no longer possible to state categorically who is the producer of ideology (the idea that wearing the alligator polo shirt is 'cool'). It could be the designer of the shirt, the manufacturer, the wearer, the TV producer and so on. Eco (1986, p. 150) concluded that 'once upon a time there were the mass media, and they were wicked...and there was a guilty party...'. But no longer. The situation is more complex. What Eco was referring to, amongst other things, was the development of marketing techniques devised much earlier in the USA that attempt to link consumers directly into the production and marketing of goods and services. According to Frank (1997) this was included in the 1960s, developing consumer scepticism about consumerism as a tool of promoting it. At the same time the commodity aesthetics of sport and sportswear have become integrated into the fashion system (Busch 1998). According to one fashion journalist, Stella McCartney, who designs a range of clothes for Adidas and Puma Rudolf Dassler, provides sports gear that 'would be wasted in the gym' (*The Guardian Weekend* 26 February 2005, p. 39). Certain forms of sport have become cool as well. We will return to these 'lifestyle sports' in Chapter 6.

5

Sport, Social Regulation and Power

Introduction

This chapter examines three main aspects of government involvement in sport in consumer culture – provision, consumer protection and promotion. Each aspect involves the operation of power, and brings the role of the state (at local, national and supranational level) in regulating sport under the spotlight. We shall argue that despite the rhetoric of globalisation the state remains a very important actor in sport (Houlihan 2003b, 2004). National squads in team games such as football, rugby and cricket are increasingly cosmopolitan, that is composed of players who qualify to compete for a particular country not by virtue of place of birth, but because of parentage, residential qualification or marriage. The same is true of national representatives in international athletic events, such as the Olympic or Commonwealth Games. Within leagues club sides are often composed of multinational teams as well – although the decision of Arsenal F.C.'s manager, Arsène Wenger, to field a completely non-British squad for a Premier League football match in February 2005 attracted considerable media comment (*The Guardian* 17 February 2005, p. 26). The 'galacticos' of Real Madrid – including Zidane, Raul and Beckham – have a common sponsor (Adidas). The German football team coach, Jürgen Klinsmann, was reported to have told his players that if they did not wear the boots of the sponsors Adidas they would not be able to play for the national team (*The Guardian* 5 May 2005, p. 33). Yet at the same time the state has become more involved in sport in the past forty years. At the elite, high performance, level the state retains a substantial role in funding and organising sport. As Houlihan (2004, p. 58) notes, 'Global sport is determined significantly by nationally set priorities.' Why is that? One answer is that increased government regulation results from intensified globalisation – 'the extension of sport beyond national boundaries does not take place by bypassing the state but requires its active participation' (Houlihan 2004, p. 69). The main questions we consider in this chapter focus on the role the state plays in the governance and regulation of sport in global consumer culture. First, we identify the main development in political philosophy influencing relations between sport and the state in the past three decades. Then we illustrate this philosophy with reference, specifically, but not exclusively, to the development of sport–state relations in the UK. Finally we identify the main contradictions and tensions that exist in the state regulation of sport as both practice and spectacle in consumer culture.

Neo-liberalism and Sport

It is conventional to imagine society as consisting of three sectors. First, there is the state, whose legitimacy ultimately relies on possession of the means of coercion. Secondly, there is the market, where profitability is the guiding principle. Thirdly, there is the voluntary sector, or civil society, where the principle of association is mutuality and the dominant form of organisation is the voluntary organisation (Wilson 1994, p. 11). It is in the last of these that sport has its origins in most of the advanced capitalist countries (Hill 2002). Yet the 'broad direction of social change has been to shrink the voluntary sector as the state expands and the market reaches into more and more areas of social life' (Wilson 1994, p. 11). It is increasingly important therefore to understand this shifting relationship between governments, the market and sport (as part of civil society). Their relationships are being redrawn and 'we are at a crucial stage of readjustment between the three sectors' (Henry 2001, p. 162). In fact, as Smart (2003, p. 167) notes, 'in practice the state has not so much been shrinking in influence as changing in form'. The state has become driven by neo-liberal economic policies in the past twenty-five years (Jessop 2002).

According to Miller et al. (2001, p. 132), 'Neoliberalism' refers to 'a belief system in which the individual pursuit of self-gain is understood to provide maximum benefits to the individual and society'. Government policies that stem from this belief system, political philosophy or ideology include 'market liberalisation, restrictive monetary policy, reduction in tariff levels, removal of the welfare net, privatization of government utilities and outsourcing'. In short, neo-liberal economic policies have shaped the development of consumer culture in the majority of advanced capitalist economies for the past three decades, and have in turn impacted on the relationship of governments to sport.

The relationship between the state and the provision of sport in consumer culture has developed gradually under the influence of issues at the nation-state level, the regional (for example, the EU) level and the international level. In the UK, for example, between 1900 and the 1950s, sport was led largely by the voluntary sector. In the 1960s and 1970s the government role increased. Since the 1980s the commercial sector has grown, especially in terms of sports goods (apparel and equipment), sport services (health and fitness clubs), the commercial sponsorship of sport, mega sports events and the televising of professional sport (Gratton and Taylor 2000, pp. 158–159, Henry 2001, pp. 177–191). Yet sport consists of diverse 'sport worlds' (Maguire et al. 2002) or communities of interest (Allison 2000). Hence there has been, and continues to be, a fragmented policy community in sport (Houlihan 1991). The three main tensions are between amateur, welfarist and commercial interests, with different values, practices and social status. Across these is the divergence between high performance, elite, sport, with an emphasis on results in national and most importantly international competitions and events, and more recreational, mass participation, sport, with equity-related objectives associated with social policy and public health policy. The balance between sport and social exclusivity and sport and social inclusivity therefore continues to underpin many of the debates about the role of the state in sport.

In addition, as we have noted earlier, some authors have argued that substantial changes have impacted on the position of the consumer in society, as there has been a shift from Fordist to Post-Fordist consumption. The consumer appears to be more dominant, producers more consumer oriented, there is greater volatility of consumer preference, greater market segmentation, a growth of consumer movements, many new products, with a shorter life, preference for non-mass forms of consumption and consumption has been aestheticised. This chapter suggests that the state has been involved in the regulation/protection of sport including its consumers and spectators in various ways. This has led at times to the sport spectator being treated as a consumer and at other times as a criminal. In the UK the government has shown concern about access to sport on television, the costs of replica football shirts and football fandom more generally through the sponsorship of 'Supporters Direct'. The latter is an organisation 'designed to offer legal and practical advice to groups of supporters who wish to form a trust in order to have more say in how their club is run' (Hamil et al. 2001, p. 1). The UK government has also supported attempts to campaign against racism and improve the involvement of minority ethnic groups in sport. At the same time in the case of football spectator violence developments in legislation have challenged some basic freedoms of movement and assembly in the UK.

As sport has increasingly been shaped by neo-liberal discourse and practice, and despite the associated policies of privatisation and withdrawal of state funding more generally, sport has received unprecedented state interest and involvement in different societies. In the USA, for example, sport has been used as an arm of foreign policy for several decades. Recent episodes include the call to the US Olympic Federation to boycott the 1980s Moscow Olympic Games after the Soviet Union invaded Afghanistan, Congressional censure of Beijing's 2000 Olympic bid and denial of a licence to broadcast the 1991 Pan-American Games to TV corporation ABC because they were to be held in Havana, Cuba (Houlihan 2002). In Australia since the 1980s, governments of apparently different political persuasion have transformed amateur sport. The Australian Institute of Sport (AIS) – sometimes referred to as ' "the gold medal factory" ' (Miller et al. 2001, p. 108) – opened in 1981 (a model that has been partially adopted in the UK since the 1990s). Then the Australian Sports Commission (ASC), with a multi-million (Australian) dollar budget, was established with responsibility for national planning and funding of sport (McKay 1991, pp. 67–89). Miller et al. (2001, pp. 108–109) note how 'The ASC was almost alone in being cushioned from 1996 budgetary cuts, and Sydney's hosting the 2000 Olympics guaranteed even more state funding.' The promotion of sport and the nation through the hosting of sports mega events has thus become a key aspect of government policy towards sport and sport has been enlisted in strategies of urban renewal and regeneration. These developments can best be illustrated with reference to one exemplar neo-liberal state: the UK.

The Neo-liberal State and Sport in the UK

Most commentators agree that since the 1980s there has been a redrawing of the relationships and boundaries between the state, market and civil society in the UK. This period has seen an apparent decline in collectivism and public policies based on equality of outcome through the creation of a social welfare safety net. It has been marked by the rise of anti-collectivism, public policies based on the encouragement of equality of access through the exercise of individual freedom and consumer choice – all values underpinning 'advanced liberalism' (Rose 1996, White 1999). In addition there has been the growth of markets and quasi-market conditions. Finally this period has witnessed the development of debates about globalisation and on a more regional basis Europeanisation. What has become clear from all these debates is that neither globalisation nor commodification are products of the 'natural motion' of capitalism. Both processes are reliant on government policy and changes in political ideology (Jessop 2002).

Alongside these changes the political projects of first Thatcherism and more recently 'The Third Way' under Prime Minister Tony Blair have drawn attention to the ideals of consumer culture in which the consumer is considered 'sovereign'. The Thatcher governments' policies of privatisation, deregulation and enterprise all influenced the formation of this new discourse concerning consumer culture. Especially important have been discourses emphasising notions such as choice and competition, which have become increasingly adopted in public services like education, health and social welfare. A second consequence of Thatcherism and 'Blairism' has been the widening gap between rich and poor, at the same time as there has been an increasing individualisation of the risks associated with living in a society governed by market-driven politics and policies (Leys 2001).

Of course, 'New Labour' in the UK is not unique. As Fairclough (2000, p. 77) noted, governments throughout Europe and North America have accepted 'the globalisation of the economy and the neo-liberal argument that it entails a drastic revision and reduction of the welfare state'. At the same time they have adopted 'a punitive stance towards those who are the victims of economic change and of the retreat from public welfare'. As Bourdieu (1999a, p. 182) suggested, 'it is impossible to understand the present state of affairs without taking into account the wholesale conversion to neoliberalism that began in the 1970s and was accomplished in the mid-1980s when Socialist leaders joined the camp'. Whilst it would be incorrect to simply call these developments 'Americanization', Manuel Castells (1998, p. 129) suggests that 'while each society will reckon with its own problems according to its social structure and political process, what happens in America regarding inequality, poverty, and social exclusion may be taken as a probable structural outcome of trends embedded in informational capitalism when market forces remain largely unchecked'. In political terms the implications, according to Bourdieu (1999a, p. 182), have been that state intervention has become seen as a form of 'totalitarianism', inequalities seen as 'unavoidable', whilst 'efficiency and modernity' are associated with 'private enterprise, and archaism and inefficiency with the public sector'.

More significantly, considering sport as an aspect of culture, at the same time as the rise of neo-liberalism, governments have increasingly moved towards what Norman Fairclough refers to as forms of 'cultural governance' (Fairclough 2000, p. 61). In the UK, interventions by government to change cultures, or ways of life, are not new. The Thatcher Government(s) between 1979 and 1990, for example, explicitly sought to create an 'enterprise culture' in which social and political well-being would be ensured not by central planning or bureaucracy but through the enterprising activities and choices of autonomous businesses, organisations and people (Heelas and Morris 1992). As Rose (1992, p. 146) noted 'enterprise' was a potent concept because it conveyed not just how organizations should operate but also how individuals should act – with energy, initiative, ambition, calculation and personal responsibility. The enterprising self was thus a calculating self, about himself or herself and on himself or herself. That the 'enterprising self' also appears to be a description of an active sports person is no coincidence. It is not unusual to find a particular kind of figure held up in high esteem. As Bellah et al. (1985 p. 39) once wrote with respect to the USA, 'A representative character provides an ideal, a point of reference and focus, that gives living expression to a vision of life, as in our society today sports figures legitimate the strivings of youth and the scientist represents objective competence.' Today perhaps some people might disagree with the second example, but few would argue with the first. Whether it is individual sports, such as tennis or yachting, or team sports such as football or rugby, youth is a key form of identification.

Under Tony Blair's New Labour, Fairclough (2000, p. 61) suggests that ' "cultural governance" – governing by shaping or changing the cultures of the public services, claimants and the socially excluded, and the general population – seems to be a more systematic part of government'. Cultural governance also 'implies an increased importance for discourses in shaping the action – managing culture means gaining acceptance for particular representations of the social world, i.e., particular discourses' (Fairclough 2000, p. 157). In this respect, sport has become a most important feature of government intervention and regulation (Green 2004). This importance has been reflected in a number of initiatives and publications. The UK Cabinet Office Strategy Unit document *Game Plan* (2002), for example, identified two main objectives for government in sport and physical activity. First, 'a major increase in participation...primarily because of the significant health benefits and to reduce the growing costs of inactivity'. Secondly, and maybe more importantly, 'a sustainable improvement in international competition, particularly in the sports which matter most to the public, primarily because of the "feelgood factor" associated with winning' (www.strategy.gov.uk/2002/ sport/report/sum.htm, accessed 22 April 2003). During the 2005 General Election the Labour Party Manifesto, *Britain forward not back*, was the only one published by the main political parties to specifically mention sport in detail. In Chapter 8, titled 'Quality of life: Excellence for all', the Labour Party looked 'Forward to Olympic gold, not back to cuts in sport and culture'. Whilst recognising the challenge of broadening participation in sport 'as wide as possible', the manifesto described support for 'the bid to bring the Olympics to London in 2012' as part of a plan to bring 'regeneration to the East End of London', creating sporting, economic and cultural legacies. Since 1999, Scotland has had its own Parliament, with responsibility devolved for certain aspects of government including sport. An amended version of the manifesto in Scotland therefore pointed out that if the bid for the 2012 Olympics were successful 'it would inspire a generation of sportsmen and women throughout the United Kingdom' and noted that Scottish business had 'already won contracts through the bid process'. In addition the Labour Party was 'studying plans to bring the Commonwealth Games to Glasgow in 2014', which would 'bring regeneration to the East End of Glasgow and leave lasting sporting, economic and cultural legacies'. Clearly the 'East End' of major British cities are considered to be in need of renewal, but whether the staging of major sports events in them is going to accomplish this remains debatable. What is not so debatable is that an uneven balance continues to be present in the politics of sport. In supporting certain sports rather than others governments help to define what is legitimate as opposed to illegitimate sport and leisure practice.

Contemporary Contradictions in Sports Provision

Speaking in 2003, the then UK Minister for Sport Richard Caborn (*The Guardian* 26 March 2003, p. 31) complained that 'There are 400 governing bodies and just 120 odd sports, and that illustrates how hard it is to find out what sports need and want. . . . My biggest problem is with the voice of sport, as it doesn't speak with one voice at all.' There are several tensions or contradictions that underpin contemporary sports policy and many stem from this state of 'disorganisation' (Roche 1993, Horne et al. 1999, pp. 193–221). One of the tensions in contemporary sports policy revolves around the dichotomy between social inclusion and social exclusion. Sports policy is focussed on both social order and health concerns. Sport is thought to help social order – primarily a concern with dealing with community decline, identity (patriotism), (anti-)racism and xenophobia – at the same time as it is expected to benefit public health. Yet these mass public and participation concerns are constantly compromised by considerations about improving elite athletic performance in international competitions and events. A second tension lies in the regulation of more commercialised sport, at a time when the government also wants to encourage markets. This raises issues of access versus commercialisation. A third tension exists between the true benefits and costs of hosting large international sports events (or mega events). Who really benefits and what are the real costs of staging mega sports events? A full audit of the *social* opportunity costs and benefits, rather than a simple *economic* analysis is required (Vigor et al. 2004).

Historical studies of the growth of state intervention into sport and leisure in Britain and other advanced capitalist countries suggests that governments have always perceived sports policy as a means to an end, rather than an end in itself. A comparison between countries suggests that national governments may have different goals, 'few of which relate to the intrinsic benefits and values of sport' (Houlihan 2002, p. 195), but they will often attempt to pursue them through sports policy. The typical *non-sporting* goals include nation-building (for example, in Canada and the former German Democratic Republic or GDR), and control of the young (for example, in France and Britain) (Houlihan 1991, pp. 40–50). In this respect, the present 'state of play' in sport policy and institutions bears the legacy of dominant ideas in the 19th century as well as a 'conventional wisdom' as to the appropriate division of labour between the voluntary, the public and the commercial sectors of sport and leisure.

Rather than providing a coherent and unified policy for sport, Roche (1993) has argued that the sports policy community in British sport had been little short of a 'disorganised shambles'. This political incoherence reflected the influence of different ideologies about sport and the lack of a central organising body for sport. Roche (1993, p. 102) identified the *gentlemanly amateur* tradition, *corporate welfarism* and the newer *market* sports interests. Each related to different political ideologies and British political parties – the amateur tradition with reluctant collectivism and traditional 'one nation' Conservatism, the corporate welfare approach with collectivism and the Labour Party and the market approach with the neo-liberalism of Thatcherism. Roche concluded that sport was one of the most 'divided, confused and conflictive policy communities in British politics' (Roche 1993, p. 78). He argued that British sports policy was disorganised because of the continuing clashes for influence over sport that the three groups he identified engaged in. Since the end of the 1990s a fourth political interest – the 'Third Way' of 'New Labour' – has been added with a specific sports policy interest of obtaining 'Best Value'. This has not made the sports policy community any more cohesive, although it has sustained the domination in sports policy of the combined ideologies of neo-liberalism and consumerism (Green 2004).

Regulating and Protecting the Sports Consumer

As noted earlier, Henry (2001, p. 162) argues that 'The relationship between the state, voluntary and commercial sectors is by no means static ... and ... we are at a crucial stage of readjustment between the three sectors.' Sport is influenced both by political institutions above and below the level of central government. These include local authorities, European organisations such as the Council of Europe (1998) and the EU itself, as well as international sports bodies such as the IOC – which some would see as the world's governing body of sport – and the FIFA.

Given the widely cited, and accepted, Council of Europe definition of sport, it is not difficult to see why sport might be viewed as a 'special case' when it comes to regulation. According to the definition, ' "Sport" means all forms of physical activity which, through casual or organised participation, aim at expressing or improving physical fitness and mental well-being, forming social relationships or obtaining results in competition at all levels' (Council of Europe 1993, Article 2). Sports can share the characteristic features of most elements of leisure production *and* consumption. Sport involves the production of experiences, skills, artefacts, objects and performances. It also involves the consumption of experiences, knowledge, artefacts, performances and goods produced by others (Haywood et al. 1995, p. 36). Sport is a source of recreation, entertainment, gambling, tourism, commercial transactions in goods and services and aspects of education (Haywood et al. 1995, p. 41). Participants consume time, space and equipment to produce performances whilst spectators produce interpretations during their consumption of sport.

Haywood et al. (1995, p. 39) argue that

> The more an activity is characterised by 'active' production...the more the attitude of the government...will be one of encouragement and financial subsidy...The more consumption-orientated the activity...the more the activity is likely to be provided by the private commercial sector, and the government to intervene to license and circumscribe it.

Whilst adopting a slightly different conception of government and governance we can nonetheless see that this view has largely been confirmed by developments in recent years.

From a Foucauldian perspective on power it is possible to consider that each form of human behaviour is subject to governance (Foucault 1981, Miller and Rose 1993, Wickham 1997, pp. 285–288). Foucault, however, considered power not to be a form of repression but a means by which human beings are created and utilised as subjects. Foucault considered power to cross all practices – both the state and private life – wherever people are ruled, administered, steered, coached or in other ways come to direct or regulate their own actions. Hence this subjectivity can be assessed in terms of strategies, tactics and procedures of regulation. From a Foucauldian perspective, then, government generally is about the way in which the self relates to power. From the 18th century onwards the capacities of individuals – as citizens, subjects and selves – has emerged as a central target and resource for authorities. Foucault (1979) refers to this as 'governmentality'. Rose (1992, p. 144) argues that 'The autonomous subjectivity of the modern self...is itself a central feature of contemporary governmentality.' We can consider this line of argument in more details by looking at changing discourses of the 'consumer' in the UK.

From Social Citizens to Citizen-Consumers

By adopting a Foucauldian perspective, we can see how the figure of 'the consumer' as such has been created through the discourses of various interests within the broader nexus of government (Miller and Rose 1997). In July 1999 the British Government published *Modern Markets: Confident Consumers* (London: Stationery Office) in which it was announced that the 'White Paper puts consumers centre stage. It recognises for the first time that confident, demanding consumers are good for business. They promote innovation and stimulate better value and in return get better products at lower prices' (quoted in Hilton 2001, p. 241). The 1999 White Paper (and subsequent legislation such as The Sale and Supply of Goods to Consumers Regulations 2002) was the culmination of decades of modern consumer protection legislation (Hilton 2001). Arguably consumerism was first officially incorporated into British competition policy with the Fair Trading Act (1973). This Act consolidated and extended UK competition law by controlling monopolies, mergers and take-overs, restrictive trade agreements and resale prices. It also established a regulatory authority – the Office of Fair Trading (OFT) – with powers to supervise all aspects of government competition policy (www.oft.gov.uk). This included the power to monitor changes to market structure and refer cases for investigation to the Monopolies and Mergers Commission (MMC) and Restrictive Practices Court (Pass et al. 2000, p. 78).

Through its interventions in issues of consumption the state thus plays an important role in shaping and defining the meaning of, and discourses about, consumerism and especially the consumer – as a rational, utility-maximising, individual, *customer*, or as an informed, socially aware, political, *activist* (Daunton and Hilton 2001, p. 5). The state provides services for consumers, sets up ideals of national taste and aesthetics, and indirectly affects the consumer through public health, child protection and macroeconomic policy (Daunton and Hilton 2001, p. 5). Whether consumers are encouraged to be advocates of public, as well as private, provision or simply shoppers in the free market is therefore largely a product of state initiatives and regulation.

Hilton (2001) argues that the politics of consumption in the UK before the Second World War were based on collectivist notions of citizenship, whereas since 1945 consumers have increasingly been encouraged to think of themselves as individual, private, economic agents. Business interests and organisations such as the Consumers' Association (CA, now known as *Which?*) have also mobilised consumers into a model of consumer politics acting as a watchdog to business rather than an alternative to it. The CA has thus become incorporated into the state apparatus along with other quangos, and its main motivation has been acquiring Value for Money rather than offering a critique of the fundamentals of free market capitalism (Aldridge 1994).

'Choice', 'value for money', 'redress', 'information' and 'education' have been the dominant words informing consumer politics under the New Labour Governments since 1997. Consumer citizenship in modern Britain has been a consequence of liberal and voluntarist traditions in state development, rather than a product of corporatist or grass roots activism as can be found elsewhere in Europe. As citizenship has been redefined with consumers at the heart of policy-making, protecting the consumer from within the market place, rather than offering a critique or a challenge to it, has become the model which applied to the consumer (or 'customer') of sport as well. We can see this with reference to the regulation of sport as commercial spectacle and sport as practice.

The Regulation of Commercial Sport

The regulation of commercial, professional, sport (sport as spectacle) in the UK has been developing in recent years. A three-year investigation by the OFT suggested that horse racing should be completely deregulated (*The Guardian* 9 April 2003, p. 29). In May 2003 the OFT reported on the Zurich Rugby Union Premiership following an investigation to establish if the 12 teams had acted as a cartel – a form of collusion between a group of suppliers aimed at suppressing competition between themselves. Whilst no action was taken, concerns continued to be expressed two years later about some Zurich Premiership sides seeking to avoid automatic relegation by offering money to clubs in the lower division (*The Guardian* 21 February 2005, Sport section, p. 21). But the most high profile cases have involved football and it is these that we will focus on.

BSkyB and Manchester United/Premier League

The transforming of the football fan into a 'customer' consumer has been one of the main aims of what King (2002/1998, p. 131) calls the 'New Directors' of English football since the 1990s. In line with this the board of directors of Manchester United accepted an offer for the sale of the club for £625 million from Rupert Murdoch's Sky satellite television company in 1998. This triggered a protest and the formation of Shareholders United Against Murdoch (SUAM) and the Independent Manchester United Supporters Association (IMUSA). The deal had to meet the satisfaction of the MMC. Other media groups started to show an interest in acquiring big name clubs – such as Arsenal and Aston Villa. At the same time, Manchester United remained one of the most widely recognised sports brands in the world.

> The official fan club has 140,000 members world wide in 200 branches and its supporters association also claims 100 million members in 2000 official fan clubs in 24 countries. There are an unprecedented 40,000 season-ticket holders and the official club magazine has a paid circulation of almost 118,000 in 30 countries. (quoted in Greenfield and Osborn 2001, p. 57)

Brown and Walsh (1999) documented the fans' campaign and the effectiveness of collective action. After 6 months (and the resignation of the Trade Secretary Peter Mandelson on a separate issue), Stephen Byers, his replacement, announced the decision on 9 April 1999 to block the bid. The MMC produced a 254-page document that stated that the take-over would have damaged the quality of British football. The MMC (1999) identified United as the strongest English football club and Sky TV would have been placed in a monopoly position.

At the same time the OFT were investigating the bundling of television rights for Premier League football. The Premier League on behalf of its clubs had packaged the rights to televise the games and sold exclusive broadcasting rights to Sky and the BBC. The investigation was heralded as brave given the influence of the Murdoch press over the Labour Government. It was assumed that the Restrictive Practices Court (RPC) would find in favour of the OFT with serious implications for the Premier League and the broadcasting deals. Sky's bid for Manchester United was interpreted as a defensive step – in case the OFT ruled that the Premier League contract signed in 1996 was unlawful, with rights reverting to clubs themselves. In the end the OFT maintained the principle of collective bargaining. After both decisions a different strategy was adopted by Sky (and other media interests). Because of Premier League rules over ownership they began to buy small (less than 10 per cent) stakes in various clubs. By April 2000, Sky TV was represented on the boards of Manchester United, Chelsea, Leeds United, Manchester City and Sunderland; NTL had interests in Newcastle United, Aston Villa and Middlesborough; and Granada was on Liverpool's board (Greenfield and Osborn 2001, p. 182).

Football Task Forces and Independent Commissions

Following the Manchester United/Sky incident the government set up a Football Task Force which in turn recommended the establishment of an independent watchdog to monitor the treatment of football fans more generally. The Independent Football Commission (IFC) supported by the government, the (English) FA and the (English) Premier League was established in March 2002. The IFC, consisting of eight people including an MP, a lord and chaired by a university professor and vice-chancellor, had a gender ratio of 6 men to 2 women. Its remit was to investigate issues such as ticketing policies, accessibility to matches, supporter involvement in clubs and merchandising. Aside from asking questions about which fans the IFC members were representative of critics of the body pointed to the fact that it can only make *recommendations*, rather than having any *statutory powers* with which to force changes in club policies.

Replica Football Shirts

English football clubs only began to seek sponsors for their shirts in the 1970s. Replica kits usually consisted of home and away strips, which changed little from year to year, and the market was predominantly for schoolboys. In the 1990s as football underwent transformations, such as the formation of the Premier League and establishment of clubs as plcs (public limited companies), replica kits became part of consumer culture. Football shirts especially, worn as a fashion item or a badge of allegiance, became another fiercely marketed commodity. Around 90 per cent of all sales of replica kit are sold in the first year after launch, and 90 per cent of those are sold between the start of the new season (August) and the end of December. By 2002 the market for replica kits was estimated to be worth £250 million (*Fair Trading* 2003). A club will usually have the same home and away strip for two seasons, with changes staggered to ensure that at least one new kit is launched each season. The exception to this is where a club changes sponsor. Hence in 2000, 'Manchester United launched five new kits after signing a £30 million sponsorship deal with Vodafone' (*Fair Trading* 2003, p. 17). Following England's 5–1 win over Germany in a World Cup qualifying match in September 2001, sales of the England replica shirt increased by £10 million.

A long-running concern of football fans therefore has been the price of replica shirts. In August 2001 the OFT began an enquiry into the sale of replica football shirts. Manchester United, the English FA and another eight companies (including sportswear manufacturer Umbro and retailers JJB Sports, JD Sport and Blacks) were investigated to find out if price fixing had occurred. The OFT found evidence that the organisations had entered into 'anti-competitive' agreements to fix the price of shirts made by Umbro (Black 2003). The setting of a minimum retail price, a breach of the 1998 Competition Act, occurred during key periods in 2000 and 2001, such as during the Euro 2000 tournament. The prices of short-sleeved shirts, the most popular item, were set at just under £40 for an adult size and £30 for a junior size. Some of Umbro's smaller retail customers were threatened with stock cancellations if they failed to comply with the agreed price (*Fair Trading* 2003, p. 16). The cartel were handed fines totalling £18.6 million for fixing the price of England, Manchester United, Chelsea, Celtic and Nottingham Forest replica shirts. JJB Sports, facing a fine of £8.37 million based on it having the highest turnover of the businesses involved, launched an appeal against the ruling in March 2004, but the judgement was upheld later that year by a tribunal (*Fair Trading* 2004).

After the ruling the prices of replica shirts fell. The chairman of the OFT, John Vickers, stated that before the OFT began its investigation 'it was very difficult to buy an adult short-sleeved England shirt for less than £39.99. By the time of Euro 2004, England shirts were widely available for as little as £25' (www.oft.gov.uk/news/press+releases/2004/162–04.htm). He claimed this was a demonstration of 'how competition law works for consumers'.

The Regulation of Sport as Practice

As already noted, the Cabinet Office Strategy Unit published its proposals for delivering the Government's objectives with respect to sport and physical activity in December 2002. *Game Plan* included plans for school sport as well as elite sports events. A national strategy for sport with Physical Education (PE) and school sport at its core was launched. This involved exhortations to get children doing more sport and financial incentives to create 'Sport

Colleges' in secondary schools (in England). Two years later, in the face of growing concerns about rising obesity rates, increased indicators of physical inactivity (such as fewer children walking or cycling to school) and declining number of active sports participants, the government announced that more funding would go into school sport, and the number of schools with 'Sports College' status would be allowed to increase from 328 to 400 by 2006 (*The Guardian* 14 and 15 December 2004, pp. 10 and 5, 9). It was expected that all school children in England would take part in 5 hours of PE per week by 2010 – as only 65 per cent took part in 2 hours of PE per week in 2004.

The moral panic over the 'obesity/health crisis' (Smith et al. 2004) has focussed attention on lifestyles rather than the environmental conditions, as we discuss in more detail in Chapter 6. Whilst hours of physical exercise have apparently fallen, time per day watching TV has increased in the past twenty years. Yet since 1982 local education authorities have been allowed to sell off school playing fields and more than 6000 have been turned into shopping malls or housing estates (*The Guardian* 16 December 2002, pp. 1, 8). In addition the government target of achieving 5 hours of PE a week by 2010 will involve only 2 hours within formal curriculum time – the rest is supposed to take place after school. Regulating sport as practice, as opposed to regulating commercial spectacle, also manifests contradictions in governmental policy.

The Influence of the European Union on Sports Policy

Henry (2001, pp. 241–249) has identified the five principal rationales for EU intervention into sport as trade, as a tool of economic regeneration, a tool of social integration, an ideological tool and as a tool of international relations. Yet when it comes to treating sport as a business, it is evident that a tension also exists at the heart of EU policy. Sports trade represented an estimated 3 per cent of GDP of Council of Europe member states in the 1990s. Since the 1970s, sport has been recognised as an economic activity according to European Community law (European Commission 1994).

One of the most significant instances of the EU treating sport like an industry was in December 1995 after the Bosman Judgement. This refers to a ruling made by the Court of Justice of the European Communities (the 'European Court') on 15 December 1995 in proceedings between the former Belgian football player Jean-Marc Bosman, the Belgian FA, RC Liege, US Dunkerque and the UEFA about the interpretation of Articles 48, 85 and 86 of the EEC Treaty. It enforced two changes that have affected all professional European football players. First, it abolished the legality of all foreign player restrictions or 'nationality clauses' on EU citizen players anywhere within the EU. Secondly, it confirmed the right of an EU citizen player to move free of any transfer fee to another country within the EU on the expiry of his contract. Until the Bosman ruling made the practice illegal European footballers were tied to their clubs even when out of contract. At the time the judgement was made, nearly every national FA in the EU enforced tight restrictions on the use of foreign players. Bosman won his fellow players freedom of movement between European clubs. Any player at the end of his contract has since been entitled to a free transfer to any club in Europe who wants to sign him. It also opened up European leagues to more non-European international players, including those from some of the newly formed professional football leagues in East Asia (Takahashi and Horne 2004).

The debate over access to televised sport reveals another tension between seeing sport as a cultural and traditional practice and a spectacular commercial enterprise. The former view of sport was exhibited in the revision of the EU *Television Without Frontiers* directive published in 1997. This stated that access via television to selected sporting events could be protected by national governments. This would enable the general population to see certain sporting events considered of national importance. The 'rationale here is that sport is more than a mere product, and that therefore its broadcasting rights cannot simply be sold to the highest bidder' (Henry 2001, p. 243). From the mid-1950s to the 1980s in Britain, competition for live sports coverage was between the terrestrial broadcasting duopoly of the BBC and ITV. Both broadcasters agreed not to compete for certain listed events (The FA and SFA Cup Finals, the whole Wimbledon championships, All Test Matches, the Derby and the Grand National, the Oxford and Cambridge Boat Race and the Olympic and Commonwealth Games). In the early 1980s the FIFA World Cup Finals were added to this list. With re-regulation of the media in the late 1980s and the 1990 Broadcasting Act, restrictions on bidding for exclusivity were lifted and satellite companies benefited – signing deals to broadcast live football, golf, cricket, snooker, darts, rugby league and some rugby union internationals. Yet governments also wanted to maintain certain sports events as shared cultural experiences – hence regulation of the media coverage of sport continued.

The English Premier League TV broadcasting rights deal concluded in 2000, to operate from 2001 to 2004, saw new rights relating to club channels and the Internet pushed through by the bigger clubs (see Chapter 3). Sky TV once more paid the largest share – £1.1 billion – for the right to broadcast 66 live games a season exclusively for four years. Some observers feared that there was a trend towards a more elite focus in football – primarily focussing on the 'Premiership within the Premiership'. The EU wanted to see the exclusivity deal with BSkyB altered in future so that a number of broadcasters could take it in turns to show live games. This arrangement had already been concluded with UEFA's Champions League. From Autumn 2001 broadcasts were shared between ITV and Sky. However, EU competition law accepted that anti-competitive practices, such as collective selling, could be exempted from law if they brought benefits (especially to the consumer). This is what the Premier League argued in the subsequent round of negotiations over broadcasting rights conducted in 2003. By December 2003 it had been agreed that BSkyB would continue as the primary source of live English Premiership football coverage for a further three seasons (2004–2007), subject to a small number of live games being allowed to be shown on a terrestrial channel. Unable to find a terrestrial broadcaster that would reach its asking price for rights to each match, by May 2004 it was evident that Sky would in fact be able to retain its monopoly to live broadcasts for another three years (Milmo 2004b).

The issue of access to televised sport illustrates one of the contradictions that continues to exist between different parts of state involvement in sport. The state regulates sport both as commerce and as part of national culture. It wants sport to be a vehicle for international success and other policy goals – such as social well-being and social order. Yet it is apparently unable or unwilling to restrict the influence of the wider market forces driving change in the sports landscape. It tends to define the sports 'consumer' very narrowly as a 'customer', rather than an 'activist', although in some areas, such as the 'Supporters Direct' initiative supported by the Government, there is a vision of the consumer as a 'stakeholder' (Morrow 1999). Nonetheless the recently formed IFC can be seen as a rather toothless shadow body. The strategy of developing such organisations can be seen as more of a populist measure rather than being of more substance. This is a product of the contradictions of contemporary sports policy in which the dominant influences are commercial market interests as opposed to other interests that contend sports policy debates. A clear example of this predominance of private over public interest can be seen in relation to the staging of major international sports events, or 'mega-events' (Roche 2000).

Promoting Major Sports Events and Locations

It is becoming increasingly commonplace to find sport reported as having a positive impact on the local community and economy. For example, the London *Evening Standard* reported that 'England victories bring £400m feelgood factor' during the 2004 European Football Championship held in Portugal (22 June 2004, p. 2). That was just a few days before England took their exit at the hands of the host country. Two years earlier a headline on the sports pages of *The Scotsman* newspaper (30 October 2002, p. 27) proclaimed 'Six Nations worth £20m per match to economy'. Yet we need to consider these proclamations very carefully. The *Evening Standard* reported that sales of champagne, ready-made pizzas and beer had increased. But does this mean that people eat more or just that they substitute their spending onto things that make watching the tournament more simple and enjoyable? How many tourists (or day-trippers) avoid Edinburgh because of the rugby internationals at Murrayfield? We always need to consider how robust is the research upon which such (mediated) claims are made.

Game Plan, the UK Government strategy for sport, was actually more cautious about the benefits of hosting large sports events following a number of well-publicised embarrassments with sport-related 'megaprojects' in recent years (Flyvbjerg et al. 2003). These have included the failed bid to host the 2006 Football World Cup Finals, the eventual inability to host the 2005 IAAF World Athletics Championship despite being awarded it, and the National/Wembley Stadium project. The last of these has taken several years longer to complete and cost many times more than previously estimated since the site was eventually agreed upon in 1997. The costs of re-building Wembley Stadium have risen from £475 million to (at the time of writing) £757 million – making it the most expensive sports venue ever built (Wray 2005).

Despite these failures the national government still wants to attract major and mega sports events to the UK and the decision was made to give the go ahead to launch a bid to host the 2012 Summer Olympic Games (*The Guardian* 16 May 2003). Governments are interested in sporting mega events because of several factors – status and the promotion of the nation, the redevelopment of specific areas of land, inward investment through tourism. Consider two of these factors. First, there is an anticipated contribution to national income through tourism generated by such events. One estimate is that sports tourism generates £1.5 billion a year in the UK, without mega events. Secondly, there are the 'identity politics' involved, that is the prestige associated with hosting mega events that much of the world witnesses through television coverage. We will consider these factors in more detail.

Contributors to Gratton and Henry (2001) explored how sport might contribute to both economic and social well-being. Economically it promises to operate as an industry around which cities can devise urban regeneration strategies. Socially sport is used for the development of urban communities, reducing social exclusion and crime. Hypothetical links exist between sport activities/facilities and work productivity, health, self-esteem, quality of life, employment and so on. What does research tell us about these hypotheses? First, and perhaps most surprisingly, not as much research has been done as might be expected given the claims made. Secondly, research is often conducted in advance on behalf of interested parties – for example, the Scottish Rugby Union commissioned the Six Nations survey referred to in *The Scotsman* in 2002. Thirdly, there has often been inadequate measurement of final and intermediate outputs as well as inputs (Jeanrenaude 1999). Gratton and Henry (2001, p. 309) conclude, 'The benefits of sport for economic and social regeneration in cities therefore remains a theoretical proposition that still requires testing.'

Cities in the USA and UK used sport strategies in response to urban decline. Hence Glasgow, Sheffield and Birmingham have invested heavily in the sports infrastructure so that each has a portfolio of major sports facilities capable of holding major sports events. Each has been designated as a National City of Sport. Cities in Australia (Adelaide, Melbourne, Brisbane and Sydney) used sport as part of an economic development strategy in response to city/state rivalry – to establish a strong tourism industry. Cities in the USA, on the other hand, placed a huge investment in the infrastructure – such as stadium developments for the big four professional team sports. Urban boosterism in the USA saw more and more cities competing to offer professional teams facilities. Teams sat back and let bidding cities 'bid up the price' (Gratton and Henry 2001, p. 311). By the end of the 1990s there were 30 major stadium construction projects in progress in the USA – nearly one-third of the total professional sports infrastructure. The total value was estimated at US$9 billion.

In the UK and Australia, sporting events have been the main stimuli for using sport for economic regeneration. In the UK, despite several failed bids (from Birmingham and Manchester) to host the Olympics in the 1980s and 1990s, other cities have still aimed to host major or mega sports events. The European Football Championships held in England – Euro 96 – was seen as a success and led to more consolidated efforts to secure the so-called 'world class' events to Britain. This was considered to pay off with the generally successfully received Commonwealth Games held in Manchester in 2002. In Australia a similar strategy has been adopted at state level – states provide cities with the funds to bid for international sports events. It was estimated at the end of the 1990s that 5 per cent of Australia's tourism income of around $16 billion was derived from major events (Gratton and Henry 2001, p. 312). Coalter et al. (2000) note, however, that there is a marked absence of systematic empirical evidence about the social impacts of sports-related projects. Most commentators appear to agree that there will be a positive outcome with respect to health promotion, crime reduction, education and employment, and general 'social inclusion' but without actually having the evidence to firmly support the view.

Perspectives on the Promotion of Major Sports Events and Locations

To be a tourist is one of the central characteristics of the 'modern' experience (Urry 2002, p. 4). Travel and tourism is the largest industry in the world 'accounting for 11.7 per cent of world GDP, 8 per cent of world exports and 8 per cent of all employment' (Urry 2002, p. 5). Yet the distribution of tourism is skewed – 45 countries account for three-quarters of all international tourism departures. Increasingly sport can be seen as part of a 'sport–media–tourism complex' (Nauright 2004). Hosting mega events can be seen as one element in this promotion of tourism. Jackson and Weed (2003) estimate that possibly 10 per cent of all tourism has a sport element. Whilst from a demand perspective participation in sport takes many different forms – from incidental, sporadic, occasional, regular, committed, to driven participants – with respect to supply, opportunities and facility provision has grown in the past two decades. The impacts of the growth of sports tourism have been both positive and negative. The economic impact of sports tourism on the UK economy, for example, has been estimated as worth £2,611 million (domestic holidays £1,640 million, overseas visitors £142 million and day trips £831 million see Jackson and Weed 2003, p. 243). In Scotland, for example, golf tourism alone is estimated to be worth £100 million annually (www. sportscotland.org.uk). The Scottish Highlands and Islands Enterprise (HIE) unit estimated in 1994 that hill walking, mountaineering and associated activities generated £160 million (supporting 6000 full-time equivalent jobs); sport shooting generated £35 million (2200 jobs); salmon fishing generated £34 million (3400 jobs); and skiing generated £14.5 million (365 jobs).

Critics note, however, that much of the work in tourism is part-time, seasonal and casual in nature. In addition, tourism has considerable ecological and environmental impacts. The staging of sports mega events and the associated construction of sports and other facilities in cities can be seen as pandering to the needs of transnational elites. The city is increasingly arranged to cater for the lifestyles and occupational necessities of an urban elite in a process that Jessop (inelegantly) calls 'glurbanization' (Jessop 2002, pp. 186–193) and Hannigan (1998) refers to as the creation of the *Fantasy City*.

Three perspectives on the re-building of Wembley Stadium identified by Houlihan (2003a) provide a good illustration of the range of opinions about the building of specialist sports facilities. Marxists focus on the commercial (especially financial) interests that loaned the money to build the new national stadium and the continued commercialisation of sport. Hence the costs of debentures and seats at the new Wembley appear to be targeted at the corporate hospitality sector rather than ordinary sports spectators. Marxists also consider the purpose of the state in constructing such objects is as a means for reaffirming national identity. Pluralists (with whom Houlihan has declared an affinity in his previous work – see Houlihan 1991) tend to consider the interplay of numerous interests – profit, regeneration, identity and sport – without focussing on one particular feature of development. Finally Houlihan argues that feminists would view the development of the stadium as another example of public resources being skewed towards the pastimes of men. In this respect the sports stadium can be seen as another 'men's cultural centre' or MCC as Kidd (1990, p. 32) once described the Skydome venue built in Toronto as a venue for the Blue Jays baseball team.

Sports mega events may generate substantial negative impacts on local residents and the environment. The residents of Montreal in Canada have still not paid off the costs of the 1976 Summer Olympic Games. The opportunities and benefits of the 2000 Olympics in Sydney were not evenly spread throughout the host city (Lenskyj 2002). Six months after the Summer Olympics held in Athens, Government ministers in Greece voiced their concern over the final costs – estimated at £6.25 billion (€9 billion). One organiser said, 'Large sums were spent on the venues' construction, but no economic viability studies were drawn up for them' (quoted in *The Guardian* 4 February 2005, p. 34). In the UK the World Student Games held in Sheffield in 1991 produced a loss of £180 million, and the resulting debt has added 'just over £100 to annual council tax bills and will not be repaid until 2013' (www.strategy.gov.uk/2002/sport/report). As the IOC insists that host cities underwrite all liabilities, opponents of the bid to host the 2012 Olympic Games in London have warned that it could add at least a similar amount to London local taxpayers bills (www.nolondon2012.org).

There is always the potential for conflict between the economic and social benefits realised from hosting sports events. Economic impact studies often claim to show that the investment of public money is worthwhile in the light of the economic activity generated by having professional sports teams or mega events in cities. Much depends on predictions of expenditure by sports tourists. Yet Crompton (2001) has shown that such studies are often methodologically flawed – 'the real economic benefit of such visitor spending is often well below that specified'. Another measure of economic impact – on the creation of new jobs in the local economy – has often been politically driven to justify the expenditure on new facilities and hence the results are equally questionable. Crompton (2001, pp. 31–32) argued that there may be positive impacts from greater community visibility, enhanced community image, the stimulation of other economic development and increases in 'psychic income' – collective morale, pride and confidence. But there have not been many research projects carried out into this, nor have the methodologies needed to investigate them been adequately developed yet. Gratton and Henry (2001, p. 312) concluded that the 'economic justification for sports-led economic regeneration strategies has not yet been proven'. Siegfried and Zimbalist (2000) (quoted in *Game Plan*, www.strategy.gov.uk/2002/sport/report) argue that:

> independent work on the economic impact of stadiums and arenas has uniformly found that there is no statistically significant positive correlation between sports facility construction and economic development. These results stand in contrast to the promotional studies that are typically done by consulting firms under the hire of teams or local chambers of commerce supporting facility development. Typically such promotional studies project future impact and almost inevitably adopt unrealistic assumptions regarding local value added, new spending and associated multipliers . . .

The UK government has published this quotation and it will be hoped that these words do not come back to haunt it. At least it would appear that the opinions of several UK sports policy analysts have been taken into account. Mega events are a part of modernity, but they cannot be seen as a panacea for its social and economic problems. There is a need for clearer sports policy objectives, more adequate monitoring and evaluation of events, and further research to collect the evidence. As Gratton and Henry (2001, p. 314) state, 'the potential benefits to social and economic regeneration of sport in the city have not yet been clearly demonstrated' in the USA, Europe or Australia. More critically Lenskyj (2000, 2002) has suggested that as the IOC has become more like a 'transnational corporation' it has increasingly exploited 'young athletes' labor and aspirations for its own aggrandisement and profit' (Lenskyj 2000, p. 195). The local mass media's economic interest in sport (mega events) turns journalists from reporters into impresarios, from potential whistle blowers into cheerleaders. The hosting and staging of sports mega events may help to create bourgeois playgrounds but the long-term benefits are unevenly shared.

Conclusion

In the past twenty years, government sports policy – concerning regulation, consumer protection and sports promotion – has developed in a context of the spread of neo-liberal economic ideology and globalisation. This has produced a change in the relationship between sport and the state. Different states use sport for different non-sports ends – economic development and social development, nation building and signalling (branding the nation) and to assist in economic and political liberalisation. As Houlihan (2002, p. 194) notes, the 'willingness of governments to humble themselves before the IOC and FIFA through lavish hospitality and the strategic deployment of presidents, prime ministers, royalty and supermodels, is a reflection of the value that governments place on international sport'. The promotion of sports mega events – the Olympics and the World Cup especially – in turn rely on two agencies. On the one hand, the media are essential since without the media sports mega events would not be able to attract the public's attention and corporate sponsorship. On the other hand, without the thousands of volunteers who work for free, the games would not be able to 'go on' (see Nogawa 2004, for an analysis of volunteers during the 2002 World Cup in Japan and Korea). The state constructs what is and what is not legitimate sports practice, and in doing so effectively determines what the sports consumers' interest is. The state also creates the framework within which partnerships between local authorities, voluntary sports and commercial organisations operate. The neo-liberal state may have 'less responsibility for direct service delivery' of sport but it has retained, if not actually expanded, its influence because of the other agencies' dependency on state resources (Houlihan 2002, p. 200, see also Green and Houlihan 2004). Hence in consumer society the state remains the place to campaign – whether it is over inequalities and social exclusion, the regulation of mega events, consumer politics, human rights or environmental risks in sport. Sociologists and other social scientists need to continue to study these developments with greater reflexivity, not as cheerleaders but as critical investigators into the use of sport by the state and corporate interests in consumer culture.

Part III

Lifestyles, Identities and Social Divisions

6

Sport, Identities and Lifestyles in Consumer Culture

Introduction

In a consumer culture consumption largely takes the form of purchasing commodities, goods obtained through market exchange rather than produced for direct use. For most of the 20th century, sport in Britain was conceived of as a form of culture largely outside the social relations of capitalist consumer culture. In the last twenty-five years this isolation has broken up. Some social scientists argue that a transformation of sport has occurred because of the increased connection between sport, the media and advertising (Hargreaves 1986, Whannel 1992, Horne et al. 1999). Television has been 'probably *the* single most influential driving force underlying the commodification of sport' (Miles 1997, p. 140)

Chandler et al. (2002, p. 47) argue that commodification, used as a synonym for commercialisation, refers to the way that 'both sport and its participants have become products for sale in the marketplace'. The neo-marxist sport sociologist, Jean-Marie Brohm (1978, p. 180), once described sport as 'an apparatus for transforming aggressive drives' of the working class. Instead of 'expressing themselves in the class struggle, these drives are absorbed, diverted and neutralised in the sporting spectacle'. Although not part of the ruling class, sport stars figure in the mediation of corporately produced goods to the consumer. As such they enter what Rojek (2000, pp. 70–74) refers to as the 'celebrity class' and what Alberoni (1972/1962) before him called the 'powerless elite'. Yet Hunter Davies, journalist and writer, suggests that involvement in sport as a fan entails a different relationship than that of a simple customer (quoted in Miles 1997, p. 129) 'Every year United fans have their ashes scattered on the turf at Old Trafford. How often do you see that happening at Tesco's?'

How does sport in consumer culture differ from other aspects of culture? We can accept that professional sport is fully incorporated into capitalist consumer culture, or would like to be so; but as other forms of physical culture – a broader notion encompassing exercise and other forms of physical activity – sport has differing degrees of relationship to commodification. It exists between the state and the market. This distinction between sport as a participatory experience and sport as a spectator event is important. As we have seen, Pierre Bourdieu (1999b) refers to this as the distinction between sport as 'practice' and sport as 'spectacle'. In popular journalism, sport as practice in consumer culture produces two dramatic figures – the couch potato and the exercise addict. On the one hand is the concern that more and more people – especially school-aged children – are watching sport rather than doing it. On the other is the less often voiced concern that some people may be over doing it – whether this is the (male) football fanatic or the female involved in several aerobic exercise classes a week. In this chapter we present evidence and argument to help you make up your mind about the veracity of these and other social stereotypes about lifestyles and ludic body styles in consumer culture.

This chapter begins by considering theoretical debates about the concept of lifestyle. Many writers have associated the notion with individualisation, the use of the body as a medium of personal expression in 'body projects' (Shilling 1993) and the aestheticisation of everyday life – all part of the contemporary social experience of consumer culture. They ask how far is consumer culture 'an important context for the development of novel relationships of individual self-assembly and group membership'? (Lury 1996 p. 256). Whilst these accounts have emphasised the creativity of lifestyles, we will argue that the body and lifestyles, through advertising and branding, have been used in the production of contemporary consumer culture as a way of life (Smart 2003, p. 73, Klein 2000a, pp. 113–115, Castells 1998, p. 340). As John O'Neill (1985, pp. 101–102) argued two decades ago, 'The consumer is not born but is produced by anxiety-inducing processes that teach him or her to want things that service needs which arise in the first place only from commercial invention.' He continued, 'Millions of consumers are conscripted to the labour of learned discontent from their earliest childhood.'

Arguably central to identity in consumer culture is the development and spread of consumer identity. Bocock (1994) notes how new patterns of consumption developed among the urban middle and working classes at the end of the 19th century. The emergence of consumer society sees the emergence of consumer identity and 'a new kind of individual who is anxious... "to preserve the autonomy and individuality of his existence in the face of overwhelming social forces"' (Bocock 1994, p. 181). These types of people have an increased awareness of style and 'need to consume within a repertory or code which is both distinctive to a specific social group and expressive of individual preference' (Bocock 1994). The person in the city 'consumes in order to articulate a sense of identity, of who they wish to be taken for' (Bocock 1994, p. 182). Consumption as a means of signification is what some writers have claimed is an attribute of postmodernity. Clearly, however, it was something recognised as long ago as the late 19th and early 20th century by sociologists such as Simmel and Veblen. This feature of consumption also forms the basis for different status groups to establish their position or rank in contrast or distinction to others.

Consumption for symbolic purposes and status value might be thought to be the preserve of the affluent in the advanced capitalist countries. Indeed substantial numbers of the world's population – including between a third and a quarter of those people who live in the advanced capitalist countries – are mainly interested in consumption for material provision rather than for 'show'. Yet the idea of consuming goods for their symbolic value as much as if not more than for their use value is not restricted to these post-industrial societies. Consumerism has spread as a global 'culture-ideology' mainly for two reasons (Sklair 2002, pp. 108ff.). First, capitalism has entered a globalising phase, and secondly the technical and social relations that structure the mass media have 'made it very easy for new consumerist lifestyles to become the dominant motif' (Sklair 2002, p. 108). Hence ' "consumerism" may influence even the symbolic life of the poor' (Bocock 1994, p. 184).

Understanding Lifestyles in Consumer Culture

For much of its history, sociology has focussed on producing and working – the wider social and economic environment – rather than consuming and playing. In the past thirty years, sociologists have begun to re-focus their analysis, including consideration of consumer culture. Advocates of the idea of post-modern culture, in line with replacing the social with the signifying, have argued that consumption is now increasingly organised by lifestyle as opposed to traditional 'ascribed identities' or modern structural social divisions and inequalities (Slater 1997, p. 202). Yet arguably many people have been structurally excluded from the postmodern experience, by immobile identities such as being female, black, disabled and old. Sociological interest in the connections between different patterns of social relationships (for example, child rearing, attitudes to social institutions such as school, education and personal health care) and the consumption of material goods and culture has often been underpinned by an understanding of social class as the key social factor. With the emergence of the concept of lifestyle the precise relationship with social class has become less clear-cut.

As Tony Veal (1993, p. 247) describes it, lifestyle is 'the distinctive pattern of personal and social behaviour characteristic of an individual or a group'. He identified four key questions for research into lifestyles (Veal 1993, p. 248): First, what are the processes by which people adopt lifestyles or, alternatively, have lifestyles thrust upon them? Secondly, what is the meaning and importance of actual or desired lifestyles to individuals – are they as important as some people believe? Thirdly, are lifestyles expressions of freedom or a contrived tool of consumer capitalism – are people heroes or dupes? Fourthly, has lifestyle replaced traditional social variables, such as social class, gender, age and so on, as the key differentiating variable in society, and what might the implication be for the analysis of leisure and sport?

David Chaney (1996, p. 38) argues that 'we need something like a concept of lifestyle to describe the social order of the modern world'. We should see the notion as offering further elaboration on Western individualism. Bourdieu (1984/1979) offered another constructive use of the concept. He argued that the objects of taste acquire their meaning, as do words, through their associations with other objects (words), and not simply in themselves. Hence Bourdieu (1984/1979, p. 88) notes that 'detective stories, science fiction or strip cartoons may be entirely prestigious cultural assets or be reduced to their ordinary value, depending on whether they are associated with avant-garde literature or music...or combine to form a constellation typical of middle-brow taste'. The same applies to sport. No matter how 'good' a sport might be, if it does not fit within the social and cultural values and meanings, or 'habitus', of someone it will not be acceptable. Bourdieu (1984/1979) argues that some people with 'cultural capital' are able to transgress boundaries and experiment (the petit bourgeois, however, are the most deferential to convention). Cultural intermediaries (including academics like Bourdieu himself) can read the struggles over taste and the 'delusions' of others. Cultural intermediaries are able to comment and offer advice through magazines and other media outlets about lifestyles and fashions. In consumer culture new expert cultural intermediaries – advertisers, designers, marketers and point-of-sale-strategists – have a major role to play in the construction of contemporary lifestyles.

The following extract from an item in the British men's magazine *Jack* illustrates the role of cultural intermediaries in positioning sportswear within the fashion system of contemporary consumer culture.

> The Italy national football shirt has long been an icon of understated chic...Puma has picked up the gauntlet by producing a shirt that is worthy of this rich sartorial heritage. Neil Barrett, the Italian-based Brit. responsible for Puma's Italia collection, is a one-time Senior Menswear Designer at Gucci and Design Director of Prada Menswear. (*Jack*, June 2004, p. 25)

Advertising and the (re)construction of the ideal body mediate the relationship between consumption and personal identities. There is a clear overlap with the impact of consumer culture on identity.

Chaney argues, however, that Bourdieu's notion of habitus is too prescriptively deterministic – not allowing for the playful adoption of styles as commentaries on people's own lifestyles. 'A central element in why there has been an increasing interest in lifestyle practices in later modernity is that an established hierarchy of cultural codes is...being over-turned by contemporary practice' (Chaney 1996, p. 67). 'De-differentiation', or a blurring of categories of taste may be occurring (Martin 1981, Featherstone et al. 1995). Rob Shields (1992, p. 8) suggests that lifestyles based on leisure spaces are inherently liminal – outside normal social space and order. In their marginality to dominant frameworks of meaning, leisure spaces are open to the liminal chaos which places social arrangements in abeyance and suggests their arbitrary, cultural, nature. Shields argues against coherence in the actor and lifestyles – 'consumption for adornment, expression and group solidarity become not merely the means to a lifestyle, but the enactment of a lifestyle' (Shields 1992, p. 16).

In short, some writers suggest that lifestyles in consumer culture may be not just (as traditionally viewed) either a distinctive mode of exploitation or a new form of structural status overlaying established class distinctions. Instead 'we may have to rethink lifestyles as distinctive ways of being that call into question our understanding of the grounded embodiments of identity and community' (Chaney 1996, p. 76). He argues that the crisis of authority in modernity not only is the 'stuff' of intellectual discourse but also 'can be seen to motivate the investments in meaning and identity that constitute so much of everyday lifestyle practice' (Chaney 1996, p. 83). Hence lifestyle sites display both the reassurance of authority and the principle of ambivalence (or anxiety) in consumer culture. Shopping malls can offer reassurance, whilst life-styles 'may be practical means of living with ambivalence' (Chaney 1996, p. 84). Lifestyles become a precondition of the cultural innovations of postmodernism and especially neo-tribal forms of association (see Hetherington 1994). The *global* rationality of cultural corporations seeking economies of scale in the manufacture of taste is opposed by *local* knowledges that diffuse, subvert and appropriate commodities and services for 'irrational' styles.

Giddens' (1991, 1992, 1994) account of sociocultural change in late modernity also argues that identity is produced by radicalised modern conditions, but identity is not completely fluid. He states that 'Modernity is a post-traditional order, in which the question, "How shall I live?" has to be answered in day-to-day decisions about how to behave, what to wear and what to eat' (Giddens 1991, p. 14). Furthermore for Giddens 'in the context of a post-traditional order, the self becomes a *reflexive project*' (Giddens 1991, p. 32). For Giddens, then, lifestyles are radically reflexive – self-aware – and 'there is a necessary openness to the meanings of any lifestyle in context' (Giddens 1991, p. 85). In short, 'the meanings of lifestyle practices are not primarily determined by "forces" in the wider society (of whatever sort)' (Giddens 1991, p. 85). The development of lifestyles and the structural changes of modernity are linked through institutional reflexivity. 'Because of the openness of social life today, the pluralisation of contexts of action and the diversity of "authorities", lifestyle choice is increasingly important in the constitution of self-identity and daily activity' (Giddens 1991, p. 5). The significance of this view for understanding sport in consumer culture is that for Giddens self-identity is an embodied project, understood by individuals in terms of their own sense of and ways of telling, personal identity and biography.

For Giddens lifestyles are more significant projects than 'leisure activities', the latter notion having been corrupted by consumerism and neo-liberalism.

The commodification of self-hood, through marketing strategies, emphasises style at the expense of meaning. Understood as existential projects, rather than the consequences of marketing projects, lifestyles have normative and political as well as aesthetic implications. For Giddens a politics that flows from this significance of lifestyle in late modernity also transforms our understanding of emancipation. He distinguishes between a tradition of *emancipatory politics* (in which activists seek to improve the organisation of collective life to enhance individual autonomy) and *life politics*. The latter does not 'primarily concern the conditions which liberate us in order to make choices: it is a politics *of* choice. While emancipatory politics is a politics of life chances, life politics is a politics of lifestyle' (Giddens 1991, p. 214). Chaney (1996, p. 86) concludes, 'Lifestyles in this view are processes of self-actualization in which actors are reflexively concerned with how they should live in a context of global interdependence.'

Lash and Urry (1987 and 1994) argue that the break-up of organised to fragmenting and disorganized capitalism is paralleled in culture. For them this situation offers a positive potential for creative autonomy – grounded in increasing reflexivity and especially aesthetic reflexivity – 'the very stuff of post-organized capitalist economies of signs and space' (Lash and Urry 1994, p. 59). For them 'reflexivity' means ways of acting that are informed by a consciousness of the self – that acts by the actor are imbued with personal awareness. There is greater choice, although greater identity risk (Lash and Urry 1994, p. 50). For Lash and Urry (and Chaney) postmodern culture means greater importance being attached to aesthetic matters in both everyday life and in 'structural concerns' (p. 69). Hence lifestyle practice and personal identity are connected and self-conscious aestheticism is no longer restricted to the avant-garde, but becomes part of the 'aestheticisation of everyday life' noted by Featherstone (1991).

Despite these confident assertions, Colin Campbell (1995, p. 113) has argued that 'there may well be good reasons for believing that it is unwise of sociologists to build theories of modern consumer behaviour around the concept of "lifestyle"'. Campbell (1995, p. 114) considers the most problematic feature of the concept of lifestyle – or the '"consumption as indicative of identity choice" thesis' as he calls it – is that it implies that consumption carries implicit meanings or messages. Rather than adopt this 'communicative act paradigm' Campbell (1995, p. 115) suggests that it is important to make three distinctions. First is that between the idea that actions are intelligible and that they have a precise, agreed meaning. Second between something (a symbol or an object) possessing a meaning and something constituting a message. Third is the distinction between receiving a message and intending to send one. Hence if some one decides to buy a particular brand of trainers and wears them whilst out shopping then it is not possible to say that everyone who sees this person will read the significance of the shoes in the same way. Just because someone may be able to read a meaning into the shoes worn by another, for many people they will just be a pair of sports shoes. Hence Campbell (1995, p. 117) is sceptical of 'the general claim that the activity of consuming should be viewed as an endeavour by individuals to indicate a chosen "lifestyle" to others'. Instead Campbell (1995, p. 117) suggests that there are no grounds for assuming that consumption involves 'an attempt by the consumer to "adopt a lifestyle" or "create an identity"'.

Others have argued that it is the notion of consumer *choice* implicit in recent social theories of lifestyle and identity, as well as in political and business rhetoric, that needs to be critiqued (Warde 2002). Choice can involve selection, picking in preference, considering fit or suitable, as well as willing or determining. The problem is that the first two meanings sometimes get conflated with the final meaning – the ability of an individual to determine his or her own fate. The latter is dependent on more systemic issues – most notably the distribution of resources, and social, political and economic power.

> Behaviour is collective and situational; and the appropriate methodological stance is collectivist or institutional. If the collective and institutional conditions of consumption are ignored, then the structure of unequal distribution of power in the various fields of consumption is also overlooked, and all actors are attributed with an equal capacity for control over their own situation. (Warde 2002, p. 19)

He continues that 'In certain fields of sociological analysis, a strong emphasis on individual agency may be beneficial. However, in others, it may be prejudicial to understanding and, in the field of consumption, this is particularly the case at present' (Warde 2002, p. 18). Warde (2002, p. 11) suggests that many 'sociologists have increasingly come to adopt the premises of a common-sense view of the world of consumption which owes much to the penetration of commercial and promotional discourse into social science'. Further this 'appears to have encouraged, a tendency to turn the benevolent aspects of consumption into a legitimisation of commercial culture and an apology for liberal capitalist markets'.

The result has been the marginalisation of alternative perspectives, including, may be especially, the production of consumption approach. This approach has been passed over in much recent sociology and the balance has swung over towards cultural (and market) populism (McGuigan 1992, Frank 2000). There have been few structural analyses of the potential political divisions over consumption. They are mostly to be found in the journalism of the anti-capitalist, 'no logo', movement (Klein 2000a). Hence there has been an apparent convergence between the concerns of social science and the market research approaches to consumer behaviour – possibly a sign of the commercialisation of mental life and the subordination of intellectual reflection to the instrumental and practical purposes of selling goods and services (Monbiot 2000).

Another way of considering the concept of lifestyle critically, consistent with the Foucauldian perspective introduced in the previous chapter, is to view it as part of a new discourse of policing the body through the neo-liberal welfare state (Howell and Ingham 2001). Through exercising smart lifestyle choices the individual becomes personally responsible for his or her own quality of life. Responsibility for health is individualised. As Howell and Ingham (2001, p. 337) state, 'The language of lifestyle is one of independence and self-sufficiency: it signifies pleasure, freedom, success and mobility.' The debate about lifestyles in contemporary society mirrors others in social science about the extent to which our actions and decisions are freely chosen or manipulated by dominant institutions, values, ideologies and discourses. Rather than treating it as an analytical concept alone it is necessary to see it as a political one. This makes it another essentially contested term.

Identities and Consumption

The new conception of identity that has emerged in sociology in the past fifteen years views identity as an ongoing project. Previously the self was either considered as 'a fully centred, unified individual, endowed with the capacities of reason, consciousness and action' or someone 'formed in relation to "significant others"' through interaction between self and society (Hall 1992b, pp. 275–276). Now the subject, rather than 'having a unified and stable identity, is becoming fragmented; composed not of a single, but of several, sometimes contradictory or unresolved identities' (Hall 1992b, pp. 275–276). This is what Stuart Hall called 'the post-modern subject' in which identity becomes more of a ' "moveable feast": formed and transformed continuously in relation to the ways we are represented or addressed in the cultural systems which surround us' (Hall 1992b, pp. 275–276). Identities are constructed but questions remain about how, from what, by whom and for what purposes?

At its simplest we can say that identity refers to how we see ourselves in relation to others. In this respect identity is about similarities and differences – drawing distinctions between 'us' and 'them'. Bechhofer et al. (1999), for example, argue that we should think of any individual's sense of national identity as not fixed but as constructed and sustained by the mundane realities of everyday life. Hence the national identity that anyone will claim to have will vary according to his or her spatial and temporal location. It also depends upon how others perceive those claims. Bechhofer et al. carried out interviews with members of the landed and arts elites in Scotland and people who lived in Berwick-on-Tweed, a small town closest to the border between England and Scotland. (Ironically, the home ground of Berwick Rangers Football Club, who play in the Second Division of the Scottish Football League, is actually located across the border in England!) Their findings suggest that place of birth does not necessarily determine people's sense of national identity. Over time this sense of identity can change for any individual. In some families children will opt for the same identity as their parents while in others they do not. In making an identity claim, some individuals implicitly or explicitly reject alternatives; they are constructing their own identity by contrasting it with other possibilities. Bechhofer et al. distinguish between *identity markers* and *identity rules*: the former are those characteristics that have symbolic importance in identity construction or recognition; the latter are the 'rules of thumb' whereby in particular circumstances the markers are actively inter-preted. For example, a lone Englishman in a Scottish bar watching a sporting event between the two countries is likely to play down his identity, out of a sense of self-preservation if nothing else!

A second study of identity formation in the UK (Hetherington 1992) suggests that traditional sources of identity – such as class, gender, locality and ethnicity – may no longer be as influential. Hetherington studied the public reaction to young people following alternative life styles in Britain in the late 1980s and early 1990s. His research focussed on 'new age travellers', groups of people who moved about the country often, living in their vehicles and taking what work they could find. In addition to studying the 'moral panic' over the travellers Hetherington explored the nature of the social relationships uniting groups of travellers. He argued that in contemporary societies the traditional bases of identity were no longer as effective, and consequently people look for alternative forms of 'sociation'. These alternative forms, 'new sociations', in his opinion, were organised around shared beliefs, styles of life and consumption practices. These 'tribe-like' groupings, of which trav-ellers are an example, are relatively unstable and require considerable effort and maintenance from their members. Hetherington offered a theory of sociality and sociation that pointed to the importance of the *emotional bases* of the collective experience of the activities involved and the forms this takes as distinctive lifestyles. Following Beck (1992/1986) he argued that this occurs through two processes: *deregulation*, or the modernisation and individualisation of modern forms of solidarity and identity formerly based on class occupation, locality and gender; and *recomposition* into 'tribal' identities and forms of sociation (along the lines indicated by Maffesoli 1996). Consumption is particularly important for holding the travellers' lifestyle together. Clothing, jewellery, hand-made objects, recreational drugs, alcohol and distinctive types of motorised vehicle all carry significance in creating solidarity. Their activities, directly and indirectly, create subsequent commercial practices – magazines, craft skills, musical and other entertainments and skills derived from living on the road.

Recent research into identity – and there has been an awful lot more – therefore suggests the following conclusions. First, that identities are claims made, contested and negotiated in particular contexts. Secondly, that identities are most likely to be contested at times of uncertainty and social change (otherwise for most of the time people do not think about who they are). Thirdly, that identities are neither fixed nor unproblematic. Identities can be considered as constructed and processed out of the mundane realities of everyday life.

Individuals construct national identities (as opposed to state identities) by using identity markers and identity rules. Postmodern theorists tend to view identities as products of lifestyle and consumption choices, whereas traditional or late modern analysts suggest that identities are still fashioned from class, gender, local and ethnic relations. 'Many collectively experienced and consumed popular cultural forms are far from a matter of individual choice' (Sugden and Tomlinson 1998b, p. 178). The debate between them is largely over the emphasis placed upon change or continuity in making sense of the present.

Body Styles, Lifestyles and Consumer Culture

How do dominant body stories or narratives available in a culture shape who we think we are (our identity) and which lifestyle we think we can develop? (Sparkes 1997, pp. 83ff.). Several social changes have contributed to the transformation of the role of exercise and sport in society. These have included shifts in the nature of work towards more sedentary forms of occupation, the development of a discourse which turns this change into a *problem*, and 'proposes as its remedy a systematised program of activities anchored in a lifestyle' (Bennett et al. 1999, p. 124). Bennett et al. (1999, p. 117) argue that a shift has also occurred with respect to the general understanding of the body since the 1980s in societies such as the UK, the USA and Australia. Like Giddens they argue that the body is now seen more as a project – rather than a given object – 'in which appearance, size, shape and even content are potentially open to reconstruction' (Sparkes 1997, p. 87). Bennett et al. (1999, p. 117) argue that two assumptions seem to underpin this shift. First, the idea 'that bodies are essentially malleable', and secondly that 'the shaping of the body is a matter of choice of lifestyle'.

Discourse about the body as personal and private has developed since the Renaissance. Today it appears obvious that it is so. There has been an individualisation and privatisation of the body in modern society. People invest more time and effort in the monitoring, control and appearance of their bodies – what Featherstone (1991) referred to as the 'look'. As a result in contemporary consumer culture the 'prime purpose of the maintenance of the inner body becomes the enhancement of the appearance of the outer body' (Sparkes 1997, p. 89). Advertisements for personal fitness machines, training devices and other equipment to help keep or get the body back into shape are regular features of weekend newspaper magazine supplements. A selection in *The Guardian Weekend Magazine* from January 2003, for example, urged readers to 'make a New Year's revolution', consider 'A New Year, A New You', and 'Get Your Sexy Body Back – Today!' (from *The Guardian Weekend Magazine* 4 January 2003).

These messages illustrate an argument put forward by several authors including David Kirk (1993). Kirk has shown how since the 1950s a number of ideas and discourses about body shape have been associated with concerns about consumerism and sedentariness and its links to heart disease. Body shape has become a critical sign of success, control, and personal worth, whilst fatness has become a metaphor for ugliness, indulgence, greed and sloth. In consumer culture those who can get their body to approximate the idealised images of youth, health, fitness and beauty can realise a higher economic exchange value than those that cannot or do not wish to.

Values and stylised images of the body are constructed and circulated through advertisements, the press, television and cinema. The emphasis is on body maintenance – like cars and other consumer goods the body requires servicing, regular care and attention to maintain maximum efficiency. People tend to transform free time into maintenance work. New technologies and disciplines are developed such as diets, exercise, chemicals and surgery that are aimed at physical transformation. The reward is an enhanced appearance and a more marketable self, rather than necessarily a more healthy body.

From a similar, Foucauldian, perspective Bennett et al. (1999, p. 115) argue that preoccupations with fat, diet and slenderness as part of exercise can be understood as 'technologies of the self' (Foucault 1988, p. 18). They suggest that diet and exercise 'are ways of working on the body but also forms of moral exercise, intimately bound up with the shaping of the self'. They continue that 'to a large extent this is also true of the playing of sport, which serves instrumental ends such as fitness and health, as well as generating pleasure in the use of the body' (Bennett et al. 1999, p. 115). As Smith Maguire (2002) argues, exercise and participation in sport can be viewed as both responsible for the production of 'docile bodies' (Foucault 1977/1975) and empowered bodies. As those involved continually self-monitor, self-discipline and constantly strive for self-improvement and transformation, consumer culture can also help to produce fitness obsessions.

Sparkes (1997) argues that various ideologies about the body exist in consumer culture, such as mesomorphism, healthism and youthism, but at the heart of them is the notion of individualism. This idea is tied to the meta-theoretical belief that individuals, rather than social structures, subcultures or other social forces, are responsible alone for their status in systems of social inequality. Ultimately this belief can lead to the view that those who do not have slim, healthy-looking, bodies are those who have chosen not to develop them. They only have themselves to blame for the consequences. This is a form of victim blaming, which also happens to fit very well with economic neo-liberalism (in Britain once referred to as 'Thatcherism'), the dominant political ideology of the past twenty-five years. The body becomes less a manifestation of identity and more of a site for its construction (Bennett et al. 1999, p. 117).

The 'Obesity Epidemic', Health and Physical Education

In a related argument Gard (2004) is critical of the increasingly widespread idea that Western societies currently face a general crisis of obesity. The most popular explanation appears to be that it is our lifestyles that are to blame. Yet Gard (2004) argues in fact that sedentary behaviour is able to coexist with physical activity. The problem as he sees it is actually lazy thinking – including the acceptance of reductionist science, leading to ineffective solutions and potentially oppressive social policies. By 'blaming', lifestyles in general attention is focussed on individuals and their lifestyles (that is, 'agents' rather than 'structures' or wider 'environments'). Often the problem is re-labelled as one of the 'diseases of affluence' or part of the problem 'modern Western lifestyles'. Yet if it is asked which people are most likely to be obese, and why, interesting social patterns emerge. In the USA African–American and Hispanic people – some of the poorest members of the society – are significantly over-represented in the overweight and obese groups. In the UK journalist Polly Toynbee (2004) has pointed out that 'Fat is a class issue.' Whilst many of the British middle class are overweight, 'most of the dangerously obese – the 22% with a body-mass index in the red zone – are to be found carless on council estates and not in the leafy suburbs where kids are driven to school in supertanker 4×4s'. She concludes that it is 'inequality and disrespect that makes people fat'.

Evans and Davies (2004) argue that in this context PE is often singled out as both the problem and the solution to contemporary body problems. PE teachers are regarded as not doing enough, whilst the school curriculum is meant to empower individuals to deal with the 'obesity epidemic'. This contradictory position is symptomatic of life in a risk society (Beck 1992/1986). The body becomes a central object of wider commercialising tendencies, whilst also offering the possibility of finding ontological security in an apparently more risky society. This situation creates the space for more claims to authority and expertise on the part of physical educators, health educators and fitness gurus (Giddens 1991, pp. 181–185).

A focus on the individual as an enterprising agent has developed as a result of these two developments. This has been underpinned by other ideologies such as 'healthism' – 'in which a hedonistic lifestyle is...combined with a preoccupation with ascetic practices aimed at the achievement or maintenance of an appearance of health, fitness and youthfulness' (Dutton 1995, p. 273). The result is another version of the view that the individual has a choice in preserving their own physical health. If people do not actively choose healthy living, then it is seen as a sign of the failure of someone to care for himself or herself. In this respect, 'healthism' places the fit or healthy body on a pedestal as one of the most desirable states of being in our society (Dutton 1995, p. 273). Associated ideas include: 'Fat is bad, therefore thin is good –

and thus the thinner you are the better. Exercise promotes fitness – therefore the more you exercise the fitter you will be. Muscularity enhances the look of the male body – therefore the bigger the muscles the more attractive you become' (Dutton 1995, p. 273). As Dutton notes, 'goals which may in themselves be harmless or even beneficial can take such a hold of the individual that they dominate, and even to some extent define, the personality' (Dutton 1995). So one of the problems with contemporary consumer culture is that the health-oriented person can become an obsessed person. As Giddens (1999, p. 46) notes, 'A society living on the other side of nature and tradition – as nearly all Western countries now do – is one that calls for decision making, in everyday life as elsewhere. The dark side of decision making is the rise of addictions and compulsions.' He adds, 'addiction comes into play when choice, which should be driven by autonomy, is subverted by anxiety' (Giddens 1999, p. 47). Conventional economics overlooks the downside of the work that is consumption – 'There are no perplexed, harassed, tired, disappointed, crazy consumers in economics' (O'Neill 1985, p. 102).

The other side of healthism is that fitness is ultimately an unattainable goal. As Bauman and May (2001, p. 101) explain, 'Fitness is about transgressing norms, not adhering to them', whereas 'Health is about keeping the body in a normal, functioning condition in order to work, earn a living, be mobile, engage in some kind of social life.' As we have already noted, however, in these circumstances it is not enough for the body simply to be fit, it also has to be seen to be fit. Hence 'the suppliers of commercial goods are eager to help the body assume such appearances and to convey the impression of fitness' (Bauman and May 2001, p. 101). Thus the body in a risk society is brought back into consumer culture through the availability of a 'wide and constantly growing choice of jogging, gym- or tracksuits and training shoes to document the body's love of exercise and its versatility' (Bauman and May 2001, p. 101). Healthism, performance and perfectibilism (Dutton 1995, p. 274) remain the three dominant ideologies constructed in contemporary consumer culture with respect to the body. Evans and Davies (2004, p. 43) argue, with respect to PE, that it is important to pay attention to the way in which 'contemporary ideals of body shape, image and the discourse of "obesity" influence the policies and practices of teachers and pupils' embodied self, identity and health'. Such ideals can easily 'divert attention both from the educational purposes of physical activity and the social and cultural conditions that shape and constrain individual lives'.

So far this chapter has focussed less on what people do with sport in consumer culture and more on what discourses of lifestyle, identity and the body in consumer culture do to people. Recently researchers have attempted to redress this by investigating empirically the balance between choice and freedom and control and constraint in the development of identities, lifestyles and the consumption of sport. We will now review some of this research.

First, we will look at sport and identity, and then we will examine research into lifestyle sports (Wheaton 2004).

Sport and Identity

Pekka Sulkunen (1997, p. 4) has suggested that 'Sports are no longer contests between nation states but between international teams and their sponsors.' To what extent is Sulkunen correct? Boyle and Haynes (2000, p. 164) argue that sport remains 'an important cultural, political and commercial marker of boundaries, identities and markets'. Much attention has been placed on the construction of national identification through the mass media. A lot of work goes into the creation of a unified patriotic collectivity, including the use of personal pronouns ('we', 'us', 'our', in contrast with 'them', 'their' and so on). That national identity is fluid and a social construct rather than a natural state has been revealed in recent years by reference to the multi-accented national teams representing not just Scotland, Ireland, Wales and England, but even such supposedly homogeneous societies as Japan. As Tudor (1998, p. 154) suggests, sports reporting and other popular cultural discourses of difference are constant contributors to the process of the search for meaning.

When it comes to considering sport and identity in consumer culture it is still necessary to see how the context of competition generates a constant concern with 'difference'. The success or failure of 'our national team' offers plenty of opportunities for inquests and reflection on the state of the nation, as well as opportunities to show support for it by buying branded products. International events offer several examples of national and other stereotyping. Anderson (1991) has demonstrated that we perceive nations as 'imagined communities', or nations of the mind complete with selective histories and constructed rituals. Tudor (1998, p. 154) argues that 'in modern societies the spectacle of international sport has come to play a striking role in articulating the "naturalness", the pre-given solidity of our imagined communities', or what Blain et al. (1993, p. 18) call 'the daily reconstitution of cultures'. Sporting contests are portrayed in the media in terms of national stereotypes as numerous studies have shown (Nowell-Smith 1978, pp. 45–59, Whannel 1983, Blain et al. 1993). Nations are products of symbolic practices – mapping, flagging and storytelling – which are all mediated. National media systems are part of the constant marking and re-marking of difference. Hence in Britain (England? Scotland?) 'sports reporting has certainly played its role in articulating and circulating the cultural frameworks which make the political discourse (of generalised xenophobic nationalism) viable' (Tudor 1998, p. 154). As Blain et al. (1993) note, 'TV and the press need a variety of Europes'.

The globalising world is marked by a crisis of governance as nation-state institutions cannot reach out transnationally or worldwide, and worldwide institutions continue to be dominated by representatives of the leading states of the world. This is a much more accurate assessment than the premature dismissal of the nation-state. First, the nation-state remains a primary source of identity building. It is where '*glocalisation*' – the combining of global and local themes in advertising – occurs. Secondly, states have been compliant with and supportive of the global reach of domestic capital for large parts of the modern era, and they still are, as they have command over the resources necessary to control domestic standards of labour, international financial transactions, and global development assistance. In this context Houlihan (2003b, p. 358) notes that sport has become a 'vehicle for the demonstration of differences' in a globalising world. Whilst economic factors dominate discussions of contemporary sport, he argues that sport/culture in general has some autonomy from these factors. He states that

> there is a danger of reading too much significance into the fact that such a high proportion of the world's population watch some part of the Olympic Games or the soccer World Cup. What is more significant is when the state intervenes to manipulate, support or impose emergent cultural trends. (Houlihan 2003b, p. 350)

Whilst we would agree with Houlihan's view, we also recognise that the actions of the state, and politics and policy in any one country, are increasingly 'conditioned, or even determined, by global economic forces' (Leys 2001, p. 1). Hence in conditions of market-driven politics, domains that were previously the preserve of the public sector 'become political flashpoints because they are also targets for global capital' (Leys 2001, p. 2). In these circumstances Leys argues that non-market spheres of life – on which social solidarity and active democracy depend – are constantly challenged by firms and capital. The latter seek ways of breaking out of the boundaries set by state regulations, including those that close off non-market spheres to commodification and profit-making. Whilst market forces attempt to gain influence over previously non-market sectors of the economy in the age of globalisation, they also transform ideological conceptions of self and identity, and sports teams and events offer a valuable vehicle for this (Jackson and Andrews 2005, Silk et al. 2005).

Lifestyle Sports and Identities

Globalisation does not mean that a sense of national identity disappears. Rather nationalism can be seen as the other side of the coin of globalisation (Bairner 2001). As global flows increase, an awareness of differences between nations and national identities also increases. Becoming aware of other cultures sharpens people' consciousness of their own domestic world and their distinctive national and cultural identities. Other identities apart from national are also developed through the consumption of sport and leisure. The relationship between personal, individual, identity and sport is therefore worth studying.

Contemporary social theorists have identified individualisation and reflexivity as central features of globalising late modernity (Giddens 1991, Lash and Urry 1994, Bauman and May 2001, pp. 152–162, Beck and Beck-Gernsheim 2002). Whether we should consider the ensuing identity politics as a goldmine or a threat (Klein 2000a, p. 115) is open to debate, as we shall see.

Belinda Wheaton (2004) argues that growing commercialisation and popularity are at the centre of debates about what she calls 'lifestyle sports'. The term itself is used by practitioners, although elsewhere the same activities have been referred to as 'new', 'whiz', 'extreme', 'alternative' or 'postmodern' sports. As the collection of essays edited by Rinehart and Sydnor (2003) suggests, 'alternative' or 'extreme' sports offer a challenge to conventional and traditional sports in some way. Wheaton (2004, p. 4) argues that the growth of 'lifestyle sports' reflects some of the developments in advanced consumer capitalism/ late modernity that we have mentioned earlier in this chapter and elsewhere in the book – especially that sport can be used as an expression of personal identity, individualisation and the increasing privatisation of consumption. At the same time, in commodified form what is sold to the consumer 'is not merely a sport or leisure activity but a complete style of life' (Wheaton 2004, p. 6).

In this respect lifestyle sports can be seen as part of the consumer activities and leisure industries of postmodern or late modern advanced capitalism. By 1999 world sales of the Quiksilver brand of surf-related products reached over US$450 million, and it was estimated in 2002 that the entire global surf industry was worth around US$2 billion (Wheaton 2004, p. 13). Lifestyle sports offer what Wheaton calls an 'alternative sportscape' although this is increasingly controlled and defined by transnational media corporations (like the US-based cable operator ESPN offering the 'X-Games' and NBC producing 'Gravity Games'). These have a 'counter-culture cachet', which 'made a mediated event like the X-Games so commercially successful' despite being derided initially as a form of 'pseudo-sport' (Wheaton 2004, p. 8).

Wheaton (2004, pp. 8–9) argues that the distinction between 'false consumer omnivores' and 'authentic members' appears in much of the media – magazines, websites, TV programmes and films and so on – concerning lifestyle sports. This is particularly marked in discussion of the component features of doing lifestyle sports – using and viewing particular media, argot, technical skills, attitude and fashion/dress sense. Wheaton argues, however, that a more productive approach is to 'investigate the meaning of, and dynamics within, these leisure subcultures, understanding how these social identities and forms of collective expression are constructed, performed and contested' since this 'recognises popular culture's significance as the basis of people's identities' (Wheaton 2004, pp. 8–9). She argues that lifestyle sport identities can form the site of identity politics around the right to be recognised.

Wheaton (2004, pp. 11–12) suggests that there are nine specific characteristics of lifestyle sports. First, they are historically recent developments – emerging in the last forty years or being adaptations of earlier residual sports. Secondly, there is an emphasis on 'grass roots' participation. Thirdly, lifestyle sports are based on the consumption and use of new objects made possible by advances in new technology and materials. Fourthly, the sports require a commitment in time, money and lifestyle 'and forms of collective expression, attitudes and social identity that develops in and around the activity' (Wheaton 2004, p. 11). Fifthly, the sports are underpinned by a participatory ideology promoting fun, hedonism, involvement, self actualisation, 'flow' and other intrinsic rewards. Thus expressivity and performativity are prioritised rather than the consumption of a spectacle to be found in mainstream sports. Sixthly, whilst participants are predominantly white, male and middle class, Wheaton contends that they are less gender differentiated than traditional sports. Seventhly, lifestyle sports are mainly though not entirely individualistic in form and attitude, although some attempts are made to create teams of individuals. Eighthly, lifestyle sports are non-aggressive and generally non-contact sports but they 'embrace and fetishise notions of risk and danger' (Wheaton 2004, p. 12). Finally the spaces in which lifestyle sports occur are new or appropriated outdoor locations or 'liminal zones' (Shields 1992, p. 7) without rigidly defined boundaries.

For Wheaton, and several of the contributors to her collection of articles, lifestyle sports are both the product of commercialisation and constantly adapting to, and contesting, it. At the same time, Wheaton and her co-authors explore the impact of the new sports on identities, especially relating to gender. They ask whether the new sports challenge or maintain the gender roles, identities and power balances to be found in traditional sports. The answers are varied. Some argue that the new sports demonstrate that gender identity, understood as scripts for living, are multiple and not fixed. Hence participants in lifestyle sports can demonstrate different and potentially transformative gender identities. For example, in adventure racing (Kay and Laberge 2004) traditional male characteristics of physical toughness and risk-taking are challenged by more female-oriented ones of team building and risk management. Others suggest, however, that there remains a strong 'fratriarchal' culture, common to more traditional sports, in surfing, that brings men together, keeps men together and degrades women (Booth 2004, p. 100). As Wheaton (2004, p. 6) adds, most – if not all – of the consumers of lifestyle sports tend to be the 'privileged white male middle class'.

Like Crawford (2004) Wheaton argues for the need to move beyond the paradigm of incorporation/resistance in studying lifestyle sports. She argues that more empirical research into how people understand the exploration of identity in the choices and tensions of consumption is required. She not only recognises the 'centrality of consumer capitalism and the media industries in their very inception and meanings of the sports practice', but also believes that by attending to participants' contestation of the discourses that accompany commercialisation she can reveal the dialectical relationship between agency and structure. The danger is, as Warde (2002) points out, is that such research can turn into a celebration of consumerism if it does not fully recognise the commercial context within which it is taking place. To consider this, we will briefly reprise a sketch of the place of sport in contemporary capitalism.

Sport in Contemporary Capitalism

For Marxists there have been several different forms of capitalism. 'Laissez-faire' capitalism in the 19th century was characterised by an unregulated market, small–medium-sized business enterprises and little state intervention. 'Organised' or 'monopoly capitalism' from the late 19th to mid-20th centuries had more regulated markets, large-scale enterprises, cartels and the growth of state intervention. Fordism was the regulatory feature of this period of capitalism. 'Disorganised capitalism' in the late 20th century featured flexible production, an emphasis on consumption and globalisation. Post-Fordism is the regulatory mode of this type of capitalism.

The neo-Marxist 'regulation school' offers an account of social change at the end of the 20th century that has informed sociologists interested in sport and leisure more generally (Henry 2001, King 2002/1998). Coates (1995, pp. 104–110) argues that Fordism augmented the *purchasing* power of consumers without significantly increasing their *market* power. Post-Fordism added to the power that consumers exercised over producers by giving them more money with which to choose, and competition from which to select a wider range of goods and services. It did not, however, constitute a major upheaval of the consumer capitalist status quo.

Under Fordism the key allocative devices linking producers and consumers were managed – big, hierarchically organised, firms provided goods in greater quantities to customers, using mass, standardised, assembly line production, and semi-/unskilled labour to customers with little experience of affluence in markets of their own design. The economic context was managed by governments keen to make purchasing and selling easier and based on nationally based macroeconomic policies (sometimes referred to as 'corporatism'). Different economic conditions prevailed from the 1980s onwards. Governments changed their role. Consumer confidence and purchasing power grew – to demand more and better things. Competition intensified and firms competed on quality and particularity, as much as quantity and cheapness. Post-Fordism thus witnessed niche marketing, up-skilling of workforces and state de-regulation under the auspices of neo-liberal economic policy and New Right political thought (in Britain called Thatcherism; in the USA, Reaganomics, as we have already noted). Although product differentiation is often very superficial and big supermarkets dominate much of the retailing market, new technologies have made it possible to stimulate and respond to increasingly varied consumer demands. Producers have had to reach out and capture markets in which product competition is intense.

Research into mass media audiences, for example, has suggested that the distinction between production and consumption has been breaking down (Ross and Nightingale 2003). As audiences become active and indeed interactive, there appears to be a transformation of the production–exchange–consumption cycle. However as Ross and Nightingale point out, inviting audiences to become more interactive is one of the best means of gaining knowledge about the audience (consumer). In the age of information capitalism (Castells 1996), knowledge/intelligence about consumers is essential and active participants, viewers and fans are the best sources of it. The opportunity to participate in the spectacle of an event may become an everyday experience as commercial interests seek to re-establish the production–consumption distinction.

In this context, sports, such as in the UK *association* football, can be seen as one of the quintessential spectacles of the contemporary era. The expansion of consumption is seen as one of the main means of increasing production and hence the accumulation of capital. Organised around the two-year cycle that separates the sport's largest mega events – the FIFA World Cup and the UEFA European Championship – considerable time and effort goes into the expansion of the football-driven economy. Products on offer in time for Euro 2004 in the UK for example, ranged from ready meals, inflatable chairs, shampoos, to watches, mini-refrigerators and tailor-made T-shirts for women. As Smith (1997, p. 180) suggests, football can be seen as the ideal sport of contemporary capitalism. He argues that football suits contemporary capitalism because

> There is no product as such, or in any traditional capitalist sense – only a short-lived event whose actual gate receipts constitute barely a small part of a top club's income. The event itself is sold for the time of its own consumption, as it were, and stands as a quintessential consumer-age product, with customers buying their own leisure time. The event is simply a performance by players who can then be used as spokesmen for endorsing other products, and which is sold to television, and which is also marginal to the big business of merchandising.

Bramlett and Sloan (2000) provide another example of a Marxist analysis of the position of the fan in contemporary sport consumption. They argue that professional team sport in the USA constitutes a distinctive economy in which team owners are capitalists, players are workers and spectators are consumers. Owners initially exploited workers until this led to conflict, unionisation and contract renegotiations that redistributed the surplus values (from gate receipts and media revenues) more evenly to players. Owners then turned to the exploitation of consumers through raising prices for tickets and merchandise. As players have become more powerful owners have sought to exploit fans even further. One example of their strategy is personal seat licenses (PSLs) in the NFL. PSLs (known as debentures or bonds in the UK) allow fans the right to buy season tickets for a price before the tickets go on sale to the wider public.

Bramlett and Sloan (2000) examine how the roles of worker, capitalist and consumer are played out in professional sport in America. The workers and the capitalists have always engaged in forms of struggle over the surpluses generated by sport. For example, the Chicago White Sox scandal in 1919, when members of the team were paid to lose the World Series baseball championship by a gambling syndicate, happened after the employers had increased the series to a 5-out-of-9 series from a 4-out-of-7 one, without an increase in pay. Players began to challenge employers through collective bargaining against the reserve clause and for free agency. Since the 1970s, in particular, there have been several work stoppages (due to either strikes by players or lockouts by employers) in all four major American professional sports (American football, baseball basketball, and, as noted earlier most recently, in NHL (ice) hockey). In the 1990s average MLB team revenue increased by nearly 31 per cent, whilst average MLB player costs per team increased from US$31.2 to US$35.4 million – a rise of only 13.4 per cent (Bramlett and Sloan 2000, p. 180).

As the business dimension of sport is increasingly elevated the spectators' ability to identify with a team and share emotional ownership with it is compromised. This is further developed by strategies that seek to exploit the sports consumer rather than the worker, including the sale of PSLs in which consumers pay for the right to buy seats. The Carolina Panthers were the first team to introduce these in 1993 as they sought to raise money for the construction of a new stadium in Charlotte (Bramlett and Sloan 2000, p. 186). The price paid for PSLs is not determined by the exploitation of the workers in the sport. PSLs have no labour directly involved in their production and are simply an added cost for the consumer.

There have been signs of reactions against commodification in sport but the launch of minority sports programmes on cable and satellite television cannot be considered as one of them. The sports featured – including snow boarding, billiards and motor boat racing – are equally susceptible to commodification as their apparel, equipment, goods and experiences are promoted, publicised and marketed as fashion. The sports market thrives on 'experiential' as well as material commodities (Lee 1993, p. 135).

Conclusion

We have noted in this chapter how ludic body styles, including, but not only, sports participation and consumption, have developed. Contemporary social theorists have identified individualisation and reflexivity as central features of globalising late modernity, affecting lifestyles and identities. Klein (2000a, p. 115) suggests that the growth of identity politics has been a goldmine for global corporations trying to promote their products to diverse markets, rather than a threat. The growth of the market for sports clothes, equipment, footwear and fitness chic, discussed in Chapter 2, has been accompanied by concerns about diet and the moulding of the body (Howson 2004, Chs 3–4). Contemporary discourses about health and fitness (Bauman and May 2001, pp. 93–108) and the care of the body and the self suggest that somaticisation and embodiment (Turner 1991, 1992, 1996, Bennett et al. 1999, Turner and Rojek 2001) have become culturally central. In turn, risks associated with this – enhancing bodily performance through the use of drugs and other aids, for example – and injuries have also increased. Risk society also gives rise to consumer addictions, including body and eating disorders such as anorexia nervosa, bulimia nervosa and obesity (Dutton 1995). Whilst these risks appear to be more individualised, research suggests that social class, gender, the life course and ethnicity remain major influences on the consumption of lifestyle sports and body styles. The next chapter looks at social divisions in participation and involvement in sport as a means of examining some of these influences in more detail.

7

Sport and Social Divisions in Consumer Culture

Introduction: Two Views of the Changing Social Context

The economic and social historian Eric Hobsbawm recounts how the 'short twentieth century' (1914–1991) saw several major social changes taking place in class structure and gender relations. We shall briefly outline these before looking at the relationship with sports participation and involvement. From the 1980s onwards in the UK and other advanced capitalist countries there has been a marked numerical decline in the industrial working class. This has been due to changes in the process of production that we have already referred to as 'Post-Fordism'. Hobsbawm (1994, p. 305) argues that this transformation was not so much a crisis 'of the class, but of its consciousness'. From being coherent and organised it became incoherent and disorganised (in this respect he shares the analysis of Lash and Urry 1987). Hobsbawm (1994, p. 306) concludes that 'conscious working-class cohesiveness reached its peak, in older developed countries, at the end of the Second World War'. The post-war economic boom, rising living standards and mass consumption that began in the 1950s 'utterly transformed the lives of working class people in the developed countries' (Hobsbawm 1994, p. 306). The availability of full employment and the emergence of 'a consumer society aimed at a genuine mass market placed most of the working class in the older developed countries, at least for part of their lives, well above the threshold below which their fathers, or they themselves, had once lived' (Hobsbawm 1994, p. 307).

Under these circumstances divisions within the working class appeared and widened from the late 1970s onwards. On the one hand, this was fuelled by the creation of the idea of an 'underclass', the resurrection of Victorian (19th century) ideas about the gap between the 'respectable' and the 'unrespectable' poor. The existence of a 'residuum' in the late 19th century implied exclusion from normal society, and a century later the same ideas were circulated. On the other hand, the impression of the collapse of unified social classes gave rise to the belief that society was underpinned by disunity in the shape of diverse communities of interest. The skilled and respectable working class supported the election of neo-liberal, right wing, governments led by Margaret Thatcher in the UK, for example. At the same time, mass migration brought about ethnic and social diversification of the working class and sowed the basis for conflicts within it. The working class became increasingly 'fragmented' (Roberts et al. 1977) as 'changes in production, the emergence of the "two-thirds society" and the changing, and increasingly fuzzy frontiers between what was "manual" and what was "non-manual" work, diffused and dissolved the formerly clear outlines of "the proletariat"' (Hobsbawm 1994, p. 310).

Changes in the involvement of women, especially married women, in the labour market, have also been significant. In the space of thirty years, from less than one-fifth to over one-half of married women now work in paid employment in the UK. More women than men are studying for undergraduate degrees in universities. The rise of 'second wave' feminism in the 1960s helped to bring more equal rights for women, as legislation and social horizons changed. These changes have brought about other issues as well that confront 'third wave' feminism, in sport and elsewhere (Hargreaves 2004). Women's autonomy and freedom are still compromised by the residual patriarchal assumptions about women's 'natural' place as wives and mothers. Many women carry the dual burden of private domestic responsibilities and public employment. A cultural backlash in the form of 'new laddism' and the fact that many of the enticing consumer cultural aspirations can only be achieved through dual incomes continue to impact on the position of men and women differently.

Sociologist Zygmunt Bauman is seen by many as one of the key theorists of consumption. His reflections on the state of society after the end of the cold war in the late 1980s and early 1990s offer an interesting contrast with Hobsbawm. Bauman (2000) refers to postmodernity as 'light' or 'liquid modernity' as opposed to 'solid modernity'. Fordism was the 'self-consciousness of modern society in its "heavy", "bulky", or "immobile"' phase (Bauman 2000, p. 56). He argues that whilst solid modernity attempted to construct a rational social order, and failed, 'light capitalism is bound to be value obsessed' (Bauman 2000, p. 61), agonising about the choice of goals or ends. Liquid modernity offers a world full of possibilities where little is predetermined. Yet here is the problem: 'the consumers' misery derives from the surfeit, not the dearth of choices' (Bauman 2000, p. 63). In these social conditions consumption replaces production as the key site of social control and social order. Hence Bauman replaces the disciplining emphasis of Foucault's early work whilst adopting his relational conception of power and freedom. The political implications of Bauman's work are also close to those of the Frankfurt School.

Bauman uses the metaphor of the race to describe contemporary consumer society. 'In the consumer race the finishing line always moves faster than the fastest of runners; but most runners forced onto the track have muscles too flabby and lungs too small to run fast' (Bauman 2000, pp. 72–73). The archetype of the race is 'the activity of shopping' (Bauman 2000, p. 73). Seduction replaces subjugation for most of the population. 'Postmodern society engages its members primarily in their capacity as consumers rather than producers' (Bauman 2000, p. 76). Identity formation and physicality acquire new meanings. Sexuality involves risk, fun, harassment and abuse. New patterns of coping with death develop. Shopping is underpinned by the desire for desiring – which is insatiable. Whereas the society of producers was based upon normative regulation, aiming at conformity and health, the society of consumers aims to seduce, but without any benchmark with which to measure conformity. Hence adequacy – being ready to go for more – or 'fitness' becomes the leading motif.

As Bauman (2000, p. 77) notes, health and fitness are not synonymous – 'not all fitness regimes are good for one's health and that what helps one to stay healthy does not necessarily make one fit'. Health relates to norms and abnormality, whereas fitness relates to being ready 'to live through sensations not yet tried and impossible to specify in advance'. Fitness implies 'the capacity to break all norms' (Bauman 2000, p. 78). Furthermore, 'The pursuit of fitness is a chase after a quarry which one cannot describe until it is reached; however one has no means to decide that the quarry has indeed been reached, but every reason to suspect that it has not' (Bauman 2000, p. 78). Hence 'life organized around the pursuit of fitness promises a lot of victorious skirmishes, but never the final triumph' (Bauman 2000, p. 78). The pursuit of fitness thus leads to a state of 'perpetual self-scrutiny, self-reproach and self-deprecation, and so also of continuous anxiety' (Bauman 2000, p. 78). In liquid modernity health becomes similar to the pursuit of fitness and uncertainty prevails. Activities like 'weight watching' remain popular and the pursuit of health itself becomes a pathogenic factor (Illich quoted in Bauman 2000, p. 80). In this respect Bauman follows a similar argument to that of Giddens (1992, pp. 65–86) over many of the contradictions of contemporary living.

The individualisation of consumption leads to the creation of groups and processes of inclusion and exclusion. Advertising has the ability to stimulate desire and assuage anxiety by provoking needs and providing product solutions. Consumption makes life a series of individualised hurdles to be solved (sometimes with expert help). This can lead to not only the formation of neo-tribes and lifestyle cliques defined by their relationship to consumption practices and identities, but also insatiability ('shopaholics' or compulsive shoppers). The twin driving forces of consumer society are pleasure and insecurity (desire and anxiety). The 'flaneur' ('stroller'), tourist, vagabond or game player replaces the pilgrim ('hopeful seeker') as the central figure of liquid modernity. Sensation-seekers replace soldier-workers as the ideal bodies (Bauman 1998). Shopping becomes 'a rite of exorcism'. Even though society is divided into 'the seduced' and 'the repressed' – the financially secure and socially included and the dependent and socially excluded – all members of society experience this world of choosing as the social ideal. Consumer society thus expresses the ambivalence of liquid modernity – in which pleasures are not only seductive, but also loaded with coercion and control – with no obvious solution to the problems it creates.

Bauman offers a dystopian vision of consumer society (Edwards 2000, p. 39). He raises important questions – to what extent does consumption plays the major role in the formation of personal and social identities? To what extent does consumption alleviate the anxiety and uncertainty induced by contemporary 'risk society'? To what extent does advertising induce more than it helps to resolve questions of identity and anxiety? Bauman's ability to write compelling social criticism is unquestioned but whether he has identified the key determinants of the problems he identifies is questionable – at least until research can be carried out to investigate his claims. In the rest of this chapter we will consider some of this research.

Social Divisions Inside the Culture of the Market

In consumer culture people tend not to talk about social inequalities or divisions, preferring to use phrases like 'social exclusion' or the need for greater 'social inclusion', even though accounts are frequently published in the press and on television about the vast gaps between haves and have-nots within society. On the day that this chapter was first drafted, for example, the BBC reported that researchers had found a stark 'north–south' divide in the UK from data contained in the 2001 census. Cultural intermediaries also continue to create classifications of consumers for use by marketing companies, which often appear to blur divisions whilst also revealing aspects of inequality. It could be argued that the concept of consumer culture itself masks the existence of capitalist relations of production and exchange. By adopting the production of consumption approach throughout this book we hope to have shown how consumer culture is a product of capitalist relations. This is not to say that only economic relationships matter, rather it is to counteract the drift of the past ten to fifteen years towards a focus on identities associated with the postmodern turn to culture.

Smart (2003, p. 163) argues that 'virtually everyone is now living inside the culture of the market'. Consumer society blurs the social distinctions by making material goods and lifestyles available to more people. Consumer society appears to individualise social experience. In the UK, for example, rising home ownership enables people to spend money by borrowing against the equity (value if sold) of their house or apartment. In the third quarter of 2002, for example, the equivalent of US$19 billion was borrowed in this way to finance consumption (Harvey 2005, p. 113). In the same year in the USA

20 per cent of GDP growth was attributed to consumers refinancing their mortgage debts for immediate consumption (Harvey 2005, p. 112). As Harvey (2005, pp. 112–113) notes, 'what happens if and when this property bubble bursts is a matter of serious concern'. So considerable risks remain and these are not evenly spread around the population. Some social groups are more exposed to risk than others. These developments are underpinned by three major features of the experience of consumption since the middle of the last century.

First, there has been a steady and general transformation in the quality of everyday life brought about by (initially) a 'Fordist regime of accumulation' (Coates 1995, p. 105). As Coates outlines it, there were 'Improvements in basic food and clothing (in the 1950s), the spread of basic consumer durables (in the 1960s), the beginning of the leisure boom (in the 1970s) and increasingly sophisticated domestic consumption and leisure experience in the 1980s and 1990s' (Coates 1995, p. 105). Secondly, however, not everyone has participated in the consumer society equally. As affluence has grown, a sizeable minority have lagged steadily behind. The gap between the highest and the lowest earners in the UK increased to its greatest in the 20th century in the 1990s. Holt and Schor (2000, pp. vii–viii) identify similar divisions in the USA, where the top 1 per cent of households owned 40 per cent of the wealth and the top 20 per cent of households were responsible for 50 per cent of consumer spending in 2000. In short, the growth of consumer culture and consumption in the UK, and elsewhere in the advanced capitalist world in the second half of the 20th century, has been marked by economic and social polarisation. The financing and organisation of consumption is the third key feature of contemporary social life under Post-Fordist principles. It was not until the 1980s that the UK experienced a credit revolution, in terms of its availability, scale and distribution. Money went 'plastic', saving became a possibility and banks and building societies grew to absorb the savings and reprocess them as credit. Personal liabilities (household debt including mortgages and credit card borrowing) reached £1 trillion for the first time in July 2004.

As we have seen in earlier chapters commodities now circulate with much greater speed (Harvey 1989, pp. 285–385). Advertising, marketing and branding techniques and strategies have helped to accelerate consumption first by promoting different and changing styles and fashions, and secondly by maintaining the propensity to consume by promising personal fulfilment through consumption. That there are limits to the accumulation and turnover of physical goods actually makes good business sense. No one wants to have unreliable goods. But there has been substantial growth in personal, business, educational, and health services, and sectors such as entertainment, leisure, sport and tourism that are all 'experiential commodities' of one sort or another. It is for these reasons that consumption has increased in significance in society as we have seen (Ritzer 1993, p. 118, Bauman 1998). As consumption has become 'the structural basis of western societies' (Lash and Urry 1994, p. 296), the corollary has been the production of new forms of social exclusion.

The Divisiveness of Social Exclusion

One form of exclusion is that faced by those people who lack the means to engage with consumer society. As Bauman (1998, p. 39) notes, 'Desiring comes free, but to desire realistically . . . requires resources.' The further implication is that in consumer society those who do not, or are unable to, consume are 'flawed consumers' and thus 'purely and simply a worry and a nuisance' (Bauman 1998, pp. 90–91). Such people become part of the consumer culture 'waste land' (see Bauman 2004b). A second form of exclusion, which focus on the idea of consumer society helps to maintain, is encountered by those who produce goods consumed in the developed world. Multinational corporations have located production in distant locations well away from shopping malls (Klein 2000a, pp. 205–206). The multinationals behave like corporate consumers searching for the best bargains where they can get their designs produced most cheaply (Klein 2000a, p. 211).

Castells (1998) also notes the unregulated nature of contemporary production relations. Work becomes more precarious and individualised, amidst rising patterns of social inequality. There is a growing global polarisation of income and wealth distribution, occurring both between and within countries (Castells 1998, pp. 161–165). A third form of exclusion exists within societies in which comfortable middle-class people experience economic security and relative social exclusion in 'a society of "risky freedom"' (Beck 2000, p. 106). Despite higher incomes, better health and much greater opportunities for women in general, British people often appear increasingly depressed, unhappy in their relationships and alienated from civil society in surveys into quality of life.

Research has confirmed the connections between income and health. The death rates for coronary heart disease are about 40 per cent higher for manual workers than non-manual workers. Life expectancy is increasing but the rich benefit more than the poor (by six years between 1972 and 1996 for the rich compared with two years for the poor). Wilkinson (1996) argues that the health of a society is not dependent on its wealth so much as the degree of inequality in a society – Greece is a poorer country than the USA but life expectancy is longer there. In the USA slightly fewer than 36 million people (12 per cent of the population) currently live below the poverty line (*The Guardian* 27 August 2004, p. 18). Of these, 12.9 million are children (17.6 per cent of the under-18 population) and 25 per cent are African–American. Wealth distribution in the USA is heavily skewed by ethnicity with white households being 11–14 times wealthier than African–American families (*The Guardian* 17 October 2004, p. 16). For our purposes what need to be examined are not so much the conditions but the systems of inequality, and how far the patterns of inequality are produced and reproduced in involvement in and consumption of sport (Abercrombie 2004). Once again we will focus on the UK.

Sport and Social Divisions of Class

A research project on *The Development of Sporting Talent 1997* (English Sports Council 1998) produced information about GB's top sportsmen and women in 11 sports – athletics, cricket (male and female), cycling, hockey, judo, netball, rowing, rugby league, rugby union (male and female), sailing and swimming. The interviewees were mostly elite or pre-elite performers – members of a senior national squad or someone who had represented below this level, at under 21 or in the 'A' squads. There were 924 interviews (approximately 500 men and 420 women) conducted between March and June 1997. Athletics produced the 'most typical elite sports people' – some one educationally well qualified, from a higher socio-economic group, who had had a family member involved in sport. Twenty-nine per cent were from the professional and managerial social class (AB), 32 per cent were from the clerical and non-manual class (C1), 28 per cent were from the skilled manual (C2) and 12 per cent were from semi- and unskilled manual classes (DE). This compared with 19 per cent AB, 34 per cent C1, 21 per cent C2 and 25 per cent DE in the GB population as a whole. Judo produced a profile 'most representative of the Great Britain population' as a whole. Excluding Judo 68 per cent of elite athletes came from non-manual social classes (37 per cent from social class AB). Amongst the Judo-ka 16 per cent were from AB, 33 per cent were from C1, 35 per cent were from C2 and 16 per cent were from DE. In rowing over 50 per cent of elite rowers were educated at private school compared to only 5 per cent of the GB population as a whole. Rugby league had the most manual/working-class profile (67 per cent were C2, D or E), whilst in rugby union – 41 per cent of elite male rugby union players and 24 per cent of elite female rugby union players were educated at private school compared to 5 per cent of the GB population. Of elite sailing athletes, 24 per cent were educated at private school compared to 5 per cent of the GB population. Sixty-one per cent were from AB, 22 per cent were from C1, 17 per cent were from C2 and none came from D or E social class backgrounds. Swimming contained the most 'upper class' profile of all the sports and 21 per cent of whom had attended private school. Sixty-nine per cent were from AB, 24 per cent were from C1 and only 6 per cent were from C2, D or E social classes.

The authors of a report that summarised the data concluded that the chances of becoming an elite or pre-elite performer were 'two times greater for individuals from professional classes than they were for those from manual classes' (English Sports Council 1998, p. 3). They also noted that the opportunity to realise sporting potential was still significantly influenced by an individual's social background. They concluded

> a precociously talented youngster born in an affluent family with sport-loving parents, one of whom has (probably) achieved high levels of sporting success, and attending an independent/private school, has a 'first-class ticket' to the sporting podium. His or her counterpart, equally talented but born in less favoured circumstances, at best has a third class ticket and at worst no ticket at all. (English Sports Council 1998, p. 13)

Their conclusions were further underscored following the Sydney Summer Olympic Games in 2000, when a survey suggested that 80 per cent of British medal winners at the games went to private schools (*The Guardian* 21 August 2004, p. 4). Collins and Buller (2003) have suggested that this situation of social inequity at a national level is mirrored at a local level. They studied an elite sport programme operated in one English region for cricket, table tennis and squash, and concluded that 'social stratification provides a filter of who gets in at the base/beginning of the selection process' for these programmes (Collins and Buller 2003, p. 438).

The supposed growth of individualisation has not greatly altered participation rates in recreational sport either. Data from Holt and Mason (2000, pp. 6–9), the *General Household Survey 1996* and **sport**scotland (2002) all show the continuance of stratified sports cultures in Britain. In the UK Collins with Kay (2003, p. 33) have shown how the gap between the professional and managerial social classes and the unskilled manual classes in terms of participation has not closed substantially since the 1960s (Table 7.1). The over-representation

Table 7.1   *Inequalities in participation in sport by social class: 1960s–1990s*

Social Class	Visiting sport centres (%)		Any sport in past four weeks (%)	
	1960s	1990s	1987	1996
A (professional)	20	40	65	63
B (managerial)	n.d.	52	52	52
C1 (junior non-manual)	44	33	45	47
C2 (skilled manual)	27	20	48	45
D (semi-skilled)	7	8	34	37
E (unskilled)	n.d.	n.d.	26	23
Total			45	46
Difference A and E	*13*	*32*	*40*	*40*

n.d. – no data.
Source: Adapted from Collins with Kay (2003), Table 3.4, p. 33.

of people from social classes AB and the under-representation of people from social classes DE in sport and physical activity continues.

Trends in adult participation in sport in England since the late 1980s (also available at www.sportengland.org) show that participation in sport has declined, and continues to vary considerably between social classes, men and women, and ethnic groups (Rowe and Moore 2004). Between 1990 and 2002 overall participation in sport declined from 46 to 43 per cent of adults (defined as people over 16 years of age). In 1990, 58 per cent of men and 39 per cent of women had participated in some form of sport or physical activity (excluding walking) during the survey periods. By 2002 the percentages were 50 and 37 per cent respectively. The most pronounced reduction was in the active participation of young adults – from 82 to 72 per cent of 16–19-year-olds and from 72 to 61 per cent of 20–24-year-olds. The most popular sports generally were swimming, keep fit/yoga (including aerobics and exercise dance), cycling and cue sports. Men preferred cue sports (15 per cent), swimming and cycling (12 per cent), and football (10 per cent). Women preferred keep fit/yoga (16 per cent), swimming (15 per cent) and cycling (6 per cent). Reflecting changes in the classification of occupations, it was found that people in the top categories of 'large employer' and 'higher managerial' were most likely to participate in sport (59 per cent) whilst those in the lowest grouping – 'routine' – participated least (30 per cent).

Rowe and Moore (2004) suggest three reasons for the decline in participation since the 1990s: people have competing demands on their time, people have a greater number of leisure choices, many of which promote more sedentary behaviour, and the quality of the sports infrastructure (for participants) has been declining. As a consequence of lack of investment over the past thirty years, 500 recreational sports centres have closed and local authorities estimate that they require £500 million to upgrade existing facilities (*The Guardian* 21 August 2004, p. 4).

Stroot (2002, pp. 137–140) discusses data collected by the United States Census Bureau in 2000 that demonstrates the relationships between income levels and participation in sport in the USA. She found that 28.3 per cent of people with annual household incomes above US$75,000 participated in 'exercising with equipment', whilst only 10.8 per cent of people with annual household incomes below US$15,000 did so. The percentage difference (in the previous example 17.5 per cent) increased in sports where the costs are greater (golf, club membership, boating). Even in popular team sports in the USA – basketball, soccer, baseball, softball (a version of baseball) and touch football – where the sports may be available through community recreation programmes and percentage differences are less, people from higher income households were more likely to participate in the sport.

Bennett et al. (1999, pp. 115–144) provide evidence of a more analytical kind regarding involvement in sport and exercise in Australia, where facilities are much more abundant than the UK. They argue that gender, class, education level and age are the four most important influences on choices and values in the context of diet, exercise and sport, but provide considerable evidence for the continuing influence of social class on participation. With respect to exercise they discuss walking, cycling, jogging, power-walking, weight-training, membership of health and sporting organisations and aerobics (Bennett et al. 1999, pp. 125–128).

In their survey and interviews they found that the ten most popular sports played (in descending order of popularity) in Australia in the 1990s were tennis, golf, swimming, walking, squash, touch football, cricket, lawn bowls, netball and aerobics (Bennett et al. 1999, p. 129). They found a considerable discrepancy between the sports that people played and watched at live venues. The top ten of these later included Australian Rules football, cricket, rugby league, tennis, swimming, motor car racing, basketball, soccer, golf and horse racing. Only cricket, tennis, swimming and golf were common to both lists. With respect to social class they found that 'Those classes like the professionals and para-professionals which had scored very high on the playing of sport score very low on watching it, whereas manual workers, who play little sport, watch it a great deal' (Bennett et al. 1999, p. 139).

In some respects Bennett et al. (1999) may have found empirical evidence for the persistence of something previously noted by Bourdieu (1978, p. 830). That it is through 'the division it makes between professionals, the virtuosi of an esoteric technique, and laymen, reduced to the role of mere consumers, a division that tends to become a deep structure of the collective consciousness, that sport produces its most decisive political effects'. The argument that sport provides different kinds of positive and negative 'cultural capital' to different groups and classes is a familiar argument of Bourdieu's. In the next section we shall look at what many consider to be an equally, if not more, important influence on sports participation and consumption – gender.

Gender, Sport and Consumer Culture

Legislative reforms in Britain thirty years ago – the Equal Pay Act (1970/ 1975) and the Sex Discrimination Act (1975) – brought about some legal support to women, but how effective has this equality package been? Reflecting on nearly thirty years of legislation reveals a mixed impact. The importance of work and family in women's (leisure) lives remains clear. Women continue to receive less pay than men, and violence at the hands of men continues. Women carry an additional burden – paid employment – with the rise of the dual income family as a necessity. Most women also retain primary responsibility for domestic work.

Lury (1996, p. 121) has noted that in much marketing and advertising it was taken for granted that the role of the consumer was a feminine one – typically women do the shopping and make the majority of consumption decisions in households. But some feminist writers have been suspicious of the concept of consumer culture for being insufficiently gender-aware (Lury 1996, Ch. 5). They argue that the broader economy should be considered in relation to the family and domestic economy – since it is there that much of the work (housework) is done on the goods bought by women in routine shopping. Lury (1996, p. 124) observes that 'The suggestion is that while there may have been changes in the commodification of objects, unless the interrelationship of these changes with the system of production and exchange that operate in domestic life are explored it is difficult to say what their impact is upon society as a whole.' The invisibility of women has been debated in the social sciences for the past thirty years. In the study of sport in society much research has looked at the under-representation of women in sport, rather than the involvement of disadvantaged women (Kay 2003, pp. 97–112). Kay (2003, p. 97) considers the links between women's experiences in sport and social exclusion. She argues that the ideology that constructs the gender order in society first 'positions women primarily as mothers and carers' and secondly 'values and rewards those roles less than that of paid work'. Such expectations of sex-appropriate behaviour remain influential in sport. Yet just as sport is a prime site for the reproduction of beliefs in the supposedly natural (that is biological) differences in the physicality (that is power) of men and women, it is also a place where these ideas could be challenged.

Wernick (1991, pp. 48–49), on the other hand, suggests that in the last quarter of the 20th century promotional or consumer culture has brought about a change in the relationship of men to advertising. There has been an extension to men of 'consumer status' and in the range of commodities aimed at them: 'Seventy years after women went through something similar, men as private people...have been targeted for economic development' (Wernick 1991, p. 49). He argues that the 'possessive individual of early capitalism has transmuted today into a more advanced variant: the promotional individual' (Wernick 1991, p. 66). Women and men are increasingly encouraged to increase their 'value as circulating tokens of exchange' rather than 'self-activating subjects' (Wernick 1991, p. 68). In the process, masculinity and femininity have become floating signifiers that can be substituted for each other (Wernick 1991, pp. 63–64). Our view is that the 'consumerisation' of men is a useful concept by which to understand this process of creating consumers for goods and services previously not widely available as commodities on the market. As several writers have noted, consumerisation has been occurring in sport with respect to spectating, and the products associated with sports sponsorship, but we can also note its development in terms of the consumption of sports goods and services such as health clubs.

Pronger (1990) has argued persuasively that since the mid-19th century sport has been one of the pre-eminent 'signs' of masculinity. The sport arena as well as the gymnasium are two of the major sites for the display and cultural reproduction of masculinities. Indeed 'the ultra-masculinity of particular sporting practices (especially those that celebrate and reward physicality and aggression) is evident as a cultural phenomenon that transcends some national and cultural boundaries' (Horne and Fleming 2000, p. v). It has been shown that manliness and forms of masculinity can be expressed in many different ways since they are a product of rich and complex cultural processes (Gilmore 1993, Gelder and Thornton 1997). Hence first and foremost in investigating masculinity is the question of the social, economic, political and cultural forces that shape manhood. In the realm of leisure, studies of femininity and women have developed since the 1980s (Deem 1986, Wimbush and Talbot 1989, Green et al. 1990) as have studies of women, sport and physical activity (Scraton 1993; Hargreaves 1994, 2000, Clarke and Humberstone 1997). These studies suggest that it is misleading to think of masculinity (or femininity) as a single undifferentiated given entity.

Connell (1993) suggested that the study of masculinity should be located historically. Industrialisation in the 18th and 19th centuries may have provided the basis for 'hegemonic' masculinity – emphasising physical strength, solidarity forged through struggles against employers and managers, and the patriarchal organisation of the home. In the late 20th century, however, it has been argued that 'hegemonic' masculinity has been threatened by Post-Fordist work practices, leading to a declining 'core' of full-time workers and an increased 'periphery' of (largely female) casualised workers (Faludi 1999). In the last twenty-five years, as young men have faced economic restructuring, including the prospect of long-term structural unemployment, their responses have either been to try harder, accept the situation or fight against it in symbolic ways. This latter, 'consumption as compensation', thesis suggests that 'Men use the plasticity of consumer identity construction to forge atavistic masculine identities based upon an imagined life of self-reliant, premodern men who lived outside the confines of cities, families, and work bureaucracies' (Holt and Thompson 2004, p. 426).

Similar to Wheaton (2004) in the previous chapter, therefore, Holt and Thompson (2004) argue that claims made about the power of messages need to be understood as filtered by active and interactive audiences and consumers. However, for Holt and Thompson social structuring continues to influence the way in which consumption occurs – hence social class will impact on how the consumption of different sports and leisure activities by men and women actually occurs as well as on its frequency. Drawing on their research in the USA, Holt and Thompson argue that there is a need to understand men's 'socially situated consumption practices, that is how men variously interpret and act on the mass culture discourse in their consumption' (Holt and Thompson 2004, p. 427).

The Gendered Consumption of Sport

Some writers suggest that one hundred years after its formation, modern sport is a 'rather less reliable ally of hegemonic masculinity' (Rowe 1995, p. 130). Others argue that sport, via its links with consumer culture, continues to play a part in the assertion and affirmation of specific hegemonic ideals of masculinity (Day 1990). Only analysis of the social meanings and interactions of specific subcultural groups and the gendered consumption of sport can reveal the nature of women's and men's practices and settle these kinds of questions (for example, Wellard 2002 and Fleming 1995).

It can be argued that the consumption of sport involves participation, as well as watching and following. Fischer and Gainer (1994, pp. 90–91) identified four themes in research into gender and sport. First, the consumption of sports helps men to develop and reinforce their masculine self-identities. Strength, muscularity, skills and knowledge are all empowering for men, but less so for women (less value). An ideal body image of slender and narrow hips (ultra-thinness) is sought by girls (often from as young as 9-years old). Men and boys have begun to exhibit body image concerns, similar to girls and young women, since the 1980s (Hargreaves 1994). Secondly, the consumption of sports promotes and reinforces a hierarchical form of social bonding among men. Competition with rather than working with men. Thirdly, through their choices in the consumption of sports, men will display a varied range of masculinities. Involvement in a wider range of sports allows men to exhibit hegemonic and subordinate masculinities, as well as women to exhibit more established femininity. Fourthly, women will experience feelings of marginalisation and possibly denigration in their consumption of organised sports. Fischer and Gainer (1994, p. 101) concluded that 'the consumption of sports is deeply associated with defining what is masculine and, concurrently, what is not feminine. It has been noted that participating in and watching sports lead to a range of masculinities, and each of them relies for its definition on being distinct from femininity.'

This conclusion is shared by historical studies of sport that have emphasised how sport was a gender distinguishing activity, related to a changing gender order, for example in the USA between the 1840s and 1890s, and in UK between the 1820s and 1880s (Whitson 1994, Burstyn 1999). The 'gendering' of sport by men involved techniques including: definition; direct control; ignoring, and/or the trivialising of women's sport or their involvement in sport. For men, sport was a primary socialising experience – into masculine identities, hierarchical social bonding and various forms of masculinity. Hence women faced marginalisation in their consumption of sport. The macho (or 'fratriarchal') culture of sport is repeatedly reinforced with every media report of the sexual misbehaviour of young male elite athletes or men associated with the administration of the sport (Booth 2004).

With regard to adults Benson (1994) argues that as sports spectators and participants women compared with men were much fewer in the mid-1960s – only 4 per cent of women watched football regularly. In recent years there has been a claim that an increasing numbers of women (and middle class) supporters are now watching football at the expense of 'traditional' football fans. Has the pattern changed? Malcolm et al. (2000) suggest that there is not much empirical evidence to support this. But further research is needed into fans. Certainly women's participation in sport grew generally between 1977 and 1986, and 1987 and 1993. Like men's, women's participation in sport fell between 1996 and 2002 in England, but at a slower rate. There appears to have been an individualisation of activity over the past fifteen years (Coalter 1999). This has involved a shift from engagement in team and partner sports towards less competitive, individual, flexible, fitness and lifestyle-oriented activities. Women's participation in sport and physical activities has grown at a faster rate than men's over this time. For example, between 1987 and 2002, in Scotland, adult women's participation rose from 50 per cent to 60 per cent (**sport**scotland 2002). Yet women's participation as a proportion of men's remains lower – at about 68 per cent – and women's participation remains segregated and confined within a much narrower range of activities than men's – as we noted earlier in the survey data from Sport England. In Scotland only 6 activities attracted more than 5 per cent of women, compared to 12 activities in which men engaged. The favourite activities for women are walking, keep fit-related activities and swimming. Each of these is relatively cheap, flexible, has limited needs for partners and can be fitted in around childcare.

The marketing of exercise – as evidenced in heath and fitness magazines as well as mainstream women's magazines – is often not for physiological fitness or psychological health, but in pursuit of physical perfection – sexual attractiveness. Women are more likely to engage in exercise – non-competitive physical activity – rather than sport. Is this related to the widespread imagery of the 'look' in consumer culture – in which appearance, fashion and physique are prioritised far more for women than sporting accomplishments? Does this leave the body – sporting or at least worked on, in the gym – as the 'last refuge of masculinity?' Or are these rigid divisions – femininity and masculinity, heterosexual and homosexual – no longer so apparent? The image making and commercialisation of the sexual body in sport has developed for both men and women athletes (Whannel 1999) but does it have an equal impact? Research by Sassatelli (1999) and Fishwick (2001) suggests that some women are able to find in exercise and health clubs an important space for self-development lacking in other parts of their lives. Yet few opportunities exist for women to work in professional sport. Sport offers women new ways of spending leisure time and exercising economic power. But it also helps to confirm and reinforce their role and position in society. It offers both liberation and constraint, challenging some social norms or conventions whilst incorporating some people into others. The recent attempt to encourage women as consumers of sportswear, as well as spectators at big events, may suggest a decline in the peripherality of sport to women compared with men. But there are many ways that women remain on the outside of sport in consumer culture. Clearly there is a need for more research into their involvement, as participants and consumers, of sport.

'Race', Consumer Culture and Sport

Studies since the 1990s have focussed on the historical and contemporary extent of racism in various British sports – athletics, basketball, cricket, rugby league and union, football, hockey, boxing and others (for example, see Chappell 2002 and the collections edited by Carrington and McDonald 2001 and Jarvie 1991). Few systematic studies into non-white peoples' participation in sport at grassroots level have been undertaken (however see Verma and Darby 1994). It is apparent that levels of participation in sport are not equal for all ethnic groups. In 1996, 46 per cent of white adults participated in one activity (excluding walking) during the previous 4 weeks, compared with 41 per cent of Black people (Caribbean, African or Black Other), 37 per cent of Indians and 25 per cent of Pakistanis and Bangladeshis (Sport England 1999a). Ethnic minorities are also under-represented in their use of local authority swimming pools (Sport England 1999b).

Analysis of sports-specific participation by ethnic minorities has not been possible due to the small sample sizes but in 2000 Sport England published *Sports Participation and Ethnicity in England National Survey 1999/2000*. This was the first large-scale survey (with 3000 non-white adult respondents) focussing on England. It found that 49 per cent of ethnic minority men compared with 54 per cent of white men participated in sport in the previous 4 weeks. Thirty-two per cent of ethnic minority women compared with thirty-nine per cent of white women participated in sport in the previous 4 weeks. Sixty per cent of 'Black Other' people (compared with 46 per cent of the total population) participated in sport in the previous 4 weeks. The survey found that 39 per cent of Black Caribbean and Indian people, 31 per cent of Pakistani people and 30 per cent of Bangladeshi people participated in sport. Compared with the general population, few ethnic minorities declared walking as a physical activity (for example, only 19 per cent of Bangladeshi women compared to 44 per cent of the total population). The findings showed differences between the participation of men and women. Swimming had a low priority – only 2 per cent of Black Other men and 5 per cent of Pakistani women – whereas football involvement amongst men was about the national average (10 per cent).

Research into the physical activity of black and minority ethnic people – in Britain as elsewhere – has tended to focus on two main themes. On the one hand are *equity issues* – to do with what Coakley (2003) calls the 'sports opportunity structure', the preserving of prejudices despite black excellence in sport, and 'stacking', the over-representation of black athletes in certain positions in team sports deemed to require less intelligence. Various anti-racism campaigns (for example, 'Let's Kick Racism Out of Football' in 1993/1994, 'Hit Racism for Six!' in cricket in 1995 and 'Football against Racism in Europe' (FARE) in 2002) have developed in response to these issues. On the other hand, research has begun to look at resistance or accommodation with racism through the consumption of sport. Whilst some black people have used sport as a route of black cultural resistance to racism and positive identity formation (Carrington and McDonald 2001), others, especially male youth in the USA, have been enticed into following their 'hoop dreams' (Brooks-Buck and Anderson 2001).

According to Brookes (2002, pp. 107ff.), research into representation has developed in the past twenty years to challenge the conceptual notion of stereotyping. The increasing commodification of sport has affected the way black people are represented in the sports media and targeted as consumers. These ideas relate to developments in the conception of identity that have emerged in the past fifteen years, especially the idea that identity is a ongoing process (see Chapter 6). The notion of the 'floating racial signifier' introduced by Stuart Hall is used by David Andrews to analyse the image of Michael Jordan in corporate advertising (1996, p. 126). This questions the value of the concept of stereotype, and suggests instead that 'racial identity is not stable, essential or consistent; it is dynamic, complex and contradictory'.

Research into black and minority ethnic groups as consumers of sport is underdeveloped in the UK, although some surveys have demonstrated the white majority among football fans. In the USA Armstrong (2004) has discussed how sportswear corporation Nike has been at the forefront of using advertisements, endorsements and sponsorship aimed at black audiences and consumers to differentiate its products from similar ones produced by other sportswear and equipment companies. Armstrong (2004) demonstrates the way that Nike targeted black audiences in the US by identifying what were considered to be appropriate symbols and images. A debate over whether black consumer purchases comprised 30 per cent (US$669 million) or 13.6 per cent (US$303 million) of Nike sales in the USA was stimulated by concerns over the exploitation of blacks by the Corporation. 'Race' has been central to many of Nike's campaigns, for example 'Spikey and Mikey' (Goldman and Papson 1998, Ch. 3). Cashmore (1997, p. 1) argues that black culture has also been converted into a commodity which certain whites are happy to consume. Blacks 'have been permitted to excel in entertainment only on the condition that they conform to whites' images of blacks'. Kusz (2004) alternatively suggests that Nike exploits black culture in order to sell their products to white youth.

Lury (1996, pp. 156ff) argues that the history of consumer culture is bound up with processes of imperialism, colonialism and the creation of the hierarchical categories of 'race'. Consumer culture has also helped to transform understandings of self and other, whiteness and blackness and 'race' itself. Images of black people helped shape the development of imperialism and consumer culture. These images were designed not for the consumption of black people but for communication between white people. As consumer culture has developed, images of black and minority ethnic people in advertising and in sport have altered. The film 'Bend it Like Beckham', released in 2002 to coincide with the World Cup in Japan and South Korea, portrayed women, Asian (Parminder Nagra) and white (Keira Knightly), as enthusiastic soccer players and fans. In the USA, where it grossed US$32 million at the box office, the film also marked a 'turning point for the sport in cinema'. At least eight more soccer films were set for release in the run up to the World Cup to be held in Germany in 2006 (*The Guardian* 1 March 2005, p. 33). As Lury (1996, p. 191) suggests, in various ways black and minority ethnic people have acted as 'key cultural intermediaries in the development of consumer culture' (Lury 1996, p. 191).

Age, Generation and the Life Course of Consumption

Childhood and youth are key periods for the construction of identity and selfhood. They are also absolutely central concerns of advertisers and marketers. Livingstone (2002, p. 116) notes how 'as traditional structures which confer identity...are being undermined, others are actively sought by young people, and these are readily addressed by the market'. She argues that young people seeking to make a life project today face a context in which leisure culture is being increasingly transformed into promotional culture. Sports fans 'play football, watch their team play, watch football on the television, buy the associated clothing and bedroom décor, and visit the football web sites' (Livingstone 2002, p. 115). In short, 'modern marketing directs flows of popular culture, identity is refashioned through consumption and the citizen (or viewer) is transformed into a consumer'. In this context being a fan – of not only pop stars but also sports stars – provides 'the "glue" which connects personal identity, social and peer relations, and taste preferences within a media-rich environment' of late modernity (Livingstone 2002, p. 115).

It might be assumed that younger consumers would spend more money on playing and watching sport whilst older consumers would spend more on reading and gambling on it. Benson's figures suggested that the young themselves did not spend more. As sportswear has become leisurewear the relationship with age has become more complex. As he writes, 'the most active consumers of nearly all types of sporting goods and services were young, male adults in their late teens, twenties or thirties' (Benson 1994, p. 125). Unlike other cultural activities, especially pop music, sport has arguably been less important in fostering distinctive youth cultures since it serves more as a bridge rather than a barrier between generations. The involvement of adults as coaches, trainers, teachers and so on could lead to resentment and rejection by some if not most young people. As Benson notes of male youth involved in sport (1994, p. 173), 'the fact that they played with adults meant that they were inculcated, more than non-participants, into an adult culture that stressed hard work, fair play, social drinking and male bonding'.

However, from the 1960s 'the distinction between sporting goods and fashion goods became blurred' and sports 'participation, consumption and youth culture became...interrelated' (Benson 1994, p. 173). England's success in the 1966 football World Cup final was a major contributor to this re-casting of sport as fashionable, throughout the UK. It became fashionable to follow football, and to wear track suits, trainers and other types of sports clothing. Yet this new relationship between sport and consumption alone did not create a distinct youth culture which transcended divisions based upon place, gender or social class.

The social construction of age and the life course – through such conceptions as 'the young' as thin and fit and 'the old' as flabby and sick – is a central feature of consumer culture and discourses of sport. Deborah Lupton's (1995, pp. 148–149) cameos demonstrate how discourses of fitness, healthism, self-discipline and asceticism can at one stage of the life course make a person feel 'attractive and vital, in control', and at another 'constitute him (or her) as lazy, unattractive, a loser, out of control' (Lupton 1995, p. 149). In other words, ideas about health, fitness, exercise and sport are 'not stable. The ways in which discourses are taken up and integrated into self-identity are at least partially contingent on the flux of individuals' positions in the workforce, in the lifecycle and the interaction of institutions such as the economy, the family, the school' (Lupton 1995, p. 149). They are also dependent on who the cultural intermediaries wish to reach with their messages. Although it is clear that some older people represent a lucrative consumption sector in their own right (Hepworth and Featherstone 1982, Featherstone and Wernick 1995, Blaikie 1999), it could be argued that young people are at the centre of debates about sport in consumer culture today.

Catching Them Young?

As we noted in the previous chapter the moral panic over the 'obesity epidemic' continues a series of concerns that have been expressed about the condition of youth, their physical and moral health and well-being, for at least the past fifty years. An alternative contemporary concern is that children and young people are being created as market segments and specifically targeted for advertising. As Antorini (2003, p. 212) noted,

> Whereas the key to the children's market used to be the products, the branding and the marketing, tomorrow's winners will be those that first find ways to make children true stakeholders of the company and so part of the company's destiny. Tomorrow's winners are those that realise that they need children to reach children.

In support of this trend Michael Moore (2002, pp. 102ff.) describes the encroachment of commercialism into US schools using data from the US-based Center for the Analysis of Commercialism in Education (CACE). The social construction of 'pester power' – 4–12-year-olds' influence on their parents purchasing decisions – in the USA, through 'cradle to grave' marketing via TV commercials, poster advertisements, logos and product placement, creates most concern (Schor 2004).

At six months of age it has been reported that babies in the US are forming mental images of corporate logos and mascots (McNeal and Yeh 1993). Brand loyalty may begin as early as 2 years of age (www.newdream.org), and by 3 years one in five American children are making specific requests for brand-name products (www.newdream.org). The children's (4–12-year-olds) market has grown so that US$8.6 billion was spent and US$31.3 billion was received from allowances and gifts in the late 1990s. In 2001 US teenagers spent US$172 billion. Market researchers estimated that 'pester power' was worth US$3000 billion in 2001 (McNeal 1998). Similar concerns are being investigated in the UK (Quart 2003). Contributors to a collection of articles edited by Lindstrom and Seybold (2003) reported on the formation of 'tweenagers' (8–14-year-olds) in 14 different countries. In addition they found that 3-year-olds could recognise brand logos and brand loyalty could be influenced by the age of two. The average British, Australian and American child would be exposed to between 20,000 and 40,000 advertisements per year. American children spent 60 per cent more time in front of a TV screen each year than they did at school. School playgrounds have become 'brand showrooms'. Brands take the place of religion in more secular societies. The coolest of all brands are the 'anti-brands' – those that dismiss phoney, false, pompous claims.

The media can be seen as central to this, especially television in America where the average child (aged 2–17 years) watches 17 hours 30 minutes of TV each week and over 20,000 TV commercials each year (over 50 per day). On average 2–18-year-olds spend 5 hours 30 minutes each day consuming media (TV, music, magazines, video games and the Internet). The increasingly commercialised school environments include brand logos on sports uniforms, textbooks and drink and fast food vending machines filled with brand names. Often children attend sponsored lessons. The response from some children is to develop critical skills as Kenway and Bullen (2001, pp. 114–116) point out in their study of Australian schoolchildren. However, whilst critical of products they are not critical of consumerism as a way of life (Kenway and Bullen 2001, pp. 119–120).

Conclusion

When 'virtually everyone is now living inside the culture of the market' (Smart 2003, p. 163), are social divisions based on traditional social categories blurred? Social experience may have become more individualised as it has become more commercialised. This creates opportunities and new risks. It also allows continuities amidst the more loudly proclaimed changes, as this chapter has suggested. Sports marketing specialists recognise that corporate sponsorship allows companies to reach 'new target markets' (Shank 2002, p. 411). Sponsors trying to reach new and 'difficult-to-capture audiences' have used the X-Games, to reach 'Generation X-ers', and another 'target market that has been neglected includes the millions of disabled Americans' (Shank 2002, p. 412). With the growth of the Paralympic Games, and in the USA programmes such as 'Sporting Chance', which provide disabled people with opportunities to participate in sport, 'marketers are now addressing this market', according to Shank (2002, p. 412). In the USA Nixon notes (2000, p. 425) that 'We have even seen athletes with disabilities on "Wheaties" cereal boxes, a site where some of the most prominent American sports heroes have been displayed'! It can be argued that the development of the Paralympic Games has involved a transformation of their purpose from making disabled people into good worker-citizens, via participation in wholesome sport, into making them good consumer-citizens through their consumption of the expanded sports spectacle. Sport may become a major conduit for the production of what can be termed 'commodity disablism' or the treatment of disability as a commodity. This will be accompanied by changes in the representation of disabled athletes in the media in all its forms. Some researchers suggest that this is already underway (Duncan and Aycock 2005).

In the next, final, chapter we summarise the contents of the book and consider how far it is possible to develop a politics of sport in consumer culture.

8

Conclusion

Review of the Book

We have attempted to show in this book how the three main features of contemporary consumer capitalism – globalisation, commodification and inequality – shape and contour contemporary sport. A global sports market has developed and in this the mass media have played and continue to play a significant role in the commodification of sport. The commodification of sport is assisted by the growth of sponsorship and the use of sport as an adjunct to advertising – particularly focussed, but not exclusively – on men as consumers. In this context the state has a role to play in regulating sport and defining 'consumer interest'. With the dominance of neo-liberal political economic discourse and a move towards 'cultural governance', the main beneficiaries of state intervention in sport have tended to be global corporations and private capital more generally. Consumerisation – the process of the construction of people with consumer values and outlooks – has impacted on personal and collective identities and the development of new lifestyles. The relationship of these developments to older social divisions in sports participation and involvement, based upon social class, gender, 'race' and age especially, have also been explored.

Part I of the book (Chapters 2 and 3) focussed attention on globalisation. Evans et al. (1996, p. 332), writing in a standard business studies textbook, argue that the impact of globalisation on consumer behaviour is to create the sensation that 'Two trends are happening simultaneously: everything is becoming the same, differences are becoming greater!' Some sociologists would agree with this, but following Sklair (2002, p. 84) we argue that globalisation is better understood as a product of 'transnational practices', which also assist in the spread of the 'culture-ideology of consumerism'. The experience of greater similarities and differences is a product of the marketisation and commodification of more aspects of everyday life. Some people experience increasing affluence and leisure as consumerism develops and these developments are the result of wider economic and political changes.

Part II of the book (Chapters 4 and 5) explored the development of the marketisation and commodification of sport through its connection with capital and especially advertising and marketing agencies. At the same time as sport has been commercialised, greater emphasis on the production of the consumer-citizen as opposed to the social citizen has taken place. The role of the state in the development of sport has increased, but political rights and entitlements of citizens have been increasingly interpreted as those of consumers' ability to make economic choices.

Part III of the book (Chapters 6 and 7) considered arguments about the supposed decline or blurring of social class, gender, 'race' and other social divisions, and the impact on sport. The growth of new lifestyles and identities forged out of consumption practices was considered. We argued that there are several continuities amidst the undoubted changes. Ken Roberts (1997) found this in his research into the changing life situations of young people in the UK. Young people's life situations had been changing and becoming more *diverse*. Class divisions were more blurred and did not determine tastes in the way that they used to in the 1960s and 1970s. Youth culture was more fragmented, and groupings that formed around particular leisure and consumption tastes could produce a sense of belonging or 'new tribes'. However, Roberts argued that although it might appear that leisure, lifestyles and consumption choices were the bases for the construction of identity by young people, this was not the case. Social class, gender and ethnicity continued to be central organising principles of young people's lives. Whilst there has been an increased emphasis on the 'politics of recognition' in the past twenty years, as interest in identities, lifestyles and the role of consumption in society have increased, we suggest that attention to the 'politics of redistribution' is still necessary in the context of contemporary social divisions (Devine et al. 2005).

Critique of Sport in Capitalist Consumer Culture

Running throughout debates about capitalist consumer culture and consumer society is a coming to terms with the collapse of the 'actually existing socialist' alternatives in the former USSR and eastern European countries, and the development of capitalism as the world's economic system. Underpinning this book, and in contrast with other recent trends in academic approach, is an emphasis on the importance of capitalism for understanding developments in the position of sport in society. As Harvey (2000, p. 87) notes, 'There are many different ways of making a profit – of gaining surplus value: whichever way works, you are likely to find increasing experiments with it – so there might be a trend towards flexible accumulation; but there are some key limits to the process.'

More business-oriented commentators on sport provide a compelling list of associated developments (Westerbeek and Smith 2003, pp. 48–49). Westerbeek and Smith (2003) identify the blurring of what is sport and what is entertainment, the vertical and horizontal integration of sport enterprises by

entertainment and media companies, an increase in venture capital and investment in transnational sports and sport properties, and the integration and
consolidation of sport, leisure, recreation, television, film and tourism into
elements of the entertainment industry, as just a few of the key trends. The
consequences include a growth in the economic effects and impacts of sport,
the ongoing increase in the value of genuinely global sport properties,
including athletes and players themselves, and the convergence of economic
power in sport ownership. These effects link up with the de-fragmentation of
sport governance and the simultaneous professionalisation and marginalisation of smaller sports and leagues – 'the gap between the sport enterprises that
are globally successful and those which remain domestically viable, will grow'
(Westerbeek and Smith 2003, p. 48). As fewer and fewer hands will own
more and more sports which are modelled according to Western sports,
the ultimate consequence will be a world-wide increase in capitalism as the
pre-eminent economic philosophy and of sport as an effective vehicle to
achieving wealth.

Whilst we might disagree with some of their futurological study, it is
undoubtedly the case that sport has become more commercialised in the
past twenty-five years. It is almost passé now to say that association football is
big business. In 1994 Sepp Blatter claimed that football was bringing in
US$163 billion annually, more than General Motors could make selling cars
(cited in Smith 1997, p. 144). Few would argue over this today. Each of the
trends identified by Westerbeek and Smith relates to the development of capitalism as the dominant economic system throughout the world. In order to
make better sense of their list of developments we argue that it is necessary to
adopt a 'production of consumption' approach to consumer capitalism.

Harvey (2000) notes that the conditions that have produced increased
consumption have a strong 'spatial fix' – contemporary geography is
composed of highly differentiated global distribution and reception of images
and information. The 'economies of signs and space' that Lash and Urry
(1994) identified require researching in terms of their uneven economic
development. First, the way Third World labour markets (in both First and
Third World countries) support First World economies of signs (Enloe 1998,
2000; Oxfam 2004). Secondly, the unevenness, directness and purposefulness
of configurations of power – its hierarchies and headquarters, and the ideological strength of TNCs and macro-institutions (the IMF, World Bank, WTO
and regional alliances such as NAFTA and the EU) and global sports organisations, such as the IOC and FIFA. Thirdly, the discursive ascendancy of
neo-liberal economic and political philosophy and corporate management
thought has contributed to the current global triumph of a (postmodern)
meta-narrative.

Franks (2000) describes these circumstances as the result of the spread of
'market populism'. By market populism Franks refers to the way in which
markets were reconceived in the USA at the end of the 1990s. The 'populist

celebration of the power and "agency" of audiences and fans' (Frank 2000, p. 282), in cultural studies (or 'cult studs' as Franks calls it), became indistinguishable from the market ideology of sovereign consumers beloved of management and business theory. Warde (2002, p. 17) also suggested some reasons to be sceptical of the celebratory perspective in studies of consumption and consumer culture. First, it is complicit in the exaggeration of the role of individual choice in consumption behaviour. Secondly, it loses sight of the 'dull compulsion to consume', its mundanity. Thirdly, it fosters a complacent suspension of critique regarding consumer culture in general. An emphasis on the creation of self-identity predominated in sociological research into consumption in the 1990s. Yet this model 'is constantly on the brink of reverting to a paradigm for understanding consumption which presumes the sovereignty of consumer choice and reduces explanation to the reasons why individuals make particular choices' (Warde 2002, p. 17). McGuigan agrees that this approach simply echoes much neo-liberal (Thatcherite) ideology about the wonders of the market economy, whilst 'some consumers are more sovereign than others' (McGuigan 1997, p. 143). Put simply, the active or interactive viewer or consumer may not be the powerful consumer. As Coates (1995) suggests, *purchasing* power is not the same as *market* power.

In the midst of consumer society, class, 'race' and gender continue to influence life trajectories. The social divisions between rich and poor continue to grow. We believe that the production of consumption approach is therefore most useful to help explore these questions for three main reasons. First, we agree with Smart (2003) that to understand the social environment of contemporary advanced societies adequately it is necessary to come to terms with the emergence of a radically transformed global capitalist free market economy. In the past thirty years, in addition to the growth of consumerism, this has seen the transformation of work and the increasing feminisation of the labour force. Secondly, although society may have moved beyond the (protestant) work ethic as its major disciplinary force, consumption increasingly operates in the service of production. Knowledge about consumers is a vital asset in information capitalism. Jobs that handle the management of economic demand, shape the conditions of consumption and thus assist in the reproduction of capitalism, such as marketing, advertising, fashion, design and other media specialities, provide a dominant role as cultural intermediaries. Thirdly, consumer culture is simply capitalistic. As Smart (2003, p. 163) suggests, 'hardly anyone's life is unaffected by the direct or indirect consequences of the global diffusion of capitalist forms of economic life'. In these circumstances, corporate brands become experiences, offering lifestyles and identities. Ironically, rather than being a threat to the established social order, the identity politics of the 1990s may have been 'a gold mine' to corporations (Klein 2000a, p. 115) since they revealed diverse market niches, without the need for additional, expensive and difficult, consumer research.

Some would argue that it is about time that 'political economy' made a comeback. This book's overall message is that to understand sport in consumer culture it is necessary to have an understanding of what creates the conditions within which consumer culture flourishes and that is the economic system (Desai 2004). Yet rather than draw on rather outdated and outmoded general models of society, we consider that the task of social science is to facilitate studies of the specifics of social and historical contexts, and thus contribute towards a better understanding of the politics of sport in consumer culture.

For a Sociology of Sport in Consumer Culture

Living within consumer society creates risks – of social exclusion and surveillance – and opportunities and dilemmas. As Bauman (1998, p. 1) notes, the 'seduced' are observed while the 'repressed', failed consumers, are kept under surveillance. Yet it has also seen the growth of new modes of community. Personal communications, 'new sociations' and friendships can flourish. Aldridge (2003, p. 109) argues that friendship is well suited to consumer society – able to withstand the collapse of old style communities and rooted in choice. In fact, 'consumer society may be the golden age of friendship' (Aldridge 2003, p. 109). In this context, leisure has become more central to life in advanced capitalist societies. There is more time for leisure, more spaces – stadia, sport centres and fitness clubs – more disposable income spent on leisure and greater amounts of interactive service work, some of it in leisure. Sport is a part of this – even as it is increasingly deployed as a promotional vehicle for consumer culture.

Research into the impact of the media on sports and peoples' behaviour has focussed on three broad areas. One concern has been the impact of television broadcasts on attendances at live sports events. Findings here have been mixed. Sometimes there appears to be an effect. It is suggested, for example, that every time a Champions League or UEFA Cup fixture is broadcast in England it costs lower level football teams (in Coca Cola League 2) up to £6000 in lost revenue (*The Guardian* 28 February 2005, Sport section, p. 13). In other studies people attend televised events to become part of the spectacle. A second area of research has been the impact on sports participation.

Following England's Rugby World Cup triumph in November 2003, there was a boom in interest and involvement in the sport. Other evidence suggests that the media impact on participation is more transitory and short term – what might be called the 'Wimbledon' effect, after the rush to the tennis courts in the UK before and slightly after the Wimbledon event in the summer. Another concern has been the impact on attitudes towards sport. Studies in the UK and elsewhere suggest that fans' views are reinforced, rather than changed, by the media coverage of their team. One way in which fans are routinely sustained with their need for more information about the objects and subjects of their admiration is through the growth of celebrity culture and the sports star.

Sport may be a means of resisting as well as subscribing to these conditions. Roger Silverstone (1999, p. 79) suggests that 'We consume media. We consume through the media. We learn how and what to consume through the media. We are persuaded to consume through the media. The media, it is not too far-fetched to suggest, consume us.' His statement provides a strong justification for considering the position of the media in constructing our relationship to sport in consumer culture as central. At the same time Silverstone identifies a, maybe what many see as the, paradox of consumption. He notes that 'The commodities that we are offered are the product of an alienating system of production on which we entirely depend, yet at the same time they offer us the raw materials for creating our own sense of ourselves' (Silverstone 1999, pp. 80–81). Just as Silverstone said of the media, much contemporary sport both is a product of an alienating system of production on which we depend, and yet also offers us the raw materials for creating our own sense of ourselves.

Many people engage in sport as a means of shaping up to the requirements of life in the 21st century. Sport is a preparation for living flexibly in a competitive capitalist world. It is also a great source of friendship/community involvement which enables people to escape (if only momentarily) from that world. For some, participation and involvement in sport in contemporary capitalist consumer culture is a 'both/and' relationship – both engagement in sport and awareness of exploitation. For others, sport is too overblown and is avoided. There is a clear gender division about sport in this regard.

The Politics of Consumer Activism in Sport

In academic life it is not surprising that studies of consumers from business and management perspectives often convey commercially exploitable knowledge. Consumers are often treated as individual, rational decision-makers. Although groups identified as 'new consumers' have different attitudes towards consumption than 'old consumers', research has been conducted into these consumers' behaviour using miniature cameras to record shopping experiences, monitor their blood pressure and heart rates in supermarkets, and electrical activity in their brains as they watch TV commercials. Kenway and Bullen (2001) suggest that in the study of consumer culture, the hybridisation of education, entertainment and advertising, children and adult's culture and the behaviour of corporations have been scrutinised, but often without the consumer's viewpoint being fully taken into account. There is a need to discuss participant's readings of the commodification of sport, and their construction of themselves as consumers of sport. How does sports consumption connect with other consumption patterns, identities and relationships? Research like that done by Crawford (2004) and the contributors to Wheaton's collection of essays (2004) provides a start in analysing what consumers do with sport as opposed to asking what sport does to consumers. But in addition to such research there is a need to recognise the limits on the capacity of sports consumers to resist, negotiate and engage with the politics of sport in consumer culture. Even sports scientists seem unaware of the potential impact that the introduction of commercially sponsored materials into their curricula and into their research programmes could make. It is in these circumstances that Monbiot (2000, p. 301) argues that there is a need for pedagogic strategies for creating critical consciousness. Sociology of all the social sciences used to conceive of itself in this light as Bourdieu suggests.

As with other consumer goods and services, there is clearly a need for different forms of consumer protection in sport. The question is who will regulate the regulators of sport? In their introduction to the 3rd edition of *Cranston's Consumers and the Law*, Scott and Black (2000) note that in the earlier editions the original author argued for 'strong public regulation as the basis for effective consumer protection'. Four influences have brought about changes that have affected consumers in the UK since the 1980s. First, new or modified national laws have been introduced. Secondly, European laws have become increasingly 'central to many developments' in UK consumer law (Scott and Black 2000, p. vi). Thirdly, direct government intervention has altered the position of the consumer. Conservative governments between 1979 and 1997 introduced some changes, and since 1997 the Labour administrations have been committed to substantial reform of consumer law. Finally the activity of the courts has also influenced consumer law in the UK. There is clearly a need for continual vigilance over the position of the sports consumer in contemporary society.

The 1960s saw the birth, or at least re-statement, of consumer rights in the USA and other advanced capitalist societies. Currently Consumers International (CI) proposes nine 'global' rights for consumers – to safety, to be informed, to choose, to be heard, to redress, to consumer education, to a healthy environment, to satisfaction of basic needs, and to privacy (Aldridge 2003, pp. 132–134). Aldridge identifies two significant forms of consumer activism: 'value for money (VFM) activism' and 'beyond VFM activism'. VFM activism involves the debate about how best to secure consumer rights – through the market, the state or voluntary agencies? Advocates of the first approach argue that the market is best left alone, regulation breeds bureaucracy and can lead to 'regulatory capture', whereby the regulator ends up acting on behalf of the producers rather than consumers. Nation-states and supra-state organisations such as the EU operate in slightly different ways with regard to the second approach. The EU tends to adopt a risk averse or precautionary approach. In this approach the consumer is viewed as a victim who cannot attend to his or her own interests without the aid of the state (for example, the new deal agreed for the rights to broadcast English Premiership football on British TV from 2004 was subject to EU approval). For some this is viewed as patronising meddling.

In the third approach, voluntary organisations act to supply consumers with objective knowledge and lobby the government on behalf of consumer rights. In the UK as we have seen, there is the Consumer's Association (CA, now known as *Which?*) and in North America there is the Consumer's Union of USA and Canada. Their publications include *Which?* (UK), *Consumer Reports* (USA/Canada) and *Protegez-vous* (French-speaking Canada). The aim of these organisations is to identify 'best buys' and ultimately 'prevent consumers from becoming victims and to enable them to be well informed rational actors' (Aldridge 2003, p. 140). Hence Aldridge argues these organisations construct consumption as work, not 'retail therapy', imaginative hedonism or 'fantasy'. A sports example is the survey carried out on behalf of the CA in the UK together with other European consumer organisations, to ask sports shoe manufacturers about their activities and policies with respect to the environment, social responsibility and company transparency (*Which*, June 2003). The CA wanted to investigate whether jogging shoes manufacturers were taking their corporate social responsibility (CSR) seriously – for example, by controlling and monitoring conditions at the factories they use. The survey concluded that most major running shoe companies out-sourced their manufacturing to overseas suppliers, to benefit from cheap production and newspaper reports of the appalling working conditions, low wages and environmental damage in these factories were quite accurate. Box 8.1 shows the companies and their websites. Why not see what the companies have to say for themselves? Then compare this with other organisations – such as the CA and Oxfam (2004).

Box 8.1 *The ethics of the sports shoe makers*

Companies with some ethical initiatives included
Adidas   www.adidas-salomon.com
New Balance   www.newbalance.com
Nike   www.nikebiz.com
Puma   http://about.puma.com
Reebok   www.reebok.com

Companies with limited ethical initiatives included
Asics   www.asics.com

Companies with no information about ethical initiatives included
Brooks   www.brooksrunning.com
Mizuno   www.mizuno.com
Saucony   www.sauconyinc.com

Source: *Which*, June 2003.

Beyond VFM, other forms of consumer activism have developed in relation to the expansion of promotional culture (Wernick 1991). As we have seen, it has been the journalist Naomi Klein (2000a) who has provided the most sustained critique of VFM consumerism in the era of neo-liberal global capitalism. Logos and the brands that they represent are the product of a 'third culture' produced by multinational corporations after the neo-liberal project of the 1980s and 1990s have starved the public sector and non-commercial events of resources. Corporate sponsors are now required to finance all mega events (Roche 2000). Commercial sponsorship and product placement (embedded advertising) has grown accordingly (Murdoch 1992, Fowles 1996, pp. 144–145). Klein argues that in these conditions brands become new lifestyle badges. But rather than being guarantees of quality, logos also become anti-competitive signs of global monopoly capitalism, exploitative relations (insecure, non-unionised, casualised and sweated, labour) in the Third World and anti-democratic practices since codes of conduct are often drafted by the companies themselves or organisations representing them (see Oxfam 2004). New challenges for 'liquid modernity' (Bauman 2000) include the way that consumption has broken free of former boundaries. Images, objects and people flow unstoppably across national border, and consumer activism has adopted to this (Kingsnorth 2003). The activities of 'culture jammers' and 'Adbusters' (Lasn 1999) using ridicule are other examples of consumer activism beyond VFM.

Some sociologists ask who actually feels guilty about purchases and lifestyles? Turner and Rojek (2001, pp. 226–228), for example, suggest that the anti-capitalist movement, connected to the 'no logo' critique, is not so important. Sports consumer politics has not usually been at the centre of anti-capitalist debates and campaigns. May be Turner and Rojek are correct and consumer politics in sport and of sport generally has usually taken the form of VFM activism. It is possible that debates surrounding the staging of global mega events can make connections with wider issues – such as human rights, democratisation and social equality – but mostly sport has been a forum for at best reformist politics rather than cultural revolution. Whichever we decide, we can agree with Aldridge that the study of consumer activism is, and will remain, an essential part of understanding the politics of sport in consumer culture.

Bibliography

AA (Advertising Association) (2002) *Advertising Statistics Yearbook 2002.* Henley: World Advertising Research Centre.

AT Kearney (2003) *The New Sports Consumer.* Chicago, IL: AT Kearney Inc., Marketing and Communications.

Abercrombie, N. (2004) *Sociology.* Cambridge: Polity.

Abercrombie, N., Hill, S. and Turner, B. (2000) *The Penguin Dictionary of Sociology.* Harmondsworth: Penguin (4th edition).

Abercrombie, N., Hill, S. and Turner, B. (1980) *The Dominant Ideology Thesis.* London: George Allen & Unwin.

Abercrombie, N. and Longhurst, B. (1998) *Audiences.* Cambridge: Polity.

Abercrombie, N. and Warde, A. (2000) *Contemporary British Society.* Cambridge: Polity (3rd edition).

Adbusters (2001) 'The smell of swoosh', *Adbusters: Journal of the Mental Environment.* No. 36 July/August (see www.adbusters.org and www.culturejammers.org).

Adorno, T. (1996/1951) *Minima Moralia: Reflections from Damaged Life.* London: Verso.

Adorno, T. and Horkheimer, M. (1977) 'The culture industry: Enlightenment as mass deception', in J. Curran, M. Gurevitch and J. Woollacott (eds), *Mass Communication and Society.* London: Arnold, pp. 349–383.

Alberoni, F. (1972/1962) 'The powerless "elite": Theory and sociological research on the phenomenon of the stars', in D. McQuail (ed.), *Sociology of Mass Communications.* Harmondsworth: Penguin, pp. 75–98.

Aldridge, A. (1994) 'The construction of rational consumption in *Which?* Magazine: The more blobs the better?', *Sociology*, Vol. 28, No. 4, pp. 899–912.

——. (2003) *Consumption.* Cambridge: Polity.

Alexander, V. (2003) *Sociology of the Arts.* Oxford: Blackwell.

Allison, L. ed. (2000) *Taking Sport Seriously.* Aachen: Meyer & Meyer.

Amateur Athletic Foundation of Los Angeles (2000) *Gender in Televised Sports: 1989, 1993 and 1999.* Los Angeles: The Amateur Athletic Foundation of Los Angeles.

Anderson, B. (1991) *Imagined Communities: Reflections on the Origin and Spread of Nationalism.* London: Verso.

Anderson, J. (2000) 'Disability sports', in R. Cox, G. Jarvie and W. Vamplew (eds), *Encyclopedia of British Sport.* Oxford: ABC-CLIO, pp. 105–107.

Andreff, W. and Staudohar, P. (2000) 'The evolving European model of professional sports finance', *Journal of Sports Economics*, Vol. 1, No. 3, pp. 257–276.

Andrews, D. (1996) 'The facts of Michael Jordan's blackness: Excavating a floating racial signifier', *Sociology of Sport Journal*, Vol. 13, No. 1, pp. 125–158.

——. (2000) 'Posting up: French post-structuralism and the critical analysis of contemporary sporting culture', in J. Coakley and E. Dunning (eds), *Handbook of Sports Studies*. London: Sage, pp. 106–137.

——. ed. (2001) *Michael Jordan, Inc.* Albany: State University of New York Press.

——. (2004) 'Speaking the "universal language of entertainment": News corporation, culture and the global sport media economy', in D. Rowe (ed.), *Critical Readings: Sport, Culture and the Media*. Maidenhead: Open University Press, pp. 99–128.

——. ed. (2004) *Manchester United*. London: Routledge.

Andrews, D. and Jackson, S. eds (2001) *Sport Stars*. London: Routledge.

Ang, I. (1985) *Watching Dallas*. London: Methuen.

Antorini, Y. (2003) 'The essence of being a child', in M. Lindstrom and P. Seybold (eds), *Brandchild*. London: Kogan Page.

Armstrong, K. (2004) 'Nike's communication with black audiences: A sociological analysis of advertising effectiveness via symbolic interactionism', in D. Rowe (ed.), *Critical Readings: Sport, Culture and the Media*. Maidenhead: Open University Press, pp. 210–228.

Baade, R. and Matheson, V. (2002) 'Bidding for the Olympics: Fool's gold?', in C. Barros, M. Ibrahimo and S. Szymanski (eds), *Transatlantic Sport*. London: Edward Elgar, pp. 127–151.

Bairner, A. (2001) *Sport, Nationalism and Globalization*. Albany, NY: State University of New York Press.

Bakhtin, M. (1984) *Rabelais and His World*. Bloomington: Indiana University Press.

Barber, B. (1995) *Jihad vs. McWorld*. New York: Random House.

Baudrillard, J. (1983/1981) *Simulacra and Simulations*. New York: Semiotext(e).

——. (1988) *Jean Baudrillard: Selected Writings* (M. Poster, ed.). Cambridge: Polity.

Bauman, Z. (1998) *Work, Consumerism and the New Poor*. Buckingham: Open University Press.

——. (2000) *Liquid Modernity*. Cambridge: Polity.

——. (2004a) 'The Consumerist Syndrome in Contemporary Society', an interview with Chris Rojek, *Journal of Consumer Culture*, Vol. 4, No. 3, pp. 291–312.

——. (2004b) *Wasted Lives*. Cambridge: Polity.

——. (2004c) 'Liquid sociality', an interview with N. Gane (ed.), *The Future of Social Theory*. London: Continuum, pp. 17–46.

Bauman, Z. and May, T. (2001) *Thinking Sociologically*. Oxford: Blackwell (2nd edition).

Bechhofer, F., Stewart, R., Kiely, R. and McCrone, D. (1999) 'Constructing national identity: Arts and landed elites in Scotland', *Sociology*, Vol. 33, No. 4, pp. 515–534.

Beck, U. (1992/1986) *Risk Society: Towards a New Modernity*. London: Sage.

Beck, U. (2000) *The Brave New World of Work*. Cambridge: Polity.

Beck, U. and Beck-Gernsheim, E. (2002) *Individualization*. London: Sage.

Belk, R. (2001/1995) *Collecting in a Consumer Society*. Cambridge: Polity.

Bellah, R., Madsen, R., Sullivan, W., Swidler, A. and Tipton, S. (1985) *Habits of the Heart*. Berkeley: University of California Press.

Benjamin, W. (1999) *The Arcades Project*. London: Belknap.

Bennett, T., Emmison, M. and Frow, J. (1999) *Accounting for Tastes: Australian Everyday Cultures.* Cambridge: Cambridge University Press.

Benson, J. (1994) *The Rise of Consumer Society 1880–1980.* Harlow: Longman.

Birkinshaw, J. and Crainer, S. (2004) *Leadership: The Sven-Goran Eriksson Way – How to Turn Your Team into Winners.* Chichester: Capstone (2nd edition).

Birley, D. (1995) *Playing the Game.* Manchester: Manchester University Press.

——. (2000) *A Social History of English Cricket.* London: Aurum Press.

Birrell, S. and Cole, C. eds (1994) *Women, Sport, and Culture.* Champaign, IL: Human Kinetics.

Black, D. (2003) 'Man United fined over football kit price-fixing cartel', *The Guardian*, 2 August, p. 7.

Blackshaw, T. (2002) 'The sociology of sport reassessed in light of the phenomenon of Zygmunt Bauman', *International Review of the Sociology of Sport*, Vol. 37, No. 2, pp. 199–217.

Blackshaw, T. and Crabbe, T. (2004) *New Perspectives on Sport and 'Deviance'.* London: Routledge.

Blaikie, A. (1999) *Ageing and Popular Culture.* Cambridge: Cambridge University Press.

Blain, N. (2002) 'Beyond "Media Culture": Sport as dispersed symbolic activity', *Culture, Sport, Society*, Vol. 5, pp. 227–254.

Blain, N., Boyle, R. and O'Donnell, H. (1993) *Sport and National Identity in the European Media.* Leicester: Leicester University Press.

Bocock, R. (1994) 'Consumption and lifestyles', in R. Bocock and K. Thompson (eds), *Social and Cultural Forms of Modernity.* Cambridge: Polity Press, pp. 119–167.

Bolchover, D. and Brady, C. (2004) *The 90-Minute Manager. Lessons from the Sharp End of Management.* Harlow: Pearson Education (Revised edition).

Booth, D. (2004) 'Surfing: from one (cultural) extreme to another', in B. Wheaton (ed.), *Understanding Lifestyle Sports.* London: Routledge, pp. 94–109.

Bordwell, M. (2002) 'Jamming culture: Adbusters' hip media campaign against consumerism', in T. Princen, M. Maniates and K. Conca (eds), *Confronting Consumption.* Cambridge, MA: MIT Press, pp. 237–253.

Bourdieu, P. (1978) 'Sport and social class', *Social Science Information*, Vol. 17, No. 6, pp. 819–840.

——. (1984/1979) *Distinction.* London: Routledge.

——. (1993) *Sociology in Question.* London: Sage.

——. (1998) *On Television and Journalism.* London: Pluto.

——. (1999a) 'The abdication of the state', *The Weight of the World: Social Suffering in Contemporary Society.* Cambridge: Polity, pp. 181–188.

——. (1999b) 'The state, economics and sport', in H. Dauncey and G. Hare (eds), *France and the 1998 World Cup.* London: Frank Cass, pp. 15–21.

——. (2000) quoted in 'La sociologie est un Sport de Combat', Film directed by Pierre Carles.

——. (2003) *Firing Back.* London: Verso.

Bourdieu, P. and Wacquant, L. (1992) *An Invitation to Reflexive Sociology.* Cambridge: Polity.

Boyle, R. and Haynes, R. (2000) *Power Play*. London: Longman.

——. (2002) 'New media sport', *Culture, Sport, Society*, Vol. 5, pp. 95–114.

——. (2004) *Football in the New Media Age*. London: Routledge.

Bramlett, M. and Sloan, M. (2000) 'The commodification of sports: The example of personal seat licenses in professional football', in M. Gottdiener (ed.), *New Forms of Consumption: Consumers, Culture and Commodification*. Lanham/Oxford: Rowman & Littlefield, pp. 177–201.

Brohm, J.-M. (1978) *Sport a Prison of Measured Time*. London: Ink Links.

Brooks-Buck, J. and Anderson, E. (2001) 'African American access to higher education through sports: Following a dream or perpetuating a stereotype?', *Widening Participation and Lifelong Learning*, Vol. 3, pp. 26–31.

Brookes, C. (1978) *English Cricket*. London: Weidenfeld and Nicolson.

Brookes, R. (2002) *Representing Sport*. London: Arnold.

Brown, A. and Walsh, A. (1999) *Not for Sale: Manchester United, Murdoch and the Defeat of BSkyB*. Edinburgh: Mainstream.

Brown, P. (2003) 'Shopping until you drop leads to misery', *The Guardian*, 17 September, p. 5.

Bryman, A. (2004) *The Disneyization of Society*. London: Sage.

Buck-Morss, S. (1991) *The Dialectics of Seeing: Walter Benjamin and the Arcades Project*. Cambridge, MA: MIT Press.

Buckingham, D. and Sefton-Green, J. (2003) 'Gotta catch 'em all: structure, agency and pedagogy in children's media culture', *Media, Culture and Society*, Vol. 25, No. 3, pp. 379–399.

Burns, T. (1995) *Description, Explanation and Understanding: Selected Writings 1944–1980*. Edinburgh: Edinburgh University Press.

Burstyn, V. (1999) *The Rites of Men: Manhood, Politics and the Culture of Sport*. Toronto: Toronto University Press.

Burton Nelson, M. (1996) *The Stronger Women Get, the More Men Love Football*. London: Women's Press.

Busch, A. ed. (1998) *Design for Sport*. London: Thames and Hudson.

Buxton, D. (1990) 'Rock music, the star system, and the rise of consumerism', in S. Frith and A. Goodwin (eds), *On Record*. London: Routledge, pp. 427–440.

Cabinet Office Strategy Unit (2002) *Game Plan*. London: The Cabinet Office (accessible at www.strategy.gov.uk/2002/sport/report).

Campbell, C. (1995) 'The sociology of consumption', in D. Miller (ed.), *Acknowledging Consumption*. London: Routledge, pp. 96–126.

Carrington, B. and McDonald, I. eds (2001) *'Race', Sport and British Society*. London: Routledge.

——. (2002) 'Sport, racism and inequality', *Sociology Review*, Vol. 11, No. 3, pp. 8–11.

——. (2003) 'The politics of "race" and sports policy', in B. Houlihan (ed.), *Sport & Society*. London: Sage, pp. 125–142.

Cashmore, E. (1997) *The Black Cultural Industry*. London: Routledge.

——. (2000a) *Making Sense of Sport*. London: Routledge (3rd edition).

——. (2000b) *Sports Culture: An A-Z Guide*. London: Routledge.

——. (2002) *Beckham*. Cambridge: Polity.

Cashmore, E. and Parker, A. (2003) 'One David Beckham? Celebrity, masculinity, and the soccerati', *Sociology of Sport Journal*, Vol. 20, pp. 214–231.

Castells, M. (1996) *The Rise of the Network Society*. Oxford: Blackwell.

Castells, M. (1998) *End of Millennium*. Oxford: Blackwell.

Central Council for Physical Recreation/CCPR (1983) *Committee of Enquiry into Sports Sponsorship: The 'Howell Report'*. London: CCPR.

Centre for Contemporary Cultural Studies, University of Birmingham (1980) *Fads and Fashions*. London: Social Science Research Council/Sports Council.

Chandler, T., Cronin, M. and Vamplew, W. (2002) *Sport and Physical Education: The Key Concepts*. London: Routledge.

Chaney, D. (1996) *Lifestyles*. London: Routledge.

——. (2002) *Cultural Change and Everyday Life*. Basingstoke: Palgrave.

Channel 4 (1991) *The Trainer Wars*. Documentary broadcast on Channel 4 Television.

Chappell, B. (2002) 'Race, ethnicity and sport', in A. Laker (ed.), *The Sociology of Sport and Physical Education: An Introductory Reader*. London: Routledge, pp. 92–109.

Clapson, M. (1992) *A Bit of a Flutter*. Manchester: Manchester University Press.

Clarke, G. and Humberstone, B. eds (1997) *Researching Women and Sport*. Basingstoke: Macmillan.

Clarke, J. and Critcher, C. (1985) *The Devil Makes Work*. Basingstoke: Macmillan.

Clarke, R. (2003) *The Business of Sports Marketing*. London: Sport Business Group Limited.

Coakley, J. (2003) *Sport in Society*. New York: McGraw-Hill (8th edition).

Coakley, J. and Donnelly, P. eds (1999) *Inside Sports*. London: Routledge.

——. (2004) *Sport in Society*. Toronto: McGraw-Hill Ryerson (1st Canadian edition).

Coakley, J. and Dunning, E. eds (2000) *Handbook of Sport Studies*. London: Sage.

Coakley, J. and White, A. (1999) 'Making decisions: How young people become involved and stay involved in sports', in J. Coakley and P. Donnelly (eds), *Inside Sports*. London: Routledge, pp. 77–85.

Coalter, F. (1999) 'Sport and recreation in the United Kingdom: Flow with the flow or buck the trends?', *Managing Leisure*, Vol. 4, No. 1, pp. 24–39.

Coalter, F., Allison, M. and Taylor, J. (2000) *The Role of Sport in Regenerating Deprived Urban Areas*. Edinburgh: Scottish Executive Central Policy Unit.

Coalter, F., Long, J. and Duffield, B. (1988) *Recreational Welfare*. Aldershot: Gower.

Coates, D (1995) *Running the Country*. London: Hodder & Stoughton (2nd edition).

Cohen, L. (2003) *A Consumers' Republic: The Politics of Mass Consumption in Postwar America*. New York: Alfred A. Knopf.

Cohen, R. and Kennedy, P. (2000) *Global Sociology*. Basingstoke: Palgrave (Ch. 13 esp.).

Cohen, S. (2003) *Folk Devils and Moral Panics*. London: Routledge (3rd edition).

Cohen, S. and Taylor, L. (1992) *Escape Attempts*. London: Routledge.

Collier, G. (2000) 'The ex-sportswriter', *Columbia Journalism Review*, January/February, (also reprinted in B. Collins ed. *The Best American Sports Writing 2001*. New York: Houghton Mifflin, pp. 334–337).

Collins, M. (2003) 'Social exclusion from sport and leisure', in B. Houlihan (ed.), *Sport & Society*. London: Sage, pp. 67–88.

Collins, M. and Buller, J. (2003) 'Social exclusion from high-performance sport', *Journal of Sport and Social Issues*, Vol. 27, No. 4, pp. 420–442.

Collins, M. with Kay, T. (2003) *Sport and Social Exclusion*. London: Routledge.

Collinson, P. (2004) 'From flowers to football-sponsors sign on for the £1bn Summer season', in *The Guardian*, 24 May, p. 3.

Connell, B. (1993) 'The big picture: Masculinities in recent world history', *Theory and Society*, Vol. 22, No. 5, pp. 597–624.

Council of Europe (1998) *The Council of Europe and Sport 1966–1998 Volume II*. Strasbourg: Council of Europe.

Council of Europe (1993) *European Sports Charter*. Strasbourg: Council of Europe.

Cowe, R. and Buckingham, L. (1998) 'Rupert's moving tax target', *The Guardian*, 5 February, p. 15.

Crabbe, T. and Brown, A. (2004) ' "You're not welcome anymore". The football crowd, class and social exclusion', in S. Wagg (ed.), *British Football and Social Exclusion*. London: Routledge, pp. 26–46.

Craib, I. (1997) *Classical Social Theory*. Oxford: Oxford University Press.

Crawford, G. (2004) *Consuming Sport*. London: Routledge.

Critcher, C. (1987) 'Media spectacles: Sport and mass communication', in A. Cashdan and M. Jordin (eds), *Studies in Communication*. Oxford: Blackwell, pp. 131–150.

Crompton, J. (2001) 'Public subsidies to professional team sport facilities in the USA', in C. Gratton and I. Henry (eds), *Sport in the City*. London: Routledge, pp. 15–34.

Cross, G. (1993) *Time and Money: The Making of Consumer Culture*. London: Routledge.

Curran, J. and Seaton, J. (2003) *Power Without Responsibility*. London: Routledge (6th edition).

Dauncey, H. and Hare, G. eds (1999) *France and the 1998 World Cup*. London: Frank Cass.

Daunton, M. and Hilton, M. eds (2001) *The Politics of Consumption*. Oxford: Berg.

Davidson, R. (2003) 'Amen!', *New Consumer*, February/March, pp. 26–30.

Davies, L. (2002) 'Consumers' expenditure on sport in the UK: Increased spending or underestimation?', *Managing Leisure*, Vol. 7, pp. 83–102.

Davis, L. (1997) *Sports Illustrated and the Swimsuit Issue*. New York: State University of New York Press.

Day, I. (1990) *'Sorting the Men Out from the Boys': Masculinity, a Missing Link in the Sociology of Sport*. Sheffield: Sheffield City Polytechnic.

De Certeau, M. (1984) *The Practice of Everyday Life*. Berkeley: University of California Press.

Deem, R. (1986) *All Work and No Play*. Buckingham: Open University Press.

Deloitte and Touche (2000) *Annual Review of Football Finance*. Manchester: Deloitte & Touche.

Department of Trade and Industry (1999) *Modern Markets: Confident Consumers*. London: Stationery Office.

Desai, M. (2004) *Marx's Revenge*. London: Verso.

Devine, F., Savage, M., Scott, J. and Crompton, R. eds (2005) *Rethinking Class*. Basingstoke: Palgrave.

Dewhirst, T. and Sparks, R. (2003) 'Intertextuality, tobacco sponsorship of sports, and adolescent male smoking culture', *Journal of Sport and Social Issues*, Vol. 27, No. 4, pp. 372–398.

Dicken, P. (1998) *Global Shift*. London: Paul Chapman (3rd edition).

——. (2003) *Global Shift*. London: Sage (4th edition).

Dodd, N. (1999) *Social Theory and Modernity*. Cambridge: Polity.

Donnelly, P. (1996) 'Prolympism: Sport monoculture as crisis and opportunity', *Quest*, Vol. 48, pp. 25–42.

——. (2000) 'Interpretive approaches to the sociology of sport', in J. Coakley and E. Dunning (eds), *Hand Book of Sport Studies*. London: Sage, pp. 77–91.

——. (2003) 'Sport and social theory', in B. Houlihan (ed.), *Sport and Society*. London: Sage, pp. 11–27.

Donnelly, P. and Young, K. (1999) 'Rock climbers and rugby players: Identity construction and confirmation', in J. Coakley and P. Donnelly (eds), *Inside Sports*. London: Routledge, pp. 67–76.

Du Gay, P., Hall, S., Janes, L., Mackay, H. and Negus, K. (1997) *Doing Cultural Studies: The Story of the Sony Walkman*. London: Sage.

Duncan, M. and Aycock, A. (2005) 'Fitting images: Advertising, sport and disability', in S. Jackson and D. Andrews (eds), *Sport, Culture and Advertising*. London: Routledge, pp. 136–153.

Dunning, E. and Malcolm, D. eds (2003) *Sport: Critical Concepts in Sociology*. London: Routledge.

Dutton, K. (1995) *The Perfectible Body*. London: Cassell.

Eco, U. (1986) *Travels in Hyper Reality*. San Diego: Harcourt Brace Jovanovich.

Edwards, T. (2000) *Contradictions of Consumption: Concepts, Practices and Politics in Consumer Society*. Buckingham: Open University Press.

Eitzen, D. S. ed. (2001) *Sport in Contemporary Society: An Anthology*. New York: Worth (6th edition).

Eldridge, J. ed. (1993) *Getting the Message*. London: Routledge.

Elias, N. (1978) *The History of Manners*. Oxford: Blackwell.

——. (1982) *State Formation & Civilization*. Oxford: Blackwell.

——. (1993/1986) 'Introduction', in N. Elias and E. Dunning (eds), *Quest for Excitement: Sport and Leisure in the Civilising Process*. Oxford: Blackwell.

Elias, N. and Dunning, E. (1986) *Quest for Excitement: Sport and Leisure in the Civilising Process*. Oxford: Blackwell.

Engel, M. (2003) 'The Jordan effect', *The Guardian*, 16 April 2003, p. 25.

English Sports Council (1998) *The Development of Sporting Talent 1997: An Examination of the Current Practices for Talent Development in English Sport*. London: English Sports Council.

Enloe, C. (1998) 'The globetrotting sneaker', in P. Donnelly (ed.), *Taking Sport Seriously: Social Issues in Canadian Sport*. Toronto: Thompson Educational Publishing, pp. 251–258.

——. (2000) 'Daughters and generals in the politics of the globalized sneaker', in P. Aulakh and M. Schechter (eds), *Rethinking Globalization(s)*. Basingstoke: Macmillan, pp. 238–246.

The Ethical Consumer (1989) 'Sports shoes', September/October, pp. 7–11.

Euromonitor (2001) *European Marketing Data and Statistics 2001*. London: Euromonitor plc.

European Commission (1994) *The Impact of European Union Activities on Sport*. Strasbourg: European Commission.

Evans, J. and Davies, B. (2004) 'Sociology, the body and health in a risk society', in J. Evans, B. Davies and J. Wright (eds), *Body Knowledge and Control*. London: Routledge, pp. 35–51.

Evans, M., Moutinho, L. and Van Raaij, W. F. (1996) *Applied Consumer Behaviour*. Harlow: Addison-Wesley.

Ewen, S. (1976) *Captains of Consciousness*. New York: McGraw-Hill.

Fairclough, N. (2000) *New Labour, New Language?* London: Routledge.

Fair Trading (2003) 'Fined', *Fair Trading*, No. 36, November, pp. 16–18.

——. (2004) 'OFT welcomes the competition appeal tribunal's judgement on replica kit price-fixing', *Fair Trading*, No. 39, November, p. 1.

Faludi, S. (1999) *Stiffed: The Betrayal of the Modern Man*. London: Chatto & Windus.

Farrelly, L. ed. (1998) *Sneakers: Size Isn't Everything*. London: Booth-Clibborn.

Featherstone, M. (1982) 'The body in consumer culture', *Theory, Culture & Society*, Vol. 1, pp. 18–33.

——. (1987) 'Leisure, symbolic power and the life course', in J. Horne, D. Jary and A. Tomlinson (eds), *Sport, Leisure and Social Relations*. London: Routledge & Kegan Paul, pp. 113–138.

——. (1991) *Consumer Culture and Postmodernism*. London: Sage.

Featherstone, M. and Wernick, A. eds (1995) *Images of Aging*. London: Routledge.

Featherstone, M., Lash, S. and Robertson, R. eds (1995) *Global Modernities*. London: Sage.

Finn, G. and Giulianotti, R. eds (2000) *Football Culture: Local Contests, Global Visions*. London: Frank Cass.

Finnegan, R. (1989) *The Hidden Musicians: Music-making in an English Town*. Cambridge: Cambridge University Press.

Fischer, E. and Gainer, B. (1994) 'Masculinity and the consumption of organised sports', in J. A. Costa (ed.), *Gender Issues and Consumer Behaviour*. London: Sage pp. 84–103.

Fishwick, L. (2001) 'Be what you wanna be: A sense of identity down at the local gym', in N. Watson and S. Cunningham-Burley (eds), *Reframing the Body*. Basingstoke: Palgrave, pp. 152–165.

Fiske, J. (1989) *Understanding Popular Culture*. London: Unwin Hyman.

——. (1993) *Power Plays, Power Works*. London: Verso.

Fleming, S. (1995) *"Home and Away": Sport and South Asian Male Youth*. Aldershot: Avebury.

Fletcher, W. (2005) 'Why advertising is booming', 'Media Guardian', *The Guardian*, 17 January, p. 14.

Flyvbjerg, B., Bruzelius, N. and Rothengatter, W. (2003) *Megaprojects and Risk*. Cambridge: Cambridge University Press.

Foer, F. (2004) 'Soccer Vs. McWorld', *Foreign Policy*. January/February (available online at www.foreignpolicy.com).

FA (Football Association)/MORI (2002) *State of the Nation: A Survey of English Football*. London: The Football Association/Market & Opinion Research International.

Foster, K. (2000) 'How can sport be regulated', in S. Greenfield and G. Osborn (eds), *Law and Sport in Contemporary Society*. London: Frank Cass, pp. 267–287.

Foucault, M. (1977/1975) *Discipline and Punish*. Harmondsworth: Penguin.

——. (1979) 'On governmentality', *Ideology and Consciousness*, No. 6, pp. 5–21.

——. (1981/1976) *The History of Sexuality Vol. 1*. Harmondsworth: Penguin.

——. (1987a/1984) *The History of Sexuality Vol. 2*. Harmondsworth: Penguin.

——. (1987b/1984) *The History of Sexuality Vol. 3*. Harmondsworth: Penguin.

——. (1988) 'Technologies of the self', in L. Martin, H. Gutman and P. Hutton (eds), *Technologies of the Self: A Seminar with Michel Foucault*. Amherst: University of Massachusetts Press, pp. 16–49.

Fowles, J. (1996) *Advertising and Popular Culture*. London: Sage.

Frank, T. (1997) *The Conquest of Cool: Business Culture, Counterculture, and the Rise of Hip Consumerism*. Chicago: University of Chicago Press.

——. (2000) 'The rise of market populism', *The Nation*, 30 October.

——. (2001) *One Market Under God*. London: Secker & Warburg.

Fraser, H. (1981) *The Making of the Mass Market*. London: Macmillan.

Gabriel, Y. and Lang, T. (1995) *The Unmanageable Consumer*. London: Sage.

Galbraith, J. K. (1958/1963) *The Affluent Society*. Harmondsworth: Penguin.

Galtung, J. and Ruge, M. (1981/1965) 'Structuring and selecting news', in S. Cohen and J. Young (eds), *The Manufacture of News: Deviance, Social Problems and the Mass Media*. London: Constable, pp. 52–63.

Gard, M. (2004) 'An elephant in the room and a bridge too far, or physical education and the "obesity epidemic"', in J. Evans, B. Davies and J. Wright (eds), *Body Knowledge and Control*. London: Routledge, pp. 68–82.

Garland, J., Malcolm, D. and Rowe, M. eds (2000) *The Future of Football*. London: Frank Cass.

Gelder, K. and Thornton, S. eds (1997) *The Subcultures Reader*. London: Routledge.

Giddens, A. (1984) *The Constitution of Society: Outline of the Theory of Structuration*. Cambridge: Polity.

——. (1986) *Durkheim on Politics and the State*. Cambridge: Polity.

——. (1990) *The Consequences of Modernity*. Cambridge: Polity.

——. (1991) *Modernity and Self-Identity*. Cambridge: Polity.

——. (1992) *The Transformation of Intimacy: Sexuality, Love and Eroticism in Modern Societies*. Cambridge: Polity.

——. (1994) *Beyond Left and Right*. Cambridge: Polity.

——. (1998) *The Third Way*. Cambridge: Polity.

——. (1999) *Runaway World*. London: Profile Books.

Gilmore, D. (1993) *Manhood in the Making: Cultural Concepts of Masculinity*. New Haven, CT: Yale University Press.

Gilroy, P. (1987) *'There Ain't no Black in the Union Jack' The Cultural Politics of Race and Nation*. London: Hutchinson.

Giulianotti, R. (1999) *Football: A Sociology of the Global Game*. Cambridge: Polity.

——. (2002) 'Supporters, followers, fans, and flaneurs', *Journal of Sport and Social Issues*, Vol. 26, No. 1, pp. 25–46.

——. (2004) 'Cash cow gets one up on 3 lions', *The Times Higher Education Supplement*, 11 June, p. 22.

——. ed. (2004) *Sport and Modern Social Theorists*. Basingstoke: Palgrave.

——. (2005) *Sport, a Critical Sociology*. Cambridge: Polity.

Goldman, R. and Papson, S. (1998) *Nike Culture*. London: Sage.

Gramsci, A. (1971) *Selections from the Prison Notebooks*. London: Lawrence & Wishart.

Gratton, C. (1998) 'The economic importance of modern sport', *Culture, Sport, Society*, Vol. 1, No. 1, pp. 101–117.

——. (2000) 'The peculiar economics of English professional football', in J. Garland, D. Malcolm and M. Rowe (eds), *The Future of Football*. London: Frank Cass, pp. 11–28.

Gratton, C. and Henry, I. (2001) 'Sport in the city; Where do we go from here?', *Sport in the City*. London: Routledge, pp. 309–314.

——. eds (2001) *Sport in the City*. London: Routledge.

Gratton, C. and Taylor, P. (1985) *Sport and Recreation: An Economic Analysis*. London: Spon.

——. (2000) *Economics of Sport and Recreation*. London: Spon.

Green, E., Hebron, S. and Woodward, D. (1990) *Women's Leisure, What Leisure?* Basingstoke: Macmillan.

Green, M. (2004) 'Changing policy priorities for sport in England: The emergence of elite sport development as key policy concern', *Leisure Studies*, Vol. 23, No. 4, pp. 365–385.

Green, M. and Houlihan, B. (2004) 'Advocacy coalitions and elite sport policy change in Canada and the United Kingdom', *International Review for the Sociology of Sport*, Vol. 39, No. 4, pp. 387–403.

Greenfield, S. and Osborn, G. (2001) *Regulating Football*. London: Pluto.

Gruneau, R. (1999/1983) *Class, Sports, and Social Development*. Urbana IL: Human Kinetics.

Gruneau, R. and Whitson, D. (1993) *Hockey Night in Canada*. Toronto: Garamond.

Guttmann, A. (1978) *From Ritual to Record*. New York: Columbia University Press.

——. (1992) 'Chariot races, tournaments and the civilizing process', in E. Dunning and C. Rojek (eds), *Sport and Leisure in the Civilizing Process*. Basingstoke: Macmillan, pp. 137–160.

Guttmann, L. (1976) *Textbook of Sport for the Disabled*. Aylesbury: HM & M Publishers.

Hall, A., Slack, T., Smith, G. and Whitson, D. (1991) *Sport in Canadian Society*. Toronto: McClelland & Stewart Inc.

Hall, S. (1973) *Encoding and Decoding in Television Discourse*. Centre for Contemporary Cultural Studies, Stencilled Paper No. 7. Birmingham: University of Birmingham.

——. (1989) 'The meaning of new times', in S. Hall and M. Jacques (eds), *New Times*. London: Lawrence & Wishart, pp. 116–134.

——. (1990) 'The whites of their eyes: Racist ideologies and the media', in M. Alvarado and J. Thompson (eds), *The Media Reader*. London: British Film Institute, pp. 7–23.

——. (1992a) 'The west and the rest: Discourse and power', in S. Hall and B. Gieben (eds), *Formations of Modernity*. Cambridge: Polity, pp. 275–331.

——. (1992b) 'The question of cultural identity', in S. Hall, D. Held and T. McGrew (eds), *Modernity and Its Futures*. Cambridge: Polity, pp. 273–325.

Hall, S. and Jefferson, T. eds (1976) *Resistance through Rituals*. London: Hutchinson.

Hamil, S., Michie, J. and Oughton, C. eds (1999) *A Game of Two Halves?* Edinburgh: Mainstream.

Hamil, S., Michie, J., Oughton, C. and Warby, S. eds (2000) *Football in the Digital Age?* Edinburgh: Mainstream.

——. (2001) 'Recent developments in football ownership', *The Changing Face of the Football Business – Supporters Direct*. London: Frank Cass, pp. 1–10.

Hannigan, D. (2005) 'Impasse in labour dispute means big freeze for whole NHL season', *The Guardian*, 17 February, p. 29.

Hannigan, J. (1998) *Fantasy City: Pleasure and Profit in the Postmodern Metropolis*. London: Routledge.

Hare, G. (1999) 'Buying and selling the world cup', in H. Dauncey and G. Hare (eds), *France and the 1998 World Cup*. London: Frank Cass.

Hargreaves, Jennifer (1994) *Sporting Females: Critical Issues in the History and Sociology of Women's Sports*. London: Routledge.

——. (2000) *Heroines of Sport*. London: Routledge.

——. (2004) 'Querying sport feminism: Personal or political?', in R. Giulianotti (ed.), *Sport and Modern Social Theorists*. Basingstoke: Palgrave, pp. 187–205.

Hargreaves, John (1986) *Sport, Power and Culture*. Cambridge: Polity.

——. (1987) 'The body, sport and power relations', in J. Horne, D. Jary and A. Tomlinson (eds), *Sport, Leisure and Social Relations*. London: Routledge & Kegan Paul, pp. 139–159.

Harkin, J. (2001) 'The logos fight back', *New Statesman*, 18 June, pp. 25–27.

Harvey, D. (1989) *The Condition of Postmodernity*. Oxford: Blackwell.

——. (2000) *Spaces of Hope*. Edinburgh: Edinburgh University Press.

——. (2005) *The New Imperialism*. Oxford: Oxford University Press.

Harvey, J. and Law, A. (2005) ' "Resisting" the global media oligopoly? The Canada Inc. response', in M. Silk, D. Andrews and C. Cole (eds), *Sport and Corporate Nationalisms*. Oxford: Berg, pp. 187–225.

Harvey, J., Law, A. and Cantelon, M. (2001) 'North American professional team sport franchises ownership patterns and global entertainment conglomerates', *Sociology of Sport Journal*, Vol. 18, pp. 435–457.

Haug, W. (1986) *Critique of Commodity Aesthetics*. Cambridge: Polity.

Haywood, L., Kew, F., Bramham, P., Spink, J., Capenerhurst, J. and Henry, I. (1995) *Understanding Leisure*. Cheltenham: Stanley Thornes (2nd edition).

Hebdige, D. (1978) *Subculture: The Meaning of Style*. London: Methuen.

Heelas, P., Lash, S. and Morris, P. eds (1996) *Detraditionalization*. Oxford: Blackwell.

Heelas, P. and Morris, P. eds (1992) *The Values of the Enterprise Culture*. London: Routledge.

Hendry, L., Shucksmith, J., Love, J. and Glendinning, A. (1993) *Young People's Leisure & Lifestyles*. London: Routledge.

Henry, I. (2001) *The Politics of Leisure Policy*. Basingstoke: Palgrave (2nd edition).

Hepworth, M. and Featherstone, M. (1982) *Surviving Middle Age*. Oxford: Blackwell.

Herman, E. and McChesney, R. (1997) *The Global Media*. London: Cassell.

Hetherington, K. (1992) 'Stonehenge and its festival: Spaces of consumption', in R. Shields (ed.), *Lifestyle Shopping*. London: Routledge, pp. 83–98.

——. (1994) 'The contemporary significance of Schmalenbach's concept of the Bund', *Sociological Review*, Vol. 42, No.1, pp. 1–25.

Hill, J. (2002) *Sport, Leisure and Culture in Twentieth-Century Britain*. Basingstoke: Palgrave.

Hilton, M. (2001) 'Consumer politics in post-war Britain', in M. Daunton and M. Hilton (eds), *The Politics of Consumption*. Oxford: Berg, pp. 241–259.

Hirsch, F. (1977) *Social Limits to Growth*. London: Routledge & Kegan Paul.

Hobsbawm, E. (1994) *Age of Extremes: The Short Twentieth Century 1914–1991*. London: Michael Joseph.

Hobson, D. (1982) *Crossroads: The Drama of a Soap Opera*. London: Methuen.

Hoch, P. (1972) *Rip Off the Big Game*. New York: Anchor.

Holt, D. and Schor, J. (2000) 'Introduction', in J. Schor and D. Holt (eds), *The Consumer Society Reader*. New York: New Press, pp. vii–xxiii.

Holt, D. and Thompson, C. (2004) 'Man-of-action heroes: The pursuit of heroic masculinity in every day consumption', in *Journal of Consumer Research*, Vol. 31, September, pp. 425–440.

Holt, R. and Mason, T. (2000) *Sport in Britain 1945–2000*. Oxford: Blackwell.

Horne, J. and Fleming, S. eds (2000) *Masculinities: Leisure Cultures, Identities and Consumption*. Leisure Studies Association Publication No. 69, Eastbourne: Leisure Studies Association.

Horne, J. and Manzenreiter, W. eds (2002a) *Japan, Korea and the 2002 World Cup*. London: Routledge.

——. eds (2002b) 'The world cup and television football', *Japan, Korea and the 2002 World Cup*. London: Routledge, pp. 195–212.

——. (2004) 'Accounting for mega-events', *International Review for the Sociology of Sport*, Vol. 39, No. 2, pp. 187–203.

Horne, J., Tomlinson, A. and Whannel, G. (1999) *Understanding Sport*. London: Spon.

Houlihan, B. (1991) *The Government and Politics of Sport*. London: Routledge.

——. (1997) *Sport, Policy and Politics*. London: Routledge.

——. (2002) 'Political involvement in sport, physical education and recreation', in A. Laker (ed.), *The Sociology of Sport and Physical Education*. London: Routledge pp. 190–210.

——. ed. (2003) *Sport & Society: A Student Introduction*. London: Sage.

——. ed. (2003a) 'Politics, power, policy and sport', *Sport & Society*. London: Sage, pp. 28–48

——. ed. (2003b) 'Sport and globalisation', *Sport & Society*. London: Sage, pp. 345–363.

——. (2004) 'Sports globalisation, the state and the problem of governance', in T. Slack (ed.), *The Commercialisation of Sport*. London: Routledge, pp. 52–71.

Houlihan, B. and White, A. (2002) *The Politics of Sports Development*. London: Routledge.

How, A. (2003) *Critical Theory*. Basingstoke: Palgrave.

Howell, J. and Ingham, A. (2001) 'From social problem to personal issue: The language of lifestyles', *Cultural Studies*, Vol. 15, No. 2, pp. 326–351.

Howson, A. (2004) *The Body in Society*. Cambridge: Polity.

Hums, M., Moorman, A. and Woolf, E. (2003) 'The inclusion of the Paralympics in the Olympic and Amateur Sports Act', *Journal of Sport and Social Issues*, Vol. 27, No. 3, pp. 261–275.

Ipsos-RSL (2003) *Sportscan Monthly News and Comment Report*. London: Ipsos-RSL Ltd.

Jackson, G. and Weed, M. (2003) 'The sport-tourism interrelationship', in B. Houlihan (ed.), *Sport & Society.* London: Sage, pp. 235–251.

Jackson, S. and Andrews, D. eds (2005) *Sport, Culture and Advertising*. London: Routledge.

Jackson, S., Andrews, D. and Scherer, J. (2005) 'Introduction: The contemporary landscape of sport advertising', in S. Jackson and D. Andrews (eds), *Sport, Culture and Advertising*. London: Routledge, pp. 1–23.

Jarvie, G. ed. (1991) *Sport, Racism and Ethnicity*. London: Falmer Press.

Jeanrenaude, C. ed. (1999) *The Economic Impact of Sport Events*. Neufchatel: CIES.

Jefferies, S. (2004) 'The tyranny of the gym' in 'G2', *The Guardian*, 5 January, pp. 2–3.

Jenkins, H. (2003) 'Interactive audiences?', in V. Nightingale and K. Ross (eds), *Critical Readings: Media and Audiences*. Maidenhead: Open University Press, pp. 279–295.

Jenkins, R. (1992) *Pierre Bourdieu*. London: Routledge.

Jennings, A. with Sambrook, C. (2000) *The Great Olympic Swindle*. London: Simon & Schuster.

Jessop, B. (2002) *The Future of the Capitalist State*. Cambridge: Polity.

Jhally, S. (1987) *The Codes of Advertising*. London: Frances Pinter.

Jollimore, M. (1998) 'Woman gets full Nike treatment', in P. Donnelly (ed.), *Taking Sport Seriously: Social Issues in Canadian Sport*. Toronto: Thompson Educational Publishing, pp. 259–261.

Just Don't Do It (1998) 'Just don't do it campaign at the University of Michigan', http://www-personal.umich...d/nike/nike101-1.htm.

Kay, J. and Laberge, S. (2004) '"Mandatory equipment". Women in adventure racing', in B. Wheaton (ed.), *Understanding Lifestyle Sports*. London: Routledge, pp. 154–174.

182 *Bibliography*

Kay, T. (2003) 'Sport and gender', in B. Houlihan (ed.), *Sport & Society*. London: Sage, pp. 89–104.

Kellner, D. (1992) 'Popular culture and the construction of postmodern identities', in S. Lash and J. Friedman (eds), *Modernity & Identity*. Oxford: Blackwell, pp. 141–177.

——. (2003) *Media Spectacle*. London: Routledge.

Kelso, P. (2005) 'Sports face three-prong test to keep public funds', *The Guardian*, 2 February, p. 32.

Kenway, J. and Bullen, E. (2001) *Consuming Children: Education-Entertainment-Advertising*. Buckingham: Open University Press.

Kidd, B. (1990) 'The men's cultural centre: Sports and the dynamic of women's oppression/men's repression', in M. Messner and D. Sabo (eds), *Sport, Men and the Gender Order*. Champaign, IL: Human Kinetics, pp. 31–43.

——. (1995) 'Toronto's skydome: The world's greatest entertainment centre', in J. Bale and I. Moen (eds), *The Stadium and the City*. Keele: Keele University Press.

King, A. (1997) 'New directors, customers and fans: The transformation of English football in the 1990s', *Sociology of Sport Journal*, Vol. 14, No. 3, pp. 224–240.

——. (2002/1998) *The End of the Terraces*. Leicester: Leicester University Press.

Kingsnorth, P. (2003) *One No Many Yeses*. London: Free Press.

Kirk, D. (1993) *The Body, Schooling and Culture*. Victoria, Australia: Deakin University Press.

Klein, N. (2000a) *No Logo*. London: Flamingo.

——. (2000b) 'The tyranny of the brands', *New Statesman*, 24 January, pp. 25–28.

Kline, S. (1993) *Out of the Garden*. London: Verso.

Kolah, A. (1999) *Maximising the Value of Sports Sponsorship*. London: FT Media/Informa Publishing.

Koppett, L. (1994) *Sports Illusion, Sports Reality: A Reporter's View of Sports, Journalism and Society*. Urbana: University of Illinois Press.

Korr, C. (1986) *West Ham United*. London: Duckworth.

Korzeniewicz, M. (1994) 'Commodity chains and marketing strategies: Nike and the global athletic footwear industry', in G. Gereffi and M. Korzeniewicz (eds), *Commodity Chains and Global Capitalism*. Westport CT: Praeger, pp. 247–265.

Kusz, K. (2004) ' "I want to be the minority": The politics of youthful white masculinities in sport and popular culture in 1990s America', in D. Rowe (ed.), *Critical Readings in Sport, Culture and the Media*. Maidenhead: Open University Press, pp. 261–275.

Laberge, S. and Kay, J. (2002) 'Pierre Bourdieu's sociocultural theory and sport practice', in J. Maguire and K. Young (eds), *Theory, Sport and Society*. Oxford: Elsevier, pp. 239–266.

Labour Party (2005) *Britain Forward Not Back*. London: Labour Party.

Labour Research (2002) 'The kids the world cup relies on', *Labour Research*, May, pp. 15–17.

LaFeber, W. (1999) *Michael Jordan and the New Global Capitalism*. New York: Norton.

Langer, J. (1981) 'Television's personality system', *Media, Culture and Society*, Vol. 3, No. 4, pp. 351–365.

Lash, S. and Urry, J. (1987) *The End of Organized Capitalism.* Cambridge: Polity.

——. (1994) *Economies of Signs and Space.* London: Sage.

Lasn, K. (1999) *Culture Jam: The Uncooling of America.* New York: Eagle Brook.

Law, A., Harvey, J. and Kemp, S. (2002) 'The global sport mass media oligopoly', *International Review for the Sociology of Sport*, Vol. 37, Nos 3–4, pp. 279–302.

Lawrence, F. (2004) *Not on the Label.* Harmondsworth: Penguin.

Lee, M. (1993) *Consumer Culture Reborn.* London: Routledge.

——. ed. (2000) *The Consumer Society Reader.* Oxford: Blackwell.

Leifer, E. (1995) *Making the Majors: The Transformation of Team Sports in America.* Cambridge, MA: Harvard University Press.

Leiss, W., Kline, S. and Jhally, S. (1986) *Social Communication in Advertising.* London: Routledge.

Lenskyj, H. (2000) *Inside the Olympic Industry.* Albany: State University of New York Press.

——. (2002) *The Best Olympics Ever? Social Impacts of Sydney 2000.* Albany: State University of New York Press.

Lewis, D. and Bridger, D. (2001) *The Soul of the New Consumer: Authenticity – What We Buy and Why in the New Economy.* London: Nicholas Brealey.

Leys, C. (2001) *Market-Driven Politics.* London: Verso.

Lindstrom, M. and Seybold, P. (2003) *Brandchild.* London: Kogan Page.

Livingstone, S. (2002) *Young People and New Media.* London: Sage.

Lodziak, C. (2002) *The Myth of Consumerism.* London: Pluto.

Lowerson, J. (1995) *Sport and the English Middle Classes 1870–1914.* Manchester: Manchester University Press.

Lowes, M. (1999) *Inside the Sports Pages.* Toronto: University of Toronto Press.

Lunt, P. and Livingstone, S. (1992) *Mass Consumption and Personal Identity.* Milton Keynes: Open University Press.

Lupton, D. (1995) *The Imperative of Health: Public Health and the Regulated Body.* London: Sage.

Lury, C. (1996) *Consumer Culture.* Cambridge: Polity.

Lyotard, J.-F. (1984) *The Post Modern Condition.* Manchester: Manchester University Press.

Mac an Ghaill, M. (1994) *The Making of Men: Masculinities, Sexualities and Schooling.* Buckingham: Open University Press.

McGuigan, J. (1992) *Cultural Populism.* London: Routledge.

——. (1997) 'Cultural populism revisited', in M. Ferguson and P. Golding (eds), *Cultural Studies in Question.* London: Sage, pp. 138–154.

McKay, J. (1991) *No Pain, No Gain? Sport and Australian Culture.* Sydney: Prentice Hall.

McNeal, J. (1998) 'Tapping the three kids' markets', *American Demographics*, April, pp. 37–41.

McNeal, J. and Yeh, C.-H. (1993) 'Born to shop', *American Demographics*, June, pp. 34–39.

McPherson, B., Curtis, J. and Loy, J. (1993) *The Social Significance of Sport.* Champaign, IL: Human Kinetics.

Maffesoli, M. (1996) *The Time of the Tribes*. London: Sage.

Maguire, J. (1999) *Global Sport*. Cambridge: Polity.

Maguire, J., Jarvie, G., Mansfield, L. and Bradley, J. (2002) *Sport Worlds: A Sociological Perspective*. Champaign, IL: Human Kinetics.

Makins, C. (1972) 'The moneybags of British sport', *New Society*, 29 December, pp. 968–970.

Malcolm, D., Jones, I. and Waddington, I. (2000) 'The people's game? Football spectatorship and demographic change', *Soccer and Society*, Vol. 1, No. 1, pp. 129–143.

Manzenreiter, W. and Horne, J. eds (2004) *Football Goes East: Business, Culture and the People's Game in China, Japan and South Korea*. London: Routledge.

Martin, B. (1981) *A Sociology of Contemporary Cultural Change*. Oxford: Blackwell.

Marx, K. (1976/1867) *Capital Volume 1*. Harmondsworth: Penguin.

Marx, K. and Engels, F. (1973/1848) *Manifesto of the Communist Party*. Moscow: Progress Publishers.

Mason, T. (1980) *Association Football and English Society 1863–1915*. London: Harvester.

——. (1988) *Sport in Britain*. London: Faber.

——. ed. (1989) *Sport in Britain*. Cambridge: Cambridge University Press.

Michie, J. and Oughton, C. (2004) *Competitive Balance in Football: Trends and Effects*. London: The Sports Nexus.

Miles, S. (1997) *Consumerism as a Way of Life*. London: Sage.

——. (1998) 'McDonaldization and the global sports store', in M. Alfino, J. Caputo and R. Wynyard (eds), *McDonaldization Revisited*. Westport CT: Praeger, pp. 53–65.

Miller, P. and Rose, N. (1993) 'Governing economic life', in M. Gane and T. Johnson (eds), *Foucault's New Domains*. London: Routledge, pp. 75–105.

——. (1997) 'Mobilising the consumer: Assembling the subject of consumption', *Theory Culture and Society*, Vol.14, No. 1, pp. 1–36.

Miller, T. (1999) 'Televisualization', *Journal of Sport and Social Issues*, Vol. 23, No. 2, pp. 123–125.

Miller, T., Lawrence, G., McKay, J. and Rowe, D. (2001) *Globalization and Sport*. London: Sage.

Milligan, A. (2004) *Brand It like Beckham*. London: Cyan Books.

Milmo, D. (2004a) 'BSkyB sells off Premier match rights', *The Guardian*, 22 April, p. 20

——. (2004b) 'Pay-TV group keeps football monopoly after rivals miss price target', *The Guardian*, 13 May, p. 21.

Mintel (2000) *Sponsorship 2000*. London: Mintel International.

Mitchell, B. R. and Deane, P. eds (1988) *British Historical Statistics*. Cambridge: Cambridge University Press.

Monbiot, G. (2000) *Captive State*. Basingstoke: Macmillan.

Moore Jr, B. (1969) *Social Origins of Dictatorship and Democracy*. Harmondsworth: Peregrine.

Moore, C. (2004) 'Inflation worries fuelled as unemployment figure drops to 29-year low', *The Guardian*, 17 June, p. 27.

Moore, M. (2002) *Stupid White Men*. Harmondsworth: Penguin (Revised edition).

Moorhouse, B. (1991) *Driving Ambitions*. Manchester: Manchester University Press.

——. (1998) 'Ending traditions: Football and the study of football in the 1990s', *International Journal of the History of Sport*, Vol. 15, No. 1, pp. 227–231.

Morley, D. (1986) *Family Television*. London: Comedia.

Morrow, S. (1999) *The New Business of Football*. Basingstoke: Macmillan.

Mort, F. (1996) *Cultures of Consumption*. London: Routledge.

Munting, R. (1996) *An Economic and Social History of Gambling*. Manchester: Manchester University Press.

Murdoch, G. (1992) 'Embedded persuasions: The fall and rise of integrated advertising', in D. Strinati and S. Wagg (eds), *Come on Down? Popular Media Culture in Post-War Britain*. London: Routledge, pp. 202–231.

Murray, B. (1984) *The Old Firm*. Edinburgh: John Donald.

Murray, R. (1989) 'Fordism and post-Fordism', in S. Hall and M. Jacques (eds), *New Times*. London: Lawrence & Wishart, pp. 38–47.

Nauright, J. (2004) 'Global games: Culture, political economy and sport in the globalised world of the 21st century', *Third World Quarterly*, Vol. 25, No. 7, pp. 1325–1336.

New Internationalist (2000) 'Fact file on sports shoes', *New Internationalist*, December, No. 330, p. 4.

New Political Economy (1999) 'Debate: The political economy of sport', *New Political Economy*, Vol. 4, No. 2, pp. 267–288.

Newspaper Marketing Agency (2004) 'Men. It's not difficult to get their attention', *The Guardian*, 23 March, p. 28 (www.nmauk.co.uk).

Nightingale, V. and Ross, K. eds (2003) *Critical Readings: Media and Audiences*. Maidenhead: Open University Press.

Nixon, H. (2000) 'Sport and disability', in J. Coakley and E. Dunning (eds), *Handbook of Sport Studies*. London: Sage, pp. 422–438.

No Sweat (2002) *What is a Sweatshop?* London: No Sweat (also see www.nosweat.org.uk).

Nogawa, H. (2004) 'An international comparison of the motivations and experiences of volunteers at the 2002 World Cup', in W. Manzenreiter and J. Horne (eds), *Football Goes East: Business, Culture and the People's Game in China, Japan and South Korea*. London: Routledge, pp. 222–242.

Nowell-Smith, G. (1978) 'TV-football-the world', *Screen*, Vol. 19, No. 4, pp. 45–59.

Office for National Statistics (2001) *Family Spending*. London: The Stationery Office.

Office for National Statistics (1998) *Living in Britain – Results from the 1996 General Household Survey*. London: The Stationery Office.

Ohl, F. and Tribou, G. (2004) *Les marches du sport: consommateurs et distributeurs*. Paris: Armand Colin.

O'Neill, J. (1985) *Five Bodies: The Human Shape of Modern Society*. Ithaca, NY: Cornell University Press.

——. (1998) *The Market-Ethics, Knowledge and Politics*. London: Routledge.

Oxfam (2004) *Play Fair at the Olympics.* Oxford: Oxfam/Clean Clothes Campaign/ International Confederation of Free Trade Unions (also downloadable from www.fairolympics.org).

PVI Europe (n.d.) *Live Video Insertion System.* Zaventem, Belgium: PVI (Princeton Video Image) Europe.

Parkin, F. (1973) *Class Inequality and Political Order.* London: Paladin.

Pass, C., Lowes, B. and Davies, L. (2000) *Collins Dictionary of Economics.* Glasgow: HarperCollins (3rd edition).

Pavitt, J. ed. (2000) *Brand New.* London: V&A (Victoria & Albert Museum) Publications.

Penney, D. ed. (2002) *Gender and Physical Education.* London: Routledge.

Polley, M. (1998) *Moving the Goalposts: A History of Sport and Society.* London: Routledge.

Pronger, B. (1990) *The Arena of Masculinity – Sports, Homosexuality, and the Meaning of Sex.* London: GMP Publishers.

Quart, A. (2003) *Branded.* London: Arrow.

Ray, L. and Sayer, D. eds (1999) *Culture and Economy After the Cultural Turn.* London: Sage.

Ratneshwar, S., Mick, D. G. and Huffman, C. eds (2000) *The Why of Consumption. Contemporary Perspectives on Consumer Motives, Goals and Desires.* London: Routledge.

Reich, R. (1991) *The Work of Nations.* New York: Knopf.

Richards, T. (1991) *The Commodity Culture of Victorian England: Advertising and Spectacle, 1851–1914.* London: Verso.

Rinehart, R. and Sydnor, S. eds (2003) *To the Extreme: Alternative Sports, Inside and Out.* Albany NY: State University of New York Press.

Ritzer, G. (1993) *The McDonaldization of Society.* Newbury Park, Ca: Pine Forge.

Ritzer, G. and Stillman, T. (2001) 'The postmodern ballpark as leisure setting', *Leisure Sciences,* Vol. 23, No. 1, pp. 99–113.

Robbins, S. and Waked, E. (1997) 'Hazard of deceptive advertising of athletic foot-wear', *The British Journal of Sports Medicine,* Vol. 31, pp. 299–303.

Roberts, K. (1996a) 'Youth and employment in modern Britain', *Sociology Review,* Vol. 5, No. 4, pp. 25–29.

——. (1996b) 'Young people, school sport and government policies', *Sport, Education and Society,* Vol. 1, No. 1, pp. 47–57.

——. (1997) 'Same activities, different meanings: British youth cultures in the 1990s', *Leisure Studies,* Vol. 16, No. 1, pp. 1–15.

——. (1999) *Leisure in Contemporary Society.* Oxford: CABI.

——. (2004) *The Leisure Industries.* Basingstoke: Palgrave.

Roberts, K., Clark, F., Clark, S. and Semeonoff, E. (1977) *The Fragmentary Class Structure.* London: Heinemann.

Robidoux, M. (2001) *Men at Play: A Working Understanding of Professional Hockey.* Montreal and Kingston: McGill-Queen's University Press.

Roche, M. (1993) 'Sport and community: Rhetoric and reality in the development of British sport policy', in J. Binfield and J. Stevenson (eds), *Sport, Culture and Politics.* Sheffield: Sheffield Academic Press.

——. (2000) *Mega-Events & Modernity.* London: Routledge.

Rojek, C. (1985) *Capitalism and Leisure Theory.* London: Tavistock.

——. (1997) ' "Leisure" in the writings of Walter Benjamin', *Leisure Studies*, Vol. 16, No. 3, pp. 155–171.

——. (2000) *Leisure and Culture.* Basingstoke: Macmillan.

——. (2001) *Celebrity.* London: Reaktion Books.

Rose, N. (1992) 'Governing the enterprising self', in P. Heelas and P. Morris (eds), *The Values of the Enterprise Culture.* London: Routledge, pp. 141–164.

——. (1996) 'Authority and the genealogy of subjectivity', in P. Heelas, S. Lash and P. Morris (eds), *Detraditionalization.* Oxford: Blackwell, pp. 294–327.

Ross, K. and Nightingale, V. (2003) *Media and Audiences: New Perspectives.* Maidenhead: Open University Press.

Rowe, D. (1992) 'Modes of sports writing', in P. Dahlgren and C. Sparks (eds), *Journalism and Popular Culture*, London: Sage, pp. 96–112.

——. (1995) 'Big defence: Sport and hegemonic masculinity', in A. Tomlinson (ed.), *Gender, Sport and Leisure: Continuities and Challenges.* Chelsea School Research Centre Topic Report 4, Eastbourne: University of Brighton.

——. (2004a) *Sport, Culture and the Media.* Maidenhead: Open University Press (2nd edition).

——. ed. (2004b) *Critical Readings in Sport, Culture and the Media.* Maidenhead: Open University Press.

Rowe, N. and Moore, S. (2004) *Participation in Sport – Results from the General Household Survey 2002.* Sport England Research Briefing Note, London: Sport England.

Sage, G. (1998) *Power and Ideology in American Sport.* Champaign IL: Human Kinetics.

——. (1999) 'Justice do it! The Nike transnational advocacy network: Organization, collective action and outcomes', *Sociology of Sport Journal*, Vol. 16, No. 3, pp. 206–235.

——. (2000) 'Political economy and sport', in J. Coakley and E. Dunning (eds), *Handbook of Sports Studies.* London: Sage, pp. 260–276.

——. (2002) 'Global sport and global mass media', in A. Laker (ed.), *The Sociology of Sport and Physical Education.* London: Routledge, pp. 211–233.

Sandvoss, C. (2003) *A Game of Two Halves: Football Television and Globalization.* London: Routledge.

——. (2005) *Fans.* Cambridge: Polity.

Sassatelli, R. (1999) 'Interaction order and beyond: A field analysis of body culture within fitness gyms', *Body & Society*, Vol. 5, No. 2–3, pp. 227–248.

Saunders, P. (1990) *A Nation of Home Owners.* London: Unwin Hyman.

Schaaf, P. (2004) *Sports, Inc: 100 Years of Sports Business.* Amherst, NY: Prometheus.

Schaffer, K. and Smith, S. eds (2000) *The Olympics at the Millennium: Power, Politics and the Games.* London: Rutgers University Press.

Schor, J. (1992) *The Overworked American*. New York: Basic Books.

——. (1998) *The Overspent American*. New York: Basic Books.

——. (2004) *Born to Buy: The Commercialized Child and the New Consumer Culture*. New York: Scribner.

Schor, J. and Holt, D. eds (2000) *The Consumer Society Reader*. New York: New Press.

Scott, C. and Black, J. (2000) *Cranston's Consumers and the Law*. London: Butterworths (3rd edition).

Scott, M. (2005) 'Chelsea leap up earnings big league', *The Guardian*, 17 February, p. 34.

Scottish Labour Party (2005) *Scotland Forward Not Back*. Glasgow: Scottish Labour Party.

Scraton, S. (1993) *Shaping up to Womanhood: Gender and Girls' Physical Education*. Buckingham: Open University Press.

Scraton, S. and Flintoff, A. eds (2001) *Gender and Sport: A Reader*. London: Routledge.

Shank, M. D. (2002) *Sports Marketing: A Strategic Perspective*. New Jersey: Prentice Hall.

Shields, R. ed. (1992) *Lifestyle Shopping: The Subject of Consumption*. London: Routledge.

Shilling, C. (1993) *The Body and Social Theory*. London: Sage.

The Shorter Oxford English Dictionary (1987) *Volume II*. Oxford: Oxford University Press (3rd edition).

Siegfried, J. and Zimbalist, A. (2000) 'The economics of sports facilities and their communities', *Journal of Economic Perspectives*, Vol. 14, No. 3, pp. 95–114.

Silk, M. and Andrews, D. (2001) 'Beyond a boundary? Sport, transnational advertising and the reimagining of national culture', *Journal of Sport and Social Issues*, Vol. 25, No. 2, pp. 180–201.

Silk, M., Andrews, D. and Cole, C. eds (2005) *Sport and Corporate Nationalisms*. Oxford: Berg.

Silverstone, R. (1999) *Why Study the Media?* London: Sage.

Sklair, L. (2002) *Globalization*. Oxford: Oxford University Press.

Slack, T. ed. (2004) *The Commercialisation of Sport*. London: Routledge.

Slater, D. (1997) *Consumer Culture and Modernity*. Cambridge: Polity.

Smart, B. (2003) *Economy, Culture and Society*. Maidenhead: Open University Press.

Smith, A., Green, K. and Roberts, K. (2004) 'Sports participation and the "obesity/health crisis"', *International Review for the Sociology of Sport*, Vol. 39, No. 4, pp. 457–464.

Smith, C. (1990) *Morality and the Market: Consumer Pressure for Corporate Accountability*. London: Routledge.

Smith, D. (2003) *The State of the World Atlas*. London: Earthscan (7th edition).

Smith, P. (1997) *Millennial Dreams: Contemporary Culture and Capital in the North*. London: Verso.

Smith Maguire, J. (2002) 'Michel Foucault: Sport, power, technologies and governmentality', in J. Maguire and K. Young (eds), *Theory, Sport and Society*. Oxford: JAI/Elsevier, pp. 293–314.

Solomon, M., Bamossy, G. and Askegaard, S. (2002) *Consumer Behaviour A European Perspective*. Harlow: Prentice Hall Europe (2nd edition).

Spa, M. de Moragas, Rivenburgh, N. and Larson, J. (1995) *Television in the Olympics*. Luton: John Libbey.

Sparkes, A. (1997) 'Reflections on the socially constructed physical self', in K. Fox (ed.), *The Physical Self*. Campaign IL: Human Kinetics, pp. 83–110.

SPORTEL (2001) *Have Broadcasting Rights for Sports Events on TV Reached a Ceiling?* Proceedings from the 12th International Symposium on Sport and Television, Monaco: SPORTEL.

Sport England (1999a) *Participation in Sport in Great Britain 1996*. London: Sport England.

———. (1999b) *Survey of Sports Halls and Swimming Pools in England 1997*. London: Sport England.

———. (2000) *Sports Participation and Ethnicity in England National Survey 1999/2000*. London: Sport England.

Sport Industries Research Centre/SIRC (2003) *Sport Market Forecasts 2003–2007*. Sheffield: Sheffield Hallam University/SIRC.

Sports Business (2001) 'Sportfacts', *Sport Business*, No. 58, June, p. 54.

———. (2003) 'Adidas relies on stars and stripes', *Sports Business International*, No. 84, pp. 18–19.

sportscotland (2001) *Sports Participation in Scotland 2000*. Edinburgh: **sport**scotland.

———. (2002) *Sports Participation in Scotland 2001*. Edinburgh: **sport**scotland.

Stebbins, R. (1992) *Amateurs, Professionals and Serious Leisure*. Montreal: McGill-Queen's University Press.

Stevenson, N. (2002) *Understanding Media Cultures*. London: Sage (2nd edition).

Stoddart, B. (1997) 'Convergence: Sport on the information superhighway', *Journal of Sport and Social Issues*, Vol. 21, No. 1, pp. 93–102.

Stroot, S. (2002) 'Socialisation and participation in sport', in A. Laker (ed.), *The Sociology of Sport and Physical Education*. London: Routledge, pp. 129–147.

Sugden, J. and Tomlinson, A. (1998a) *FIFA and the Contest for World Football*. Cambridge: Polity.

———. (1998b) 'Sport, politics and identities: Football cultures in comparative perspective', in M. Roche (ed.), *Sport, Popular Culture and Identity*. Aachen: Meyer & Meyer, pp. 169–192.

———. eds (2002) *Power Games*. London: Routledge.

———. (2003) *Badfellas*. Edinburgh: Mainstream.

Sulkunen, P. (1997) 'Introduction: The new consumer society-rethinking the social bond', in P. Sulkunen, J. Holmwood, H. Radner and G. Schulze (eds), *Constructing the New Consumer Society*. Basingstoke: Macmillan, pp. 1–18.

Sulkunen, P., Holmwood, J., Radner, H. and Schulze, G. eds (1997) *Constructing the New Consumer Society*. Basingstoke: Macmillan.

Szymanski, S. and Kuypers, T. (1999) *Winners and Losers*. London: Viking.

Takahashi, Y. and Horne, J. (2004) 'Japanese football players and the sport talent migration business', in W. Manzenreiter and J. Horne (eds), *Football Goes East:*

Business, Culture and the People's Game in China, Japan and South Korea. London: Routledge, pp. 69–86.

Thompson, J. (1990) *The Media and Modernity.* Cambridge: Polity.

Tomlinson, A. ed. (1995) *Gender, Sport and Leisure: Continuities and Challenges.* Eastbourne: Leisure Studies Association.

——. (1996) 'Olympic spectacle: Opening ceremonies and some paradoxes of globalization', *Media, Culture & Society*, Vol. 18, No. 4, pp. 583–602.

Toohey, K. and Veal, A. (2000) *The Olympic Games: A Social Science Perspective.* Oxford: CABI.

Toynbee, P. (2004) 'Inequality is fattening', *The Guardian*, 28 May.

Tudor, A. (1998) 'Sports reporting: Race, difference and identity', in K. Brants, J. Hermes and L. van Zoonen (eds), *The Media in Question, Popular Cultures and Public Interests.* London: Sage, pp. 147–156.

Turner, B. (2005) *The Pits: The Real World of Formula One.* London: Atlantic Books.

Turner, B. S. (1991) 'The discourse of diet', in M. Featherstone, M. Hepworth and B. S. Turner (eds), *The Body: Social Process and Cultural Theory.* London: Sage, pp. 157–169.

——. (1992) *Regulating Bodies.* London: Routledge.

——. (1996) *The Body and Society.* London: Sage (2nd edition).

Turner, B. S. and Rojek, C. (2001) *Society & Culture.* London: Sage.

Understanding Global Issues (1999) *Advertising: The Attempt to Persuade.* Cheltenham: Understanding Global Issues Ltd.

——. (2000) *Globalized Sport: Media, Money and Morals.* Cheltenham: Understanding Global Issues Ltd.

Urry, J. (1995) *Consuming Places.* London: Routledge.

——. (2002) *The Tourist Gaze.* London: Sage (2nd edition).

Vamplew, W. (1988) *Pay Up and Play the Game.* Cambridge: Cambridge University Press.

Veal, A. (1993) 'The concept of lifestyle: A review', *Leisure Studies*, Vol. 12, pp. 233–252.

Verma, G. and Darby, D. (1994) *Winners and Losers: Ethnic Minorities in Sport and Recreation.* London: Falmer Press.

Vigor, A., Mean, M. and Tims, C. eds (2004) *After the Gold Rush.* London: Institute for Public Policy Research.

Wagg, S. ed. (2004) *British Football and Social Exclusion.* London: Routledge.

Walby, S. (1997) *Gender Transformations.* Cambridge: Polity.

Walker, D. (2003) 'Buy now, pay later', *The Guardian*, 29 August, p. 27.

Wann, D., Melnick, M., Russell, G. and Pease, D. (2001) *Sports Fans.* New York and London: Routledge.

Warde, A. (2002) 'Setting the scene: Changing conceptions of consumption', in S. Miles, A. Anderson and K. Meethan (eds), *The Changing Consumer: Markets and Meanings.* London: Routledge, pp. 10–24.

Wellard, I. (2002) 'Men, sport, body performance and the maintenance of "exclusive masculinity"', *Leisure Studies*, Vol. 21, No. 3–4, pp. 235–247.

Wenner, L. ed. (1998) *MediaSport.* London: Routledge.

Wernick, A. (1991) *Promotional Culture*. London: Sage.

Westerbeek, H. and Smith, A. (2003) *Sport in the Global Market Place*. Basingstoke: Palgrave.

Whannel, G. (1983) *Blowing the Whistle: The Politics of Sport*. London: Pluto.

——. (1986) ' "The unholy alliance": Notes on television and the re-making of British Sport 1965–1985', *Leisure Studies*, Vol. 5, No. 1, pp. 22–37.

——. (1992) *Fields in Vision*. London: Routledge.

——. (1999) 'Sport stars, narrativization and masculinities', *Leisure Studies*, Vol. 18, No. 3, pp. 249–265.

——. (2000) 'Sport and the media', in J. Coakley and E. Dunning (eds), *Handbook of Sport Studies*. London: Sage, pp. 291–308.

——. (2001) 'Punishment, redemption and celebration in the popular press: The case of David Beckham', in D. Andrews and S. Jackson (eds), *Sport Stars*. London: Routledge, pp. 138–150.

——. (2002a) *Media Sport Stars*. London: Routledge.

——. (2002b) 'David Beckham, identity and masculinity', *Sociology Review*, Vol. 11, No. 3, pp. 2–4.

——. (2003) 'Celebrity and vortextuality in media sport' talk delivered at BSA Sociology of Sport meeting on 'Sporting Icons', University of Leicester, 7 February.

——. (2004) Book review of Sandvoss (2003) in *British Journal of Sociology*, Vol. 55, No. 3, pp. 481–482.

Whannel, G. and Philips, D. (2000) 'A cultural enterprise? The spread of commercial sponsorship', in G. Whannel (ed.), *Leisure Consumption and Participation*. Leisure Studies Association Publication No. 64, Eastbourne: Leisure Studies Association, pp. 45–59.

Wheaton, B. ed. (2004) *Understanding Lifestyle Sports*. London: Routledge.

Which (2003) 'The ethics of the shoemakers', *Which*. June.

Which (2001) 'Fitness centres: What are the choices?', *Which*. January.

White, M. (1999) 'Neo-liberalism and the rise of the citizen as consumer' in D. Broad and W. Antony (eds), *Citizens or Consumers*. Halifax, Nova Scotia: Fernwood Publishing, pp. 56–64.

Whitson, D. (1994) 'The embodiment of gender', in S. Birrell and C. Cole (eds), *Women, Sport and Culture*. Champaign, IL: Human Kinetics, pp. 353–371.

——. (1998a) 'Olympic sport, global media, and cultural diversity', in R. Barney, K. Wamsley, S. Martyn and G. MacDonald (eds), *Global and Cultural Critique: Problematising the Olympic Games*. London, Ontario: University of Western Ontario, pp. 1–9.

——. (1998b) 'Circuits of promotion: Media, marketing and the globalization of sport', in L. Wenner (ed.), *MediaSport*. London: Routledge, pp. 57–72.

Whitson, D. and Gruneau, R. (1997) 'The (real) integrated circus: Political economy, popular culture, and "major league" sport', in W. Clement (ed.), *Understanding Canada*. Montreal and Kingston: McGill-Queen's University Press, pp. 359–385.

Whitson, D., Harvey, J. and Lavoie, M. (2000) 'The Mills report, the Manley subsidy proposals, and the business of major-league sport', *Canadian Public Administration*, Vol. 43, No. 2, pp. 127–156.

Wickham, G. (1997) 'Governance of consumption', in P. Sulkunen, J. Holmwood, H. Radner and G. Schulze (eds), *Constructing the New Consumer Society*. Basingstoke: Macmillan pp. 277–291.

Wilkinson, R (1996) *Unhealthy Societies*. London: Routledge.

Williams, G. (1995) New Times, *New Statesman*, "Whose news" Supplement, 24 March, p. 9.

Williams, G. (2000) *Branded?* London: V&A (Victoria & Albert Museum) Publications.

Williams, J. (1999) *Is It All Over? Can Football Survive the Premier League?* Reading: South Street Press.

Williams, R. (1977) *Marxism and Literature*. Oxford: Oxford University Press.

——. (1980) 'Advertising: The magic system', in *Problems in Culture & Materialism*. London: Verso, pp. 170–195.

——. (1981) *Culture*. London: Fontana.

——. (1985) *Towards 2000*. Harmondsworth: Penguin.

——. (1990) *Television: Technology and Cultural Form*. London: Routledge (2nd edition).

Wilson, J. (1994) *Playing By the Rules: Sport, Society and the State*. Detroit: Wayne State University Press.

Wimbush, E. and Talbot, M. eds (1989) *Relative Freedoms*. Buckingham: Open University Press.

Woodward, K. (2002) *Understanding Identity*. London: Arnold.

Wray, R. (2005) 'Wembley contractor's profit kicked into touch', *The Guardian*, 25 February.

Zizek, S. (2005) 'The empty wheelbarrow', *The Guardian*, 19 February, p. 23.

Zukin, S. (1991) *Landscapes of Power*. Berkeley California: University of California Press.

Index